PENGUIN BO
THE GREAT UPRISING

Pramod K. Nayar teaches at the Department of English, University of Hyderabad. He is the author of *Reading Culture: Theory, Praxis, Politics* (2006), *Virtual Worlds: Culture and Politics in the Age of Cybertechnology* (2004) and *Literary Theory Today* (2002). His forthcoming work includes a study of aesthetics in English non-fictional writings on India, a book on postcolonial literature, and a new edition of *The Trial of Bahadur Shah Zafar*. He is the editor of *The Penguin 1857 Reader*.

The Great Uprising
India, 1857

PRAMOD K. NAYAR

PENGUIN BOOKS

PENGUIN BOOKS
Published by the Penguin Group
Penguin Books India Pvt. Ltd, 11 Community Centre, Panchsheel Park,
New Delhi 110 017, India
Penguin Group (USA) Inc., 375 Hudson Street, New York, New York 10014, USA
Penguin Group (Canada), 90 Eglinton Avenue East, Suite 700, Toronto,
Ontario, M4P 2Y3, Canada (a division of Pearson Penguin Canada Inc.)
Penguin Books Ltd, 80 Strand, London WC2R 0RL, England
Penguin Ireland, 25 St Stephen's Green, Dublin 2, Ireland
(a division of Penguin Books Ltd)
Penguin Group (Australia), 250 Camberwell Road, Camberwell,
Victoria 3124, Australia (a division of Pearson Australia Group Pty Ltd)
Penguin Group (NZ), 67 Apollo Drive, Rosedale, North Shore 0632,
New Zealand (a division of Pearson New Zealand Ltd)
Penguin Group (South Africa) (Pty) Ltd, 24 Sturdee Avenue, Rosebank,
Johannesburg 2196, South Africa

Penguin Books Ltd, Registered Offices: 80 Strand, London WC2R 0RL, England

First published by Penguin Books India 2007

Copyright © Pramod K. Nayar 2007

All rights reserved

10 9 8 7 6 5 4 3 2 1

ISBN-13: 978-0-14310-238-0   ISBN-10: 0-14310-238-9

Typeset in *Perpetua* by SÜRYA, New Delhi
Printed at Saurabh Printers Pvt. Ltd, Noida

This book is sold subject to the condition that it shall not, by way of trade or otherwise, be lent, resold, hired out, or otherwise circulated without the publisher's prior written consent in any form of binding or cover other than that in which it is published and without a similar condition including this condition being imposed on the subsequent purchaser and without limiting the rights under copyright reserved above, no part of this publication may be reproduced, stored in or introduced into a retrieval system, or transmitted in any form or by any means (electronic, mechanical, photocopying, recording or otherwise), without the prior written permission of both the copyright owner and the above-mentioned publisher of this book.

This one is for my first critic
(*you* know, don't you?)

Contents

Map: Places Connected with the 1857 Uprising viii

Acknowledgements x

Preface, and a Cautionary Note xii

Chronology: India 1857–59 xvi

Prologue: Raj 1

One: The Gathering Storm 39

Two: The Summer of Discontent 62

Three: The Retreat of the Native 143

Four: The Raj Rises Again 178

Appendix 1: The Fiction of 1857 234

Appendix 2: British India, A Chronology 252

Bibliography 258

Index 272

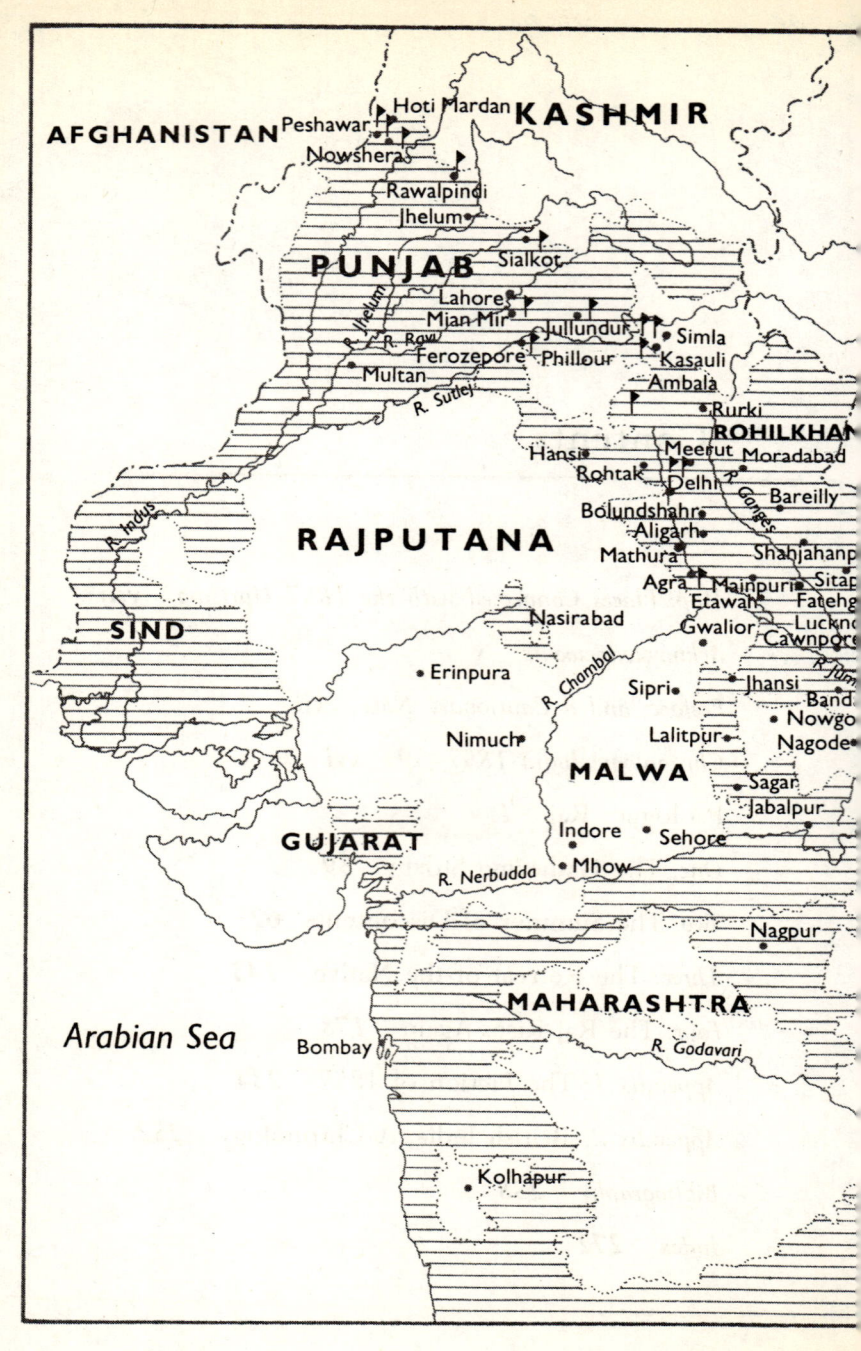

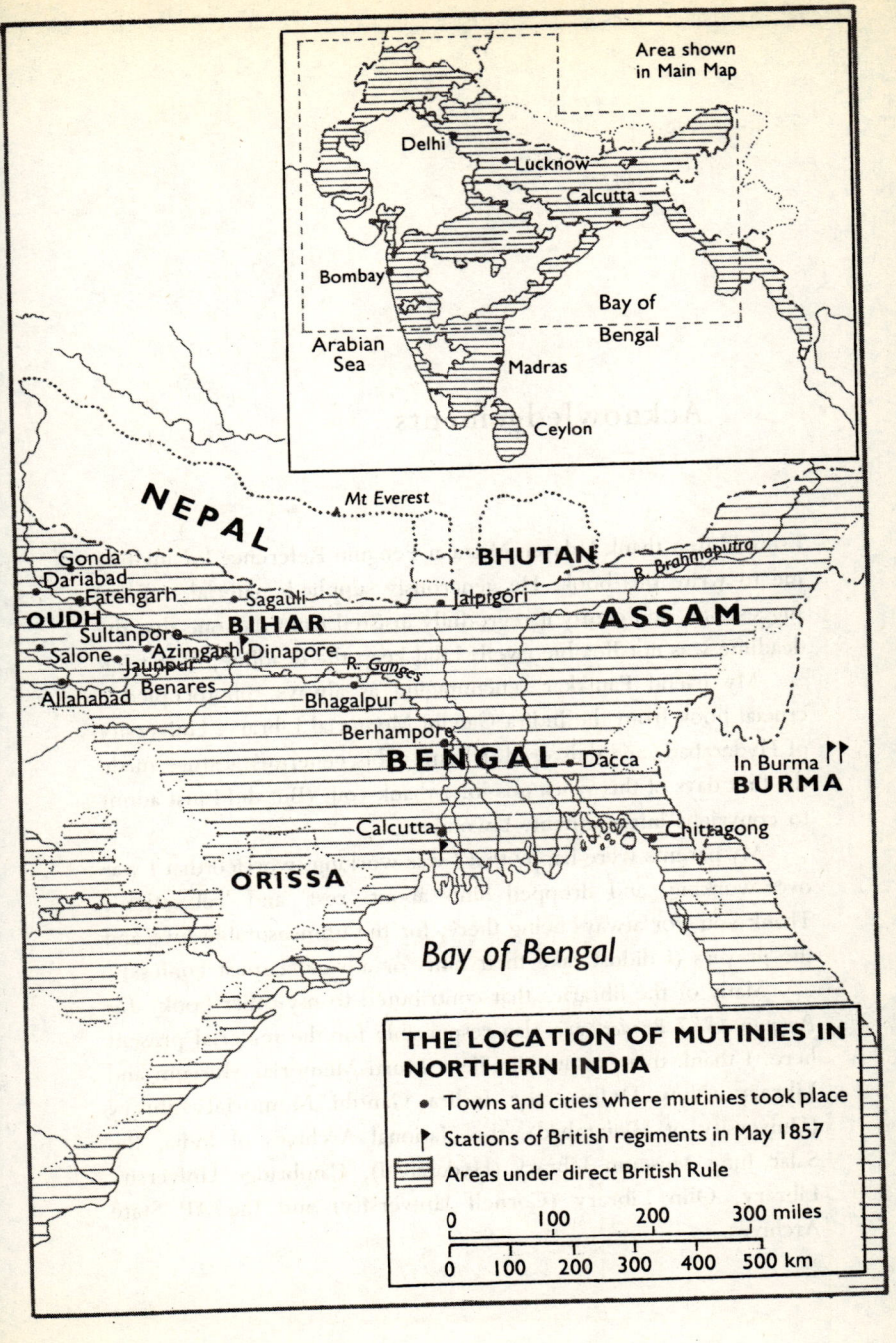

Acknowledgements

I should first thank Udayan Mitra at Penguin Reference for inviting me to write this book. He generously supplied material, offered suggestions, and gently if regretfully insisted from day one that the deadline was not flexible (well, I did keep the deadline, didn't I?)!

My friend Panikkar, encouraging as always, photocopied a crucial book from the Indira Gandhi Memorial Library, University of Hyderabad, *and* delivered it home—his generous gesture made the first days of this work possible: thank you. (But did I just admit to copyright infringement, I wonder...)

My parents were happy that I was working, worried that I was over-working, and dropped hints about 'rest' and 'relaxation'. Thank you, for always being there, for the immeasurable love and the prayers (I didn't take their hints or advice, I must confess).

Many of the libraries that contributed to my other book, *The Penguin 1857 Reader*, are also responsible for the material present here. I thank them again: the Teen Murti Memorial Museum and Library (New Delhi), the Indira Gandhi Memorial Library (University of Hyderabad), the National Archives of India, the Salar Jung Museum Library (Hyderabad), Cambridge University Library, Olin Library (Cornell University) and the AP State Archives.

Prof. Sudhakar Marathe, helpful as always, for mentioning in passing, in his characteristic 'surely-you-know-this' tone (he knew I didn't!), the Christina Rossetti poem on Jhansi: thank you very much.

Noella took time off from her usual, vigorous reading, pushed her younger brother out of the room saying she had 'work to do', and read through the first three chapters overnight and offered her comments: thank you, Noella (but this printed line is not your *only* reward!).

Anna is my long-standing manuscript-reader-in-chief. It is now routine to thank her for her insights, proofing and encouraging comments (sometimes anguished ones at my sentence constructions)—but it remains a privilege to say it again: thank you!

W.J. Surresh of Asian Educational Services, Chennai, supplied crucial books after just one phone call. I am very grateful for his efficiency and service.

Thank you, Niyati, for the copy of *Majha Pravas*.

I would like to thank my father-in-law, Sri Anil Khadakkar, for translating sections of *Majha Pravas*.

Nandini, with characteristic affection and concern, ensured that the study door was shut (while she *wrote* in the other room!) during the writing. Thank you, for putting up with me, my demonic work-loads. And being there, even when you were away!

Pranav, bouncing around the house, deserves thanks for ensuring that I took my eyes off the screen (or out of the printed word) to see something fascinating in whatever he brought in.

Archana Shankar at Penguin for her meticulous job with the editing, which makes this a better book—thank you.

Preface, and a Cautionary Note

The Mutiny, India 1857, has never really slipped out of imaginations, either Indian or British. Fifty years after the events, G.R. Hearn's travel guide, *The Seven Cities of Delhi* (1906), provided an itinerary for travellers wishing to see the Mutiny sites around Delhi, just so that they would be familiar with the 'story of this strenuous struggle by which India was saved'. And 150 years after the stirring events of 1857, Holts Tours (London), specializing in Battlefield Tours, advertises an Indian Mutiny tour: Delhi, Meerut, Lucknow, Kanpur, Agra (*Battlefields and History*, pp. 48–49. Website: www.holts.co.uk), although it has the grace to admit that there were 'appalling atrocities committed by both sides'.

But why and how does the Mutiny have this effect? What exactly *was* the Mutiny?

This book explores the scale and multiple dimensions of the events of 1857 that have sustained popular, historiographic and literary imaginations for over a century.

The book is situated somewhere between the dry-as-dust historical tract, the dramatic narrative of a momentous event, and a scholarly (please note the footnotes, which reveal its aspirations to the scholarly) work. It is a popular account of the most fascinating years in British India before the arrival of Gandhi. It introduces characters and places, events and times; it seeks to capture some of the great drama. The drama that was India 1857.

The bibliography is fairly extensive, and should provide the reader with more texts, should she be interested in exploring further. It includes a large number of first-person narrative accounts of 1857, and should be of particular interest to those who want to read experiential accounts. Finally, I have provided a short section on the fiction of the Mutiny. This might be of interest to those who would like to know how literary texts from the time saw and represented the events.

*

The events of 1857 are open to interpretation. The term 'Mutiny' carries a pejorative connotation from the Indian standpoint. Other terms such as 'the first war of Independence' or 'nationalist struggle' have been proposed, used and contested. 'Uprising' seems to be yet another popular choice. Was 1857—and notice how a date becomes the name of an event, not unlike 9/11—truly 'national' when it did not touch southern India? Was it military in character, or was it civilian and popular too? 1857 meant, and continues to mean, different things to different people.

I have retained the use of the term 'Mutiny', fully aware that it runs the risk of sounding like a Western (Euro-American) account of 1857, which this is most emphatically *not*. However, the choice was dictated by the indisputable fact that it is the most common, and therefore recognized, appellation (along with 'sepoy revolt') for the years 1857–58, from school textbooks to scholarly works. Ideally the term ought to be placed in quotes—as many scholarly works continue to do—to indicate the questionable relevance and implicit politics of the term. But using the quote marks throughout would be tedious and irritating. **I, however,**

request the reader to *assume* the quote marks exist, that the term is not simple or decisive in its meanings. The 'Uprising' in the title is a deliberate shift away from the West-centric 'Mutiny', even as the rest of the book uses the commonest term.

I have also retained the use of British spellings like Cawnpore (Kanpur) and Oudh (Awadh) so that it remains close to the original.

Massacres, violence and brutality were common to both sides in the story. There was Satichaura and Bibighar on the side of the Indians: brutal, excessive, unpardonable. But, equally unpardonable were the British, who destroyed entire villages and executed natives without ascertaining their participation in the Mutiny. Euro-American narratives on/of the Mutiny focus on Nana Sahib's disposition and violence. James Neill, who left behind him as a penalty for mutiny, entire villages empty of human life, does not attract the same attention. If Meerut saw officers being shot dead, Delhi saw three princes stripped and killed in full view of the populace. If no single European was left alive in Meerut after 12 May, 5,000 natives died within Jhansi's walls, for the sole reason that they stood by their queen.

Too often British actions have been seen only as retaliatory, a direct response to the cruelties of Nana Sahib and the natives. *What is ignored, crucially, I believe, is that James Neill's massacre of villagers in Allahabad preceded the Cawnpore massacres (Allahabad was in the first weeks of June 1857, well before Satichaura on 27 June, and Bibighar almost a month later).* Even Christopher Hibbert mentions Allahabad after Cawnpore, thus suggesting a cause–effect sequence, when it was not really so. Michael Edwardes, who is one of the few to acknowledge the 'madness of Colonel Neill' (the title of one of the chapters in his *Red Year*, 1973), locates Neill after Cawnpore. Saul David places Allahabad, Benaras and Neill's actions *after* the chapter 'Satichaura Ghat'. P.J.O. Taylor, an exception, however, believes that Neill's 'conduct en route [to Cawnpore and Lucknow] is said to have provoked the massacres in Cawnpore'. V.D. Savarkar, in his Indian version of 1857, draws attention to this awkward historiography when he states: 'Neill's barbarities were not a revenge of Cawnpore, but the Cawnpore bloodshed was the result of and revenge of Neill's inhuman brutalities'.

Neither side of the story is innocent, neither entirely evil. Neither murder nor mutilation can be justified or explained as 'rebellion' or 'retribution'.

Innocent people, Indian and British, did lose their lives and property. Remembering it all is traumatic, but also politically charged. And this is the reason why Edward Thompson in *The Other Side of the Medal* (1925) recommended that we stop publishing Mutiny narratives.

For, as the poet Eliot put it: after such knowledge, what forgiveness?

PKN

Hyderabad
2006–07

Chronology: India 1857–59

1857
January
- 22   Dum-Dum encounter between sepoy and khalasi, first rumours about greased cartridges

February
- 26   19th Native Infantry (N.I.) at Berhampore refuses cartridges

March
- 29   Mangal Pandey's actions at Barrackpore
- 31   19th N.I. disbanded

April
- 8   Mangal Pandey hanged
- 24   3rd Light Cavalry, Meerut, refuses cartridges

May
- 6   Seven companies of 34th (Mangal Pandey's company) disbanded at Barrackpore
  83rd Light Cavalry court-martialled
  93rd Light Cavalry disarmed, imprisoned
- 10   Indian troops free imprisoned comrades, shoot officers at Meerut
- 11   Meerut mutineers arrive at Delhi, Europeans killed in Delhi
- 13   Bahadur Shah Zafar proclaimed new Mughal emperor; partial mutiny at Ferozepur

16	Canning's Proclamation
20–23	Mutiny at Agra
22	Peshawar garrison disarmed
27	George Anson, Commander-in-Chief, dies
28	Mutiny at Nasirabad (Rajputana)
30	Mutiny at Lucknow; Wilson defeats Delhi mutineers at Hindan river
31	Mutinies at Shahjahanpur and Bareilly

June

3	Mutinies at Sitapur, Nimuch
4	Mutiny at Benares
5	Mutinies at Cawnpore, Jhansi
6	Mutiny at Allahabad;
4–6	Neill's massacres at Benares and Allahabad
6	Cawnpore siege begins
7	Mutiny at Jullundur
8	Barnard defeats rebels at Badli-ki-Serai
10	Mutiny at Nowgong
14	Mutiny at Gwalior
17	Patrick Grant arrives as Commander-in-Chief
25	Nana offers terms to Wheeler at Cawnpore
27	Satichaura Ghat massacre
30	Henry Lawrence defeated at Chinhat; Lucknow siege begins

July

1	Nana Sahib proclaimed Peshwa
5	Barnard dies, Birjis Qadr crowned king of Oudh
12	Havelock defeats rebels at Fatehpur
15	Havelock wins at Aong and Pandu Nadi; Bibighar massacre at Cawnpore
16	Havelock defeats Nana Sahib near Cawnpore
25	Mutiny at Dinapore, Kunwar Singh begins actions
31	Canning's Resolution

August
- 2 Eyre defeats Dinapore rebels
- 13 Havelock returns to Cawnpore, Colin Campbell arrives at Calcutta
- 14 John Nicholson arrives at Delhi Ridge
- 17 William Hodson defeats rebels at Rohtak
- 24 Nicholson defeats Nimuch rebels at Najafgarh

September
- 9 John Colvin dies in Agra fort
- 14 Battle for Delhi begins
- 20 Delhi cleared of rebels
- 21 Zafar surrenders
- 22 Zafar's sons/grandson shot dead by Hodson
- 23 Nicholson dies
- 25 First relief of Lucknow by Havelock and Outram

October
- 10 Greathed's column defeats rebels at Agra

November
- 17 Second relief of Lucknow by Campbell
- 24 Havelock dies
- 26/27 Tatya Tope defeats Windham at Cawnpore

December
- 6 Campbell defeats Tope, takes Cawnpore
- 15 C.S. Stuart takes Indore

1858

January
- 2 Campbell defeats Nawab of Farrukhabad and Bakht Khan at Khudaganj
- 27 Trial of Bahadur Shah Zafar begins

February
- 3 Hugh Rose relieves Sagar

March
- 2 Campbell moves to relieve Lucknow
- 9 Zafar found guilty

chronology: india 1857–59

   21   Lucknow taken
   22   Rose tackles Jhansi

April
    1   Rose defeats Tope at Betwa
    3   Rose captures Jhansi, Rani Lakshmibai escapes
   19   Whitlock defeats Nawab of Banda
   21   Kunwar Singh wounded
   23   Kunwar Singh defeats Le Grande at Jagdishpur

May
    5   Campbell defeats Khan Bahadur Khan at Bareilly
    7   Rose defeats Tope and Rani Lakshmibai at Kunch
   22   Rose defeats Rao Sahib and Rani Lakshmibai at Kalpi
   31   Rebel army at Gwalior defects, Scindia flees to Agra

June
   12   Hope Grant defeats Beni Madho at Nawabganj
   15   Maulvi of Faizabad killed
   17   Rani Lakshmibai killed in battle
   19   Rose takes Gwalior

August
    2   India Bill transfers powers to British Crown

October
    7   Zafar, the last Mughal emperor, leaves Delhi

November
    1   Victoria's Proclamation

1859

January
    3   Bala Rao, Oudh rebels driven into Nepal
   21   Holmes defeats Tope and Firoz Shah

April
    7   Tatya Tope betrayed, captured
   18   Tatya Tope executed

Prologue: Raj

The 'Raj' really took shape after 1764, with the decisive victory of the East India Company (EIC) at Buxar. 'Raj' connotes 'rule', and as such is a term that is more suitable to describe nineteenth-century India, where the East India Company assumed and consolidated political power, and transformed itself from a trading unit into an administrative one. But the Company's role in Indian economy, politics and social life dates back to nearly 150 years before Buxar.

In order to situate the events of 1857 in context we need to understand the development of this massive administrative, political and military leviathan called the Raj. The leviathan, as is the case most of the time, began life with a small idea—of trade—and a tiny whiff—of spices.

Company

In 1498 an intrepid explorer Vasco da Gama arrived from Portugal at the port of Calicut in what is now Kerala state. The Portuguese who arrived in the wake of Vasco da Gama, picked the west coast town of Goa as their headquarters. In addition to trade they managed another set of tasks: spreading the gospel and religious conversions. The Dutch arrived in India in 1595. They headed farther east to Java and other places, and were soon making tidy profits trading in spice.

The first Englishman to step on to Indian soil may have been Thomas Stephens. Having reached India in 1579, he spent the next forty years as a Goa-based missionary. In September 1599 some London merchants petitioned Queen Elizabeth for permission to trade with the East Indies. Elizabeth agreed, and signed a charter granting this permission, which they received on 31 December 1599. When the EIC started out to India they were a trading Company with a monopoly of all trade with the East, though this monopoly did not include conquest or political colonization.

In 1608 William Hawkins arrived at Surat and met Emperor Akbar to secure trading concessions. After two years, Hawkins returned to England, unsuccessful in his efforts. The two successive 'ambassadors' after Hawkins did something unusual. Sir Henry Middleton seized Indian trading vessels at sea and ransomed them. Thomas Best, who kept a detailed account of his voyage, engaged Portuguese ships in battle and defeated them, thus reasserting English sea-power. In a sense, these two were gesturing at future events—the British would not tolerate competition in trade, and would engage in war if necessary, even though the official policy prohibited war.

In 1612 the English set up a trading post at Surat, marking a more permanent English presence in India. Sir Thomas Roe, ambassador from the court of James I, met Emperor Jahangir in 1615. Roe was instrumental in extracting rights for the free movement of English goods and people through India. The English were allowed to set up factories at specific Mughal ports (mainly Surat, Gujarat). 'Factories' were actually warehouses, where resident agents—the 'factors'—collected goods until they were loaded on the ship.

In 1640 the Company moved to the East Coast of India. It acquired some land at Madras and set up its establishment here, in what was to eventually become Fort St. George. In 1660 the Company sought to strengthen its relations with the Crown of England by offering £ 3,000 worth of silver plates to the monarch. And in 1662 it loaned him £ 10,000 (over the years the loan amount totalled upwards of £ 150,000). Bombay was included as an item of dowry when Catherine of Braganza married Charles II in 1661. When William and Mary took over the throne of England in 1688 the Company's fortunes appeared under threat. Finally, by 1690, the Company had a colony in Bengal—on the Hoogly, near Calcutta (as the English called it). This settlement became the basis for Fort William. By the end of the seventeenth century there were three Presidencies in India: Madras, Bengal and Bombay. A new company was set up by the House of Commons in 1698. The two companies merged in 1709.

The Company paid for Indian products in silver bullion, tin, lead and quicksilver and made tidy profits through the seventeenth century. Not restricting itself to spices, the Company sold Indian products such as indigo, saltpetre (used to make gunpowder), Indian textiles (calico, muslin, chintz) and spices in Europe. Pepper and other spices were obtained from Malabar. Sugar came from Madras, indigo dye from Gujarat and silk from Bengal.

All this settlement and acquisition meant a certain degree of conflict, of course. Muslim officers did not, for instance, make it easy for the Hooghly settlement to operate their boats. Sivaji, the Maratha king, attacked Surat in 1664, and ransacked most of the port. Such skirmishes were part of the early trading settlements. In 1675 the Surat factory finally received orders that its employees were to be trained in military disciplines, so that they could defend the factory in the event of such attacks. Four companies of British troops arrived in Bombay in 1662—it would be such troops that the Company government would turn to 200 years later, during the Mutiny.

A Court of Directors was set up in London and corresponded with the Presidencies directly. The Presidencies developed law courts and civic corporations, with their own rituals and ceremonial processions. Further, the English began to build their own quarters and segmented the Indian town, separating 'white' from 'black' towns.

A Greater Company

With the Act of Union between England and Scotland sealed in 1707, the East India Company became a British rather than an English company.

Towards the end of the seventeenth century more and more Englishmen came out to India in search of prosperity. Though there had been a Company embargo against private trading by its employees, practically every one of them indulged in it to supplement their incomes.

By the mid-eighteenth century the essential structures of an imperial power, the Raj, were in place in India. Since communication with England and the Parliament was often difficult and delayed, the 'man-on-the-spot' became the sole authority in decision-making. While the Company itself was dependant on the renewal of its Charter by the British Parliament, its servants were more or less independent masters in India. The Company, increasingly seen as an 'engine' of revenue generation by the British Government, agreed to pay the English government £ 400,000 annually. Trade expanded and the government, landed gentry and financial powers furthered the growth of the Company's territories.

The Company continued to recognize the authority of the Mughal emperor—it struck coins in his name, used Persian as the official language and administered justice in courts based on Hindu and Muslim laws. The Company followed the policy of least intervention. War and any other form of civil disturbance were regarded as being against English and Company interests. However, it became clear by the mid-eighteenth century that the Company would have to war with its European rivals and deal with native threats in order to maintain its profits.

> By 1750, Bengal alone accounted for 75 per cent of the company's procurement of Indian goods.

Soon the Company had to face almost continuous war: Plassey (1757), Buxar/Baksar (1764), Mysore (1767–69, 1780–84, 1790–92, 1799). First the French attacked and captured Madras in 1746. Later, the French Governor François Dupleix intervened in the succession disputes involving the Nawab of Carnatic and the Nizam of Deccan. What the French and British did was to back specific successors to the thrones here so that a puppet king, favourable to them, would be in power. The man involved in the winning battles at Arcot during this period was Robert Clive. After his victory at Arcot, Clive went to England, only to return to India in a few months. This time the problem was with Siraj ud-Daula, the Nawab of Bengal. In June 1756 Siraj ud-Daula attacked the Company settlement, and captured it with little trouble (he was accompanied by over 30,000 foot soldiers, and 20,000 horsemen). Later, after the victory, he put the captured English soldiers into a small room. This event—much of its actual details disputed and unproven—was the infamous Black Hole. J.Z. Holwell, who was one of the survivors, wrote the story of the Black Hole in which he claimed that, of the 146 people put inside the cell, only twenty-three survived.

In any case the events indicated that the Nawab was likely to be a major problem for the Company. Robert Clive, the Arcot hero, was sent to Bengal to resolve the problem. Clive began by promoting Mir Jafar as the successor to Siraj ud-Daula. In the battle of Plassey, Clive defeated the Nawab and placed Mir Jafar in his stead. This event marked the most significant moment since Queen Elizabeth delivered the charter to the Company. It marked the transformation of the Company from a mere trading house to a political power. It also meant a radical change in the lives of the Company servants. Most of them made their fortunes in the form of gifts, rewards and protection money received from native rulers and businessmen. To provide one instance: the House of Commons investigating the Bengal problem computed that presents paid to Company men amounted to nearly £ 2,238,575 between 1756 and 1765. In 1765, after a treaty with the Mughal emperor, the Company secured the diwani (revenue collecting rights) for Bihar, Bengal and Orissa, though the actual collection was left to the Nawab's officials. This meant that the Company was a *deputy* to the Mughal emperor. However, the Company remained wary of assuming administrative responsibilities. Another effect of the Plassey success was the organization of the Company's armies. Robert Clive realized the need for a strong army, and began recruiting Indian soldiers, though it was Stringer Lawrence who, in 1748, first began the drive to create a permanent Indian army for the Company. These sepoys were recruited from Rajput and Brahmin communities in the Oudh–Bihar region (there were, however, attempts made to recruit from the hill tribes, especially after the Company extended its territories into the mountainous Jungle Terai in the 1770s and the Ceded and Conquered Districts in the early 1800s).

> By 1790 the Indian Army had 100,000 men. It had 154,000 in 1824 and 214,000 in 1856.

The Company's army soon began to include diverse social groups. Clive, Hastings and others ensured that the religious sentiments of the various communities were respected, and celebrations such as the Ram Lila were granted official recognition.

Company officials during the seventeenth century began to acquire huge fortunes as a result of their work in India. These men, with their lavish lifestyles and arrogance, were called the 'Nabobs' (after the Indian 'Nawab'). One of the best known and most influential of these was Warren Hastings. Hastings first arrived in India in 1750 as a writer for the Company. Later, he returned to India in the capacity of Second Member of the Madras Council in 1769. In 1772 he was appointed Governor of Bengal. Around this time the Company had discovered that they could not trust the Nawab's officials to collect revenues. It was decided that the Company would have to rely on its own resources for revenue collection. European District Collectors were placed in charge of revenue collection, while the revenue collecting rights were auctioned. This was known as the 'farming system,' which ultimately failed because the farmers only sought to extract as much revenue as possible without worrying about the production process.

By this time the Company was also heavily in debt, and Parliament passed the Regulating Act of 1773 in order to rescue the situation. This prohibited private trade by Company revenue and justice officials, and banned the 'gift' system. Hastings was also made the Governor General of the Indian holdings of the Company. The 1773 Act is important because it was the first intrusion by the English Government into the Company affairs in India. The Board of Control, with six members, created by the 1784 Act, governed the Company Directors. With the 1784 Act the Company's administration was brought under more direct government control.

Under Warren Hastings, who sought to codify laws and systematize the judicial processes in India, an English judge was placed alongside a Hindu pundit (for Hindu law) or a maulana (for Muslim law) to dispense justice.

> N.B. Halhed's translations of a digest of Hindu laws—compiled by eleven pundits at Hastings' orders—in 1776 were designed to facilitate the European judge's interpretation and administration of these laws.

Every district had a diwani adalat (or civil court) and a faujdari adalat (criminal court). Muslim laws were applied in criminal justice and Muslim and Hindu personal laws in deciding on personal matters. Civil courts were presided over by European District Collectors. With increasing crime in 1770s, the faujdars—derived from the Mughal police system—were replaced by English magistrates.

With Hastings, imperial responsibility becomes a reality. The Amending Act of 1781 defined the jurisdiction of the Supreme Court. Lord Cornwallis (1785–93) played a decisive role in consolidating the administrative structures of the Company, and kept Indians out of the administration (thereby reversing Hastings' policy). He sought to protect private property, introduce the famous British 'rule of law', and is known primarily for his 'Permanent Settlement' of Bengal. Cornwallis divested the zamindars of their police duties in 1793. He divided districts into thanas, which were units of police administration, of about thirty square miles, each under a daroga, appointed by the magistrate. In most cases the daroga functioned in close alliance with the local zamindar (and created a new nexus).

> The daroga system was extended to Madras in 1802, but was finally abolished in 1812.

The Charter Act of 1793 renewed the Company's charter for another twenty years, and gave it possession of all territories in India. Further, a code of regulations for internal government was drafted. This regulation took into account the rights, person and property of the Indian people, and asked the courts to regulate their decisions in accordance with this code. It stipulated that laws should be printed with translations in Indian languages, so that Indians—the 'subject-population' could be made aware of their rights and responsibilities.

With Lord Wellesley (1798–1805), things moved into a proper imperialist mode. Wellesley began by initiating (and winning) major battles—first against the French and then against Tipu Sultan. With this, British rule extended into south India, marking the expansionist phase of British presence. It stopped being one of several powers and began to acquire the dimensions of an empire. Mughal power had by now completely declined, and India now consisted of feudal states and British territory. Wellesley also contributed to the future of British rule in India through another act. He was instrumental in setting up Fort William College in Calcutta in 1802. Among its staff were British Orientalists and Brahmins, training students in Persian, Sanskrit and Indian mythology. Eventually Fort William College also served another purpose: by 1818 it had the largest collection of Oriental material anywhere in the world with a total of 11,335 printed and manuscript sources, and thus became a centre for language and culture research. From this would emerge the great literary and cultural period now called the Bengal Renaissance (which produced, among others, Rammohan Roy).

Wellesley was recalled in 1805, at a time when Napoleon was

threatening to recast European geopolitics. Wellesley went back to become the Duke of Wellington, and defeated Napoleon. If Wellesley had stayed on in India, Napoleon may well have won and world history would have been radically different.

Edmund Burke and William Pitt (Sr.) regarded India as civilized and cultivated, if anachronistic and stagnated. They believed that Britain should not tamper with Indian religion, even though it was savage and primitive. These conservatives saw India as a subject of study, as a profession. However, the British also did not want a return to the acknowledged glorious past of India (which would mean a return to pre-Plassey India, minus British power). People like Thomas Munro sought, instead, an India governed according to its own cultures and institutions, but under the guardianship of the British. This conservative attitude towards India was to change drastically in the first decades of the nineteenth century, the period of 'reform', when the administrators felt that India could not be allowed to run the way it had for centuries. What it needed, they argued, was a strong, firm hand to lead them out of the darkness of their culture.

The British were afraid that their systems of governance would somehow reproduce the despotic rule of the Indians. Frequent calls for the reform of Company rule were made from the last decades of the eighteenth century. A Select Committee of Parliament was appointed in 1772 to inquire into the India affairs. The main focus of such committees, speeches and calls for reform of the Company was three-fold: the relationship between the British government/Parliament and the Company, the form of control to be exerted by authorities (both the Company's and the government's) over the Company, and the centralization of power over the distant possession.

Edmund Burke, whose speeches at the impeachment of Warren Hastings (1786) were replete with images of the deleterious effects of British presence in India, led the movement for better control over the Company's functioning. The impeachment was an attempt to prevent the (further) misuse of Company authority in India. Burke and the others were against arbitrary rule—such as Hastings'—which relied on one man's morality and intellect to dispense justice. That is, Burke and the conservatives never saw the Company presence itself as unwarranted: what they opposed was the random and individualist processes of governance that, according to them, was a replication of the despotic rule of Indian kings of yore. According to the conservatives, a strong and fair system of government, discipline and sense of justice were urgently required. The rule of law, the codification of legal procedures, and the establishment of an effective judiciary, it was believed, could prevent the simple replacement of an Indian despotism with a British one. Thus, by the end of the eighteenth century the administrative and political infrastructure of the Raj was in place. In the nineteenth century this infrastructure was consolidated, and Company administrators, reformers and statesmen embarked on a project of recasting India itself.

Raj

In the first decades of the nineteenth century Britain was involved in numerous wars and treaties across the subcontinent: with Nepal, the Marathas, and against tribes such as the Pindaris. Wellesley extended the borders of British India northwards into the Ganges valley. He managed to neutralize the Peshwa of Poona in 1802 and conquered Delhi in 1803. Through the Subsidiary Alliance system, more territory was acquired. In this system the Indian prince/ruler secured protection from enemies by maintaining the Company's troops—at his own expense—in his territory. Arcot, Oudh and Hyderabad were all controlled through this scheme. Eventually, with the Company demand for payment being incessant, the native states were driven into bankruptcy. Local princes were often propped by the Company in a form of governance known as 'indirect rule'.

There were two distinct trends in the Company's administrative policies. Lord Cornwallis, working with Bengal's Permanent Settlement scheme, sought to introduce the rule of law and private property rights. Thomas Munro modified Cornwallis' Permanent Settlement by suggesting that revenues be collected directly from peasants and not the landlords. This 'Ryotwari Settlement', Munro suggested, would make the tiller of the soil more interested in developing the land. Cornwallis and Philip Francis believed that the new system was an improvement on both the despotic Indian and the European feudal ones. Munro believed that while the rule of law was a sound principle, such a system had to be modified to suit the Indian context, especially in the sense that certain elements of the Indian method of personal government needed to be maintained. Mountstuart Elphinstone, John Malcolm (who became Governor of Bombay), Charles Metcalfe (Resident at Delhi) and others mark this phase of the Raj with their benevolent paternalism, where the Indian system of personal government would be used, but by knowledgeable and 'sympathetic' Englishmen such as Thomas Munro. Metcalfe was one of the first to define the Indo-British relationship as one of mutual respect, exhorting the British, all the while, to render justice and promote the happiness of the country.

By 1820 a sense of permanence had also entered the British mindset. They were now confident of their presence in India, and the role that had been *ordained* for them. While there were rival views of what they were actually *meant* to do—witness the differing opinions of Cornwallis and Munro, for instance, on the district judge and the district collector (Cornwallis elevated the former, and Munro gave more importance to the latter)—they were never in doubt that Britain was meant to be in India. Britain was also bolstered by the boom in its own industry (now driven by steam), the successes in the Napoleonic wars, and the overall supremacy of its economy.

Commercially, India was crucial to England. The English Parliament ended Company monopoly in 1813, and asserted the ultimate sovereignty of the Crown over the Company and its possessions. There was a major shift in terms of trade around the first decades of the nineteenth century. By 1815 Indian textiles could not compete with British machine-made goods. British textiles began to flood Indian markets, and colonial economy—exporting raw material from the colony, importing manufactured goods at high prices—made its first major appearance. Weavers all over India, but especially in Dacca and Murshidabad, were ruined as a result.

> Opium was now a major trade product with China and provided up to 15 per cent of the Indian government's total revenues by 1830.

But revenues were also generated by other means—such as the 'Home Charges' (these were funds claimed by the Company as the cost of maintaining its offices, pensions and debts).

The reformist agenda had a particular teleology: Orientalism. The 'Orientalist' phase may be identified as the prominent mode of the last decades of the eighteenth century. Three institutions were set up in this period: the Calcutta Madrassa (1781), the Asiatic Society of Bengal (1784) and the Sanskrit College in Benares (1794). These institutions were created to promote the study of Indian languages and scriptures. The work of the Asiatic Society (especially its influential publication, the *Asiatic Researches*) and its scholars provided a certain image of India to the West: India had once possessed a magnificent and highly advanced civilization, but had unfortunately degenerated over the centuries. By arguing that Indian culture had degenerated, the British justified the Raj as a mechanism of preservation. The British task was to prevent further decay, and to enable development and progress. It is this Orientalist view of a degenerate India that enabled the next stage in British conceptualization and 'action' in India—that of reform.

The 1820s marked the start of the age of liberal reform in British India, and can be said to cover the period between Bentinck and Dalhousie. The liberal attitude upheld that humanity could be improved through religion, education, law and free trade. What distinguishes this phase from the earlier one was the aggressive schemes for large-scale social transformation. The period is significant for the large number of legislative and administrative measures—some of them experimental—for the 'reform' and 'improvement' of India.

> The India Act stipulated that £ 10,000 be spent on education in India. In 1833, £ 20,000 was earmarked for schools.

In keeping with the liberal belief that the truth of religion could improve mankind, the Act also lifted the prohibition on English missionary activity in India. This was perhaps the most significant development of the first decades of the nineteenth century—the evangelical Raj. With the lifting of the ban, missionaries flooded in—with Thomas Middleton as the first bishop. A few years prior to this, Wellesley had discovered the Baptist leader William Carey's talent for Indian languages. Wellesley appointed Carey to the teaching staff at Fort William College. With the start of the Serampore presses there was a large production of tracts in Bengali, Marathi, Urdu and other languages. Britain was increasingly clear as to its mission in India, though it had not yet begun to think of an empire (the idea of an empire was, during the 1830s, still associated with despotism and aggression; and the American War of Independence had further called into question any such dream).

> With the 1832 Reform Act and the Act of 1833, the Company was left with only political functions.

Indian possessions of the Company were deemed to be held in trust for the Crown by the Company (this notion was reiterated with the 1853 Act, which also renewed the charter). The Governor General of Bengal was now the Governor General of India, with control over civil, military and revenue matters.

Charles Grant was one of the earliest to point to a possible evangelical mission in India when he suggested that Indians as a race had become degenerate and base. This meant that Britain not only had the duty to provide justice to Indians, but also to ensure their moral improvement.

> The London Missionary Society, set up in 1795, dispatched its first missionary, Nathaniel Forsyth, to India in 1798.

The missionary move to improve India was closely aligned with the widespread popularity among British administrators (such as William Bentinck) of the utilitarian philosophy of Jeremy Bentham. Utilitarianism was closely aligned with the agenda of reform. James Mill and other thinkers of this period argued that nineteenth-century India was in the same state as ancient India. They therefore proposed that Britain's task was to free India from its present stagnant state. What was essential to this process of reform was a clear set of laws and system of rights. An efficient British administration would ensure the greatest happiness of the greatest number. James Mill's son, John Stuart Mill, believed that Britain could prepare India for self-government. Indeed, this was Britain's primary task in India. Indians could be taught to pursue the common good through proper education and laws (both, of course, given by the British). That is, India could be transformed only by *British* institutions. This sentiment was echoed by no less a thinker than Macaulay who argued, in a tone of universal liberalism, that 'the public mind of India may expand under our system till it has outgrown that system.' Part of the requirement for this transformation was English education for the Indian.

> The 4,000 Indian Christians in the Punjab in 1880s grew to 163,000 by 1911. In Uttar Pradesh, the Methodists grew to 104,000 between 1901 and 1911. India also boasted of the largest number of foreign missionaries in any non-Christian country: 5,200.

Led by the Clapham Sect—Charles Grant (Jr), William Wilberforce, Josiah Pratt, Zachary Macaulay, William Bentinck and others—the British began their campaign to improve India. Indian reform was driven by people who saw it as their duty—thus marking the first stirrings of what Kipling would (in)famously describe as 'the white man's burden'. It was led essentially by 'Sahibs'. The Sahibs were a category of Englishmen distinct from the Nabobs in terms of class origins and attitudes. Most of them came from upper-class English families. The Sahibs respected Moghul culture, and preferred to treat Indians, as a whole, with a degree of admiration for being an ancient, but at present degraded, civilization.

Reform followed a dual route: spreading the gospel and English education among Indians. Curiously this was also the age of massive imperial expansion. Dalhousie's 'Doctrine of Lapse', which enabled the British to take over any kingdom or principality without heirs, was largely responsible for the expansion. But it is also to Dalhousie's enterprise that we can trace the arrival of railways and telegraph.

Appalled at the so-called barbarism of Hinduism, the British sought to first introduce Christianity and then English education. Joshua Marshman, William Carey's colleague at Serampore, was one of the first to draw up proposals for public education in India. In 1818 he started *Dag Darsan*, a magazine for Indian youth, to be distributed free to students at Hindu College (Calcutta). Later Horace H. Wilson set up the Sanskrit College in Calcutta to teach Indian poetics, grammar and law. However, all these figures pale into comparison beside William Bentinck. Fervently arguing for a reformed India under British rule, Bentinck initiated measures against corruption in the Company, public works (including the start of the building of the Grand Trunk Road and steam ships on the Ganga), abolished flogging, and proceeded to enact legislations on various issues. Among the latter was the ban on the purchase/sale of slaves between one administrative district and another (1832), the ban on Sati (1829) and the campaign against thugi.

Thugi or thuggee was a form of banditry accompanied by the killing of the victim. The Thugs would travel with the victims, as fellow travellers. They would befriend the travellers and, when the time was appropriate, strangle them using a scarf or handkerchief. Colonel W.H. Sleeman, who campaigned against this, would become known as 'Thugi Sleeman'. Sleeman's contemporary, Philip Meadows Taylor, would write a novel, Confessions of a Thug, *and in the twentieth century, John Masters would write* The Deceivers.

> In five years, 1831–37, more than 3,000 men were convicted of thugi. It had been estimated that over 40,000 people were killed by Thugs each year.

The campaign against thugi was a combination of evangelical beliefs and administrative policies. Such reforms and active intervention in the lives of the Indians meant, in effect, that Britain was asserting its imperial control over the subjects of its empire. They were also seen as part of the evangelical mission—to conquer and reform their imperial subjects. The Indians had to be 'redeemed', and Britain was ordained to spread the light and influence of truth. What this meant was that while the British sought to reform India, its opinions about India progressed from respect to horror, and from admiration to revulsion, especially during the 1830s and '40s. Reform was deemed imperative for the improvement of such a culture. However, there were warning voices such as Elphinstone's and Charles Metcalfe's, recommending that Indian reform should proceed very circumspectly. Others, including Hastings in the last decades of the eighteenth century, recommended that Company regulations and systems remain close to native customs and traditions.

Alongside William Bentinck was the learned and strongly opinionated Thomas Babington Macaulay (his father Zachary had been at the forefront of the anti-slave trade movement). Macaulay firmly believed that Indians had degenerated into barbarians. Arriving in India in 1834, he met Bentinck and proceeded to make his moves. He fought for the abolition of press censorship, and the abolition of privileges of the Europeans over Indians in law (especially in matters of appeals to higher courts), before turning his eyes to Indian education. Having dismissed Indian (Sanskrit or Persian) education as worthless, he proceeded to plead for an

English education in his (in)famous Minute of 1835. Bentinck made him the President of the Education Committee, through which Macaulay was able to plead for the introduction of European literature in Indian education. A few years later, forty seminaries for the purpose of teaching English were opened. The Calcutta Book Society sold over 30,000 English texts. At the new Hoogly College, the difference in numbers was startling: 1,100 enrolled for English, and 300 for Oriental. Macaulay was also instrumental in drawing up the penal code—which India continues to use to this day—in which he suggested the right to property for women, something Britain would not itself introduce for another forty-five years. This system of laws was meant to transplant into Indian soil, if not the actual *English* laws, at least the English spirit of objective, impartial scheme of justice and the codes of judicial procedure. Liberal Macaulay wanted a more anglicized education for Indians, while the utilitarians believed that vernacular education was more suitable for India.

Though the term 'imperialism' is perhaps more appropriate as a descriptive for the last decades of the nineteenth century, imperialist moves were underway much earlier. By 1837 (when Victoria becomes Queen), almost the entire Indian subcontinent was under British governance.

> Fifty thousand British personnel, in an amazing feat, ruled over 90 million Indians when Victoria became Queen.

In 1839 the British launched an offensive against Dost Mohammed in Afghanistan. Their presence in the area was short-lived, however, and the 1842 British retreat was to be one of the great catastrophes of conquest. In 1843, Britain, under the leadership of Charles Napier, occupied Sind, and later, after the death of Ranjit Singh, the Punjab in 1849.[1] Karl Marx wrote in 1853 that it was after 1849 that an 'Anglo-Indian empire' was truly established.

More and more Victorians began to believe in an 'imperial destiny' of sorts. Merchants, evangelicals and politicians were beginning to see the enormous economic, social and moral benefits of an imperial Britain. Combined with a liberal reformist zeal—such as the drive against slavery—the Victorians began an era of expansion and consolidation, which took Britain to the status of an imperial power in a quarter of a century, climaxing in the 1870s and '80s.

> In 1850 the total exports to India from Britain and Ireland were £ 8,024,000, of which cotton goods alone amounted to £ 5,220,000 more than one-quarter of the foreign cotton trade.

In terms of military might, the Company army had been divided, since 1839 into three presidency forces, in Madras, Bombay and Bengal. It was paid for by the Company (and was popularly known as 'John Company'), though it was in effect the Crown's army. Control over the provinces often depended, however, not only on the might of the army, but on the effectiveness of what came to be seen as 'personal rule'. Personal rule was embodied in figures such as John and Henry Lawrence, and John Nicholson. This was characterized by a strong sense of personal

---

[1] Napier was also instrumental in creating a separate police department with its own officers, in Sind in 1843. This model was later introduced into Punjab in 1849, Bombay in 1853 and Madras in 1859. However, it was not until the Police Act of 1861 that the basic structure of a police establishment was outlined, a structure that remained until the end of the Raj.

sacrifice and example, an unwavering faith in their divinely ordained mission (which came to be called 'muscular Christianity'), courage, and a passion for justice. The Lawrences, for example, would travel throughout the province, supervising, disbursing justice, and generally assuring people that the Raj was taking care of them.

Christianity in the 1850s was increasingly seen as a distinguishing feature of Englishmen and women. The liberals practised religious tolerance and eschewed any interference in the customs and beliefs of their subjects. What did not change was the British effort at educating Indians. This was partly because the educated classes had not joined the mutineers. As a gesture towards the princes, the British introduced the system of *sanads* (patents), guaranteeing India's princes the right to adopt heirs. Canning's regime introduced the durbars, where Indian princes, officials and landlords were bestowed titles, lands and money. It created the Star of India, a kind of Indian knighthood, to honour the most (loyal and) influential princes.

The ruling class in England may have seen themselves as inheriting the mantle of the Roman Empire (Kipling's poem, 'A British-Roman Song' hailed the 'Imperial fire of Rome' which had devolved as a divine dispensation, 'on us, thy son'). The high imperialist mode—embodied in figures such as Auckland, Hardinge and Ellenborough—laboured under what Francis Hutchins (1967) has aptly called the 'illusion of permanence', drawing upon ideas of British invincibility and supremacy. By the 1850s, Britain was in control of the land from the Khyber to the Irrawady. However, midway through this imperial expansion, 1857 came along.

*

There were moments of unrest and rebellion prior to 1857. One of the first was the Moplah uprising in 1840s' Malabar. The

Moplahs, peasants and cultivating tenants were badly hit by the new arrangements when the British took over the area in 1792. The British recognized the janmi (holder of *janmam* tenure) as absolute owners of the land, with the right to evict tenants. The janmis were 'high-caste' Hindus while the Moplahs were Muslims. Riots broke out in 1849, 1851 and 1852, and later in 1870. In 1855–56 the Santhals protested against the brutal oppression by non-Santhal zamindars, the local police and the European collectors. The resultant insurrection almost erased Company presence from the region.

> In counter-insurrection measures against the Santhals 15–20,000 tribals were killed and 30–50,000 arrested.

Numerous changes were effected in post-1857 India (some of which are detailed below, and the rest in later chapters).

The Indian Civil Service grew. The Englishman was now a 'competitionwallah', a civil servant who had passed an exam to get into the Indian Civil Service. After it became an open competition in 1853—that is, not restricted to Haileybury students—schools such as Cheltenham, Marlborough, Clifton and Bedford contributed candidates in large numbers to it. The English middle-class was the single largest contributor. The Civil Service became famous as one of the most efficient and incorruptible services in the world, though this is not to say that all its officers were wonderful human beings. What remained unchanged was that the Indian Civil Service was effectively closed to Indians (though the Charter Act of 1833 had envisaged Indians sharing the responsibility of governing India). The Proclamation of 1858 had stated that there would be no interference in the religions of the Indians, and that Indians would be given equal opportunity to be part of the administration.

> As late as 1870 there was only one Indian among the 916 members in the Civil Service—from the Tagores in Bengal. And by 1915 Indians were still a minority: 5 per cent of the ICS.

The opening up of the Service was a lot slower, even though men like Elphinstone, among others, recommended its Indianization (the Police Commission of 1902 opened up the police force to educated Indians).

Benjamin Disraeli, the Prime Minister of England, went on to emphasize the commercial, political, philanthropic and religious roles of an imperial power. The liberals argued that projecting Britain as an imperial power meant drawing a line of continuity from India's earlier (despotic) rulers to the (benevolent) British ones.

Commercially, India was of supreme importance to the Empire; by 1880 India was the largest single customer for British manufactured goods.

> By the time of the First World War India took more British exports than Canada, Australia and South Africa put together.

Along with its role as a market, India was also being steadily exploited for its other resources. Indigo was the first major British commercial 'venture' in India, when the British established indigo plantations in Bengal. The plantations were set up and run through extortion contracts with Bengal peasants and West Indian planters. The conditions on these plantations—and later in tea and jute ones—were terrible, and flogging for petty offences was considered a standard punishment. Until the arrival of artificial dye (manufactured by Germans) in 1897, indigo trade flourished.

With the Napoleonic wars, the British began to produce silk in Bengal, and by the mid-nineteenth century, it started extensive rice cultivation for export to Europe. Jute, raw cotton and tea soon became major products in the nineteenth century.

> By 1875 there were 113 tea gardens in Darjeeling alone, producing 4 million pounds of tea. By 1882 there were twenty jute mills with a 20,000-strong labour force.

Cotton, of course, had been available in England for a long time. With England's industrial revolution and the arrival of the power loom in Lancashire, the production of cotton in England increased, and ended the monopoly of Dacca muslin (whose producers could not compete with the cheaper production of Lancashire power looms). Instead, with the decline in exports of cotton from the United States, British exports of raw cotton from India increased. Cotton planting increased massively as a result.

> Between 1863 and 1865 £ 36.5 million worth of raw cotton was exported to England from India.

A few Indians also started their own cotton mills by the mid-nineteenth century. The British government was also involved in two major battles during the post-1857 period. The first was the Afghan War (called the Second Afghan War) in 1878–80. It then saw action in 1885 in the Third Burmese War. There were also tribal uprisings (such as Gilgit, 1891) that required army movement and action, especially near the Afghan borders.

Part of the impact of such cultivation and industrialization of India was the development of its transport, irrigation and communication infrastructure. The British began by restoring several irrigation canals, built by the Mughals, which had fallen into disrepair. The construction of massive buildings was itself an attempt to impose British imperial presence on the Indian landscape. Adapting Grecian and other European models, the British constructed the Mutiny Memorial Hall and Pachaiyappa's Hall in Madras, the Lawrence and Montgomery Halls in Lahore, and other such buildings. The buildings in European style were meant to convey, as several critics have argued, a sense of legacy—of the Greek or Roman Empire upon the British.

British Life in India

The British lived mainly in cantonments and civil lines. Many of them had come out to India to make a career and fortune because their prospects in Britain were rather slim. And once they came out to India, they discovered power.

The English tried to maintain some sense of Englishness even in their new context. Sir Thomas Roe, the first official ambassador from Britain, for instance, insisted that they dine at tables and eat with appropriate cutlery, while being served by men in suitable livery. Their habits of excessive drinking and propensity for meat even during the Indian summer, however, meant that they invariably fell ill. It was said that the Englishman's life in India was limited to 'two monsoons' because cholera and a variety of fevers (malaria being the most common) took many lives. In fact Calcutta and Bombay with their humid climate and mosquitoes became two of the worst spots in British India.

> It is estimated that 57 per cent of EIC men died of sickness in Bengal between 1707 and 1775 and 74 per cent between 1747 and 1756.

India was becoming a health nightmare for the English. Plague and other diseases even necessitated separate Commissions to propose counter-measures in the nineteenth century.

The 'Nabobs' of the eighteenth century returned to England and acquired lands and titles. Their lavish lifestyles, acquired in India, drew attention to them. They went back to England with blacks or Indians as servants, and became 'gentry'. The name was popularized by Samuel Foote's satirical play, *The Nabob* (1768).

Most men of the senior-officer cadre led very comfortable and relaxed lives, even when they were hard-working men. Most had a *chotta hazri* (a light breakfast) before going out for a morning ride. The servants would be given their tasks for the day. Later, around 8 a.m., there would be a full breakfast. Some time after this was allotted to answering letters and looking at papers. They were then dressed by their servants, and left for work around 10 a.m. For the men, work in summer was almost impossible. The heat induced a lethargy that was insurmountable. Lunch-time (or dinner as it was often called), around 2 p.m., saw the men coming home. A short siesta, and some might return to work. Most did not. The evenings were devoted to sport. Some played billiards, other engaged in more community-oriented events like races, balls and dances. There would be the occasional social call, especially for the unmarried men. Then a meal and off to bed. Sundays would invariably mean church, and more formal get-togethers. During their leave they went shooting and hunting in the jungles, in the Himalayan foothills and the central lands (a large number of shikar accounts from the nineteenth century survive). The Club became a typical Raj phenomenon along with the Dak Bungalows and Circuit Houses. The men would meet to play cards, billiards or to drink, as the Club rapidly became the centre of the local European society.

Some men found an interest in nautch-girls and local

entertainments like jugglers or magicians, as captured in Charles Doyley's *The European in India* (1813). Since many men did not find English wives, they often acquired local women—either as wives or concubines (their pay varied: they got Rs 5 per month if they had an English wife and Rs 2.50 if they had a native one). The salaries of junior staff did not allow wives. Visits to local prostitutes was a common phenomenon, and eventually the government had to regulate these through legislation when sexually transmitted diseases became rampant among the troops.[2]

Here is a description of a day in the life of a Sahib from the late-eighteenth century:

> About the hour of seven in the morning, his durvan [door-keeper] opens the gate, and the viranda [gallery] is free to his circars, peons, harcarrahs [messengers] chubdars [constables] huccabadars and consumas [or stewards] writers and solicitors. The head-bearer and jemmadar enter the hall, and his bed-room at eight o' clock. A lady quits his side, and is conducted by a private stair-case either to her own apartment, or out of the yard. The moment the master throws his legs out of bed, the whole posse in waiting rush into his room, each making three salams, by bending the body and head very low, and touching the forehead with the inside of the fingers, and the floor with solicitors of his favour and protection. He condescends, perhaps, to nod or cast an eye towards the solicitors of his favour and protection. In about half an hour after undoing and taking off his long drawers, a clean shirt, breeches, stockings, and slippers are put upon his body, thighs, legs and feet, without any great exertion on his own part than if he were a statue. The barber

---

[2] See Kenneth Ballhatchet (1980).

enters, shaves him, cuts his nails, and cleans his ears. The chillumjee and ewer are brought by a servant whose duty it is, who pours water upon his hands and face, and presents a towel. The superior then walks in state to his breakfasting parlour in his waistcoat; is seated; the consumah makes and pours out his tea, and presents him with a plate of bread or toast. The hair-dresser comes behind, and begins his operation, while the houccaburdar softly slips the upper end of the snake or tube of the hucca into his hand; while the hair-dresser is doing his duty, the gentleman is eating, sipping and smoking by turns. By and by his banian presents himself with humble salams and advances somewhat more forward than the other attendants. If any of the solicitors are of eminence, they are honoured with chairs. These ceremonies are continued perhaps till 10 o'clock [...] If he has visits to make, his peons lead and direct the bearers; and if business renders his presence only necessary, he shows himself, and pursues his other engagements until two o'clock when he and his company sit down perfectly at ease in point of dress and address, to a good dinner, each attended by his own servant ... As it is expected that they shall return to supper, at 4 o'clock they begin to withdraw without ceremony, and step into their palanquins; so that in a few minutes, the man is left to go into his bedroom, when he is instantly undressed to his shirt; and his long drawers put on; and he lies down in his bed, where he sleeps till about 7 or 8 o'clock, then the former ceremony is repeated and clean linen of every kind as in the morning is administered [...] After tea he puts on a handsome coat, and pays visits of ceremony to the ladies; he returns a little before 10 o'clock; supper being served at 10. The company keep together till between 12 and 1 in the morning, preserving great sobriety and decency; and when they depart our hero is conducted to his bedroom, where he finds a female companion to amuse him until the hour of 7 or 8 the next morning. With no greater exertions than these do the Company's servants amass the most splendid fortunes.

(From William MacKintosh, 1782)

Englishwomen had slightly different lifestyles. The women began arriving in British India in the latter decades of the seventeenth century (the first records date to 1670s). Often referred to cruelly as the 'fishing fleet' because many of them were coming out to find eligible husbands, the women found life in India in sharp contrast to the ones they had led in Britain. They did not have much role to play in the political field, since that was a 'masculine' job in the rigid social order of British India. They had to face an enormous amount of hardship, in terms of acquiring the local language, dealing with recalcitrant native servants (whose notions of caste-related purity and taboo they did not understand), the harsh climate and complete boredom. Yet they also had the luxury of numerous servants to do their every bidding, including the care of their children (in fact the native ayah is a constant presence in English writings on India). The children, growing up in the company of ayahs and other native servants (which, in many cases, included a syce to help with their pony rides), often acquired Hindustani as their everyday language. Children were usually sent to Britain to study, usually around the age of seven or eight years. Summers were spent in hill-stations like Simla, Nainital and Mussoorie.

The women usually took a round of their houses in the morning, issuing orders to servants, or inspecting gardens on which many spent a great deal of effort, trying to cultivate lawns in the proper English style. Then there would be the ritual letter-writing (for which we must be grateful, for they present some of the most reliable historical accounts of the everyday life and politics of the Raj) to friends and relatives in Britain. In the afternoons, most women stayed indoors. Later they would dress, usually elaborately, and set out on some social event—a formal dinner, a social call, a play, or simply a walk. Senior ladies often took an interest in marriage alliances for the younger ones. Many of them—Emily Eden, Maria Graham—however, found the social activities tedious and their countrymen dull.

Housing posed its own problems. The heat in summer was intense, and even with the use of tatties and punkahs, unbearable. Those who could, went away to the hill-stations where the weather was much cooler. The higher cadres acquired better houses, and places like Chowringhee, Calcutta, were full of magnificent mansions, each fitted and furnished with luxurious chandeliers, carpeting, marble halls and paintings. Even in these homes, house-keeping was not an easy chore. Insects of all kinds abounded, as did servants, who seemed to have no notions of privacy—something most Memsahibs complained about. The English women were almost completely dependent upon native servants, and many acquired a smattering of the local language to communicate with them. But the Memsahib in general, had almost nothing to do. 'You could very easily get bored', confessed one. Instructional language books were written exclusively for these memsahibs. Many women complained that they could not trust their servants, especially the cook, who most English women suspected of stealing the food. Flora Annie Steel and Grace Gardiner warned in their *The Complete Indian Housekeeper and Cook* (1888):

> A few days of absence or neglect on the part of the mistress, results in the servants falling into their old habits with the inherited conservatism of dirt.

Instructing the servants was a major chore, and numerous guide books were written for the women (the most popular was Flora Annie Steel and G. Gardiner's). But, in most cases, the servants ensured that the women had absolutely nothing to do. Some of the ladies took interest in social activities. Lady Canning, for instance, set about beautifying Barrackpore's Viceregal gardens, and is even credited with inventing a new kind of sweet (called 'Lady Cannings'). Others, like Fanny Parkes, went hunting. Some commentators, like Maud Diver, believed that India changed the English woman irrevocably. Diver commented:

> Those who live for any length of time in India have to reckon with that insidious tendency to fatalism—to accept men and things as they find them, without enthusiasm, and without criticism—which lurks in the very air they breathe.

The memsahibs (as E.M. Forster was to note in his writings) were arrogant, often unhappy members of the Raj. They rarely made direct contact with India—often the only Indians they knew were servants—and tried to reproduce English habits, mannerisms, and even gardens in India. They also spent a good deal of time, according to Maud Diver's *The Englishwoman in India* (1909), in trying to keep their children from developing a 'promiscuous intimacy' with the native servants, who worshipped the 'baba-log'; the children of the whites clearly grew up believing they belonged to a superior race. The memsahibs' exact contribution to the empire has been the subject of a great deal of scrutiny—were they active supporters of the empire ideal? Did they see the empire as a means of escaping the rigid patriarchal structures in Britain by 'doing' something on their own in the colony? They did indeed try very hard to retain some measure of 'Englishness'. For instance, they were constantly trying to replicate the prevalent fashion 'back home'.

The servant population of an average English house in India ranged from eight to ten (for the lower cadres) to about sixty for the higher, though several had a larger number. Part of the reason for the large numbers was the caste hierarchy that prevented native servants from doing all kinds of jobs. The Englishman discovered that only particular castes would cook, just as not every servant would handle leather (a point noted by several residents and travellers). A detailed listing of servants is available in Spear's magnificent social history, *The Nabobs* (1963).

G.O. Trevelyan provides a detailed summary of a particular class of English men and women in British India (*The Competitionwallah*, 1866):

> During the ten months in the year the collector resides at the station. The Government does not provide its servants with house-room; but they seldom experience any inconvenience in finding suitable accommodation, for the native landlords make a point of reserving for every official the residence which had been occupied by his predecessor ... The life of a collector in the Moffusil is varied and bustling even in the hot weather. He rises at daybreak, and goes straight from his bed to the saddle. Then off he gallops across fields bright with dew to visit the scene of the late dacoit robbery; or to see with his own eyes whether the crops of the zemindar who is so unpunctual with his assessment have really failed; or to watch with fond parental care the progress of his pet embankment. Perhaps he has a run with the bobbery pack of the station, consisting of a superannuated foxhound, four beagles, a greyhound, the doctor's retriever, and a Skye terrier belonging to the assistant-magistrate ... They probably start a jackal, who gives them a sharp run of ten minutes, and takes refuge in a patch of sugar-cane;

whence he steals away in safety while the pack are occupied in mobbing a fresh fox and a brace of wolf-cubs, to the remarkably full field of sportsmen, with one pair of top-boots amongst them. On their return, the whole party adjourn to the subscription swimming bath, where they find their servants ready with clothes, razors, and brushes. After a few headers, and 'chota hasree', or 'little breakfast', of tea and toast, flavoured with the daily papers and scandal about the commissioner, the collector returns to his bungalow, and settles down to the hard business of the day. Seated under a punkah in his verandah, he works through the contents of one dispatch-box, or 'bokkus', as the natives call it, after another; signing orders, and passing them on to the neighbouring collectors; dashing through drafts, to be filled up by his subordinates; writing reports, minutes, digests, letters of explanation, of remonstrance, of warning, of commendation. Noon finds him quite ready for ... the favourite meal in the Moffusil, where the teatray is lost amidst a crowd of dishes, fried fish, curried fowl, roast kid and mintsauce, and mango-fool. Then he sets off on his buggy to Cutcherry, where he spends the afternoon in hearing and deciding questions connected with land and revenue. If the cases are few, and easy to be disposed off, he may get away in time for three or four games at rackets in the new court of glaring white plaster, which a rich native has built, partly as a speculation, and partly to please the Sahibs. Otherwise, he drives with his wife on the race-course; or plays at billiards with the inspector of police; or, if horticulturally inclined, superintends the labours of his Mollies. Then follows dinner, and an hour of reading or music. By ten o'clock he is in bed, with his little ones in cribs, enclosed within the same mosquito curtains as their parents.

The ladies, poor things, come in for all the disagreeables of up-country life. Without plenty of work, India is unbearable. That alone can stave off langour and a depth of ennui of which a person who has never left Europe can form no conception. In a climate which keeps every one within doors from eight in the morning till five in the evening, it is, humanly speaking, impossible to make sufficient occupation for yourself, if it does not come to you in the way of business. After a prolonged absence from home, reviews and newspapers become uninteresting. Good novels are limited in number, and it is too much to expect that a lady should read history and poetry for six hours every day. What well-regulated female can dress an object in a society of a dozen people, who know her rank to a title, and her income to a pice; or music, when her audience consists of a Punkah-wallah and a Portuguese Ayah? Some ladies, as a matter of conscience go very closely into the details of household affairs; but after a time they come to the conclusion that it is better to allow the servants to cheat within a certain margin, for the sake of peace and quietness; for cheat they will, do what you may. Oh! The dreariness of that hour in the middle of the long day, when the children are asleep, and your husband has gone to tiffin with the judge, and the book-club has nothing but Latham's 'Nationalities of Europe' ... and the English post has come in yesterday, with nothing but a letter from your old governess, congratulating you for being settled among the associations of the Mahommedan conquerors of India, and asking you to take some notice of her nephew, who is in the office of the Accountant-General of Bombay. It is very up-hill work for a lady out here to keep up her spirits and pluck, and her interest in general subjects. The race-week, the visit to her sister in the Punjab, the hope of being ordered down to Calcutta, the reminiscences of the sick-leave, and the anticipations of the furlough, are the consolations of a life which none but a very brave or a very stupid woman can endure long without suffering in mind, health, and tournure. If a lady becomes dowdy, it is all up to her; and the temptations to dowdiness in the Moffusil cannot be well exaggerated...

The native servant was not always treated well. Flogging was common, and kindness a rarity, as the *Times* correspondent William Russell noted with considerable shock. By the 1820s the idea of the superiority of their race altered their perceptions of the natives. They now began to regard the native cultures with contempt. This cultural misunderstanding (and often non-understanding) was to prove crucial in the decades to come. Most men and women assimilated the stereotypes of the untrustworthy native, the lustful Indian male and the evil native religions. This in turn fuelled their attitudes towards natives: indifference, anger, distrust, often in equal mix. What they did not realize was that the natives were alert to this change in attitudes.

The British in India followed a strict hierarchy, as specified in the 1841 rules of 'Precedence in the East Indies'. The Governor General was followed by the Governors of the Presidencies of Bengal, Madras, Bombay and Agra. Then came the Chief Justice of Bengal, the Bishop of Calcutta, and then their counterparts in Madras and Bombay. The Army was also hierarchy-conscious, where the Company's soldiers and Royal officers jostled for priority. Even civilians were hierarchized according to their service. Among the non-civil servants in India there were the noncommissioned troops, the business civilians (termed 'boxwallahs', a term once used to describe British travelling salesmen in India) and missionaries. 'Visiting', evening drives, polo, extended dinner parties, the 'calling cards' were all integral to the rituals of social life. The socializing was governed by the order of precedence, and it was the memsahibs who observed that the codes were observed Charles Allen (1978).

The men often went hunting. In this the local Rajas, who often had to make all the arrangements for the Sahib and his entourage, supported them. On the other side of the gender barrier, memsahibs such as Fanny Parkes (1850) visited zenanas, and met the native women—records of these meetings are often the highlight of the English woman's travelogue/memoir. They were greeted with elaborate courtesy and seem to have enormously enjoyed their visits.

In most cases in the eighteenth century, there was little social interaction with the Indians. The English met munshis and other native assistants, and socialized with their own kind. This varied, and on the Western side, the Indians, especially the banias, were able to deal with the Europeans on a more equal footing. Through the eighteenth century, even if there was segregation, it was not informed by racial prejudices or dislike. The European objections to Indian culture—Hindu and Muslim—concerned their so-called superstitions and practices (such as the purdah and sati).

From the mid-eighteenth century things began to change. As the British presence in India grew in extent and strength, a sense of superiority began to emerge. Paradoxically this was simultaneous with rigorous attempts to understand Indian culture (the 'Orientalist' phase, already mentioned). An increasing rejection of Indian culture, and Indians, begins to appear in English writings from the 1750s. There was also, again paradoxically, increased social interaction with the aristocrats and higher echelons of the native society (though this rarely extended to interaction with native *women* of the same class).

With the progress of the Raj—the imperial British presence in India—in the 1820s and 1830s, there was an increasing segregation of the English from the Indians. White Town and the Cantonment were often worlds unto themselves, each with its own hierarchies and social life. By the late-eighteenth century, according to Percival Spear, the visitor to Madras or Bombay would never enter Black Town. The British officers paid almost no attention to the native vakils or assistants. Where once the munshi used to be at least acknowledged we now see a distancing. In 1810, an English writer commented: 'Europeans have little connexion with natives of either religion.' While the Nabobs of the eighteenth century heartily adopted native modes of dress and food, the Sahibs (as the later, nineteenth-century Britons in India were called) refused to have anything native about them. A lady travelling through India in the 1820s wrote: 'it was the extremity of bad taste to appear in anything of Indian manufacture—neither muslin, silk, flowers nor even ornaments, however beautiful.' The British withdrew, separated themselves, even as a heightened racism emerged.[3]

The Raj had stopped listening to the natives.

*

1857 marked one of the first sustained (and popular, as Rudransghu Mukherjee has argued) opposition to British policy, administration and rule in India, even though it was widespread mainly in northern India and was marked by the non-participation of Gurkhas, Sikhs, Rajputs and several native princes. With evangelicalism, English education and laws, and now weaponry, the Indians began

---

[3] See Bolt (1971) and Stepan (1982).

to feel that their culture and ways of life were severely interfered with.

Later, perhaps building on the incipient nationalism generated by 1857, came the Indian National Congress, and all the threats the Mutiny held out—of the imminent nationalist fervour, the unification of the natives against a common foe, and the eventual collapse of the Raj—returned to haunt British presence in India. This time it would be more organized and sustained. This time it would spread across the subcontinent. This time there would be no native brutality.

This time there would be: Gandhi.

One
The Gathering Storm

India 1757. A brilliant soldier, Robert Clive, who had arrived in India after suicide attempts and a failed youth in Britain, and was perhaps schizophrenic, wins a decisive battle at Plassey.

India 1857. Sepoys of the Company's army rebel against their British officers, and the country witnesses its first major insurrection against foreign rule.

The two moments are separated by exactly one hundred years. Clive's victory in 1757 decided the course of the British experience of India. It transformed the East India Company—originally a rag-tag band of merchants and mercenaries seeking adventure and fortune—into a ruling authority. And of course, once the Company acquired political power it set about making large-scale social, political and economic changes in the subcontinent. It now ruled about two-thirds of the subcontinent as the agent of the British government. Native princes and rulers suddenly discovered that their political activities were subject to scrutiny, and occasionally downright interference.

Power, administration and learning developed another tongue—English. Missionaries, both European and native, preached in churches, ramshackle buildings and under trees, across the subcontinent. Grey iron and steel added a different shade to the landscape in the form of railway lines, bridges and other structures. Traditional rites and rituals were suddenly classified as evil, and prohibited in the name of 'reform'. Massive buildings flying the Union Jack higher than any native flag proclaimed the power of the Raj. Powerful feudal landlords woke up to find they owned little or no land to lord over—there were new lords now. Tribals, locals and native cultural artefacts found themselves the subject of detailed anthropological and literary analysis in ponderously written tomes and at sepulchral-toned intellectual meetings.

The subcontinent, William Shakespeare would have said, was 'translated'.

The natives were puzzled, angered and alarmed. The British were certain, confident and aggressive.

Their confidence and certainty depended, to a large extent, on the Company's army stationed in barracks in towns and cities from the North-West Provinces to Rangoon. More accurately, it depended on the loyalty and efficiency of the *native* troops in the Company's army.

> At the time of the Mutiny the Bengal Army had seventy-four native regiments—fifty-four of these revolted.

This native component of the Company's army heard the same rumours as the civilian population. They had similar anxieties though they may not have expressed discontent or anxiety or participated in the debates about the Raj. For the native troops to be affected and disillusioned it required a more direct cause, something that affected their lives directly. But they too, placid and obedient in their crowded barracks and disciplined on the parade grounds, felt the weather changing.

the gathering storm

> By 1857 the total strength of the Company army in India was 280,000. Of this there were 235,000 Indians and about 45,000 Europeans.

The breeze was gentle at first—it rustled through their thick uniforms as they took orders from their British officers, protected the Residency or accompanied the sahib or memsahib to the city. The breeze wafting across the plains of northern India would visit several spots, contributing something through each of its whispers. This whispering breeze spread news, rumour and anxiety, even as anxiety drove the breeze harder onward. The breeze of 1857 did not dissipate. It did not disappear. It became something else entirely, shaping lives, cities, histories. It shaped a different empire.

> *An early insurrection occurred at Vellore in 1806. Vellore prison was where the sons of Tipu Sultan had been imprisoned, after their father's death. Did the presence of the princes, scions of the ruler of Mysore, help channellize the mutiny in 1806? Did the princes become potential symbols of hope for natives—that their own (native) kings could perhaps replace the usurping British? There is a parallel from 1857: the sepoys briefly installed the Mughal emperor Bahadur Shah Zafar on the throne. It says something about nineteenth-century Indian communal harmony that in these cases both Hindu and Muslim sepoys voluntarily (neither the princes nor Zafar were in power) paid allegiance to Muslim rulers. It is also interesting that armed resistance in both cases centred around the figure of a Muslim king.*

*

Numerous rumours and items of bad news winged their way across northern India. Predominant among them was the 'news' that the British government, now fully in power, was planning to undertake massive conversions, of both Muslims and Hindus, to Christianity. This particular rumour was an extremely disturbing one for the natives not only because it touched on questions of faith, but also because it was seen as a betrayal of trust—thus far the British had refrained from interfering in the religion of the natives.[1] In fact, even the Army respected the caste system, and sepoys were allowed to cook their meals separately and wear caste marks. Mrs R.M. Coopland, who kept an account of the siege of Gwalior, wrote: 'their religion and caste are attended to ... even their festival days are kept.' After the 1813 Act more missionaries entered India, and itinerant preachers were now stationed everywhere across the country.

> *It is the peculiar and bounden duty of the Legislature to promote, by all just and prudent means, the interests and happiness of the inhabitants in India; and that for these ends, such measures ought to be adopted as may gradually tend to their advancement in useful knowledge, and to their religious and moral improvement.*
>
> *—Resolution of the English Parliament, 14 May 1793*

The activities of the multitasking Serampore missionaries, (headed by William Carey, who translated the Bible into Bangla, installed a printing press in Serampore and wrote on Indian

---

[1] The anxiety may have been further flamed by the conversion of Dr Chaman Lal and Master Ramachandra (the latter a Mathematics teacher at Delhi College). Mufti Sadruddin Azurda, the chief Muslim judge in Delhi, asked students to leave Delhi College after this incident.

flowers) ranged from education to proselytizing. Some Army officers, such as Colonel S.G. Wheler of the 34th Native Infantry at Barrackpore (a unit that will go down in history for another reason), openly sought the conversion of his sepoys.

> Sepoy comes from the Persian 'sipahi'.

The rumour of imminent conversion was fuelled by other actions. In the drive to modernize India, the British had introduced trains, telegraphs and roads. In order to lay tracks or widen the roads, the construction often required demolition of places of worship. The Indians believed that the demolition of temples and mosques to prepare for metallic monsters (the train) or snaking wires (the telegraph lines) was unacceptable. The train, when the common Indian could afford it, erased caste differences: 'upper-caste' shoulders rubbed against 'lower-caste' ones, items of luggage scraped together without respecting the 'purity' of their owners' castes. It seemed to suggest to the Indians a total lack of concern about the natives' faith. Britain, argued Karl Marx, was engaged in a double mission: 'one destructive, the other regenerating, the annihilation of old Asiatic society, and the laying of the material foundations of Western society in Asia'. That is, it was destroying an entire way of life, even as it 'united' India through the telegraph, the railway, a free press and other Western 'imports'.

> There were three Presidency armies—Bengal, Bombay and Madras. By 1857 the Bengal Army was notorious as the most ill-disciplined of the three.

English education, launched by Lord Macaulay's notorious Minute of 1835 and put in place by Charles Wood and others after 1850, was, according to the natives who went to these new schools, no respecter of alternative systems of belief. While earlier the British officers and Orientalists (a group of scholars, led by Sir William Jones, who founded the Asiatic Society in Calcutta in 1784) were respectful of and interested in native festivals, literature and the arts, the new breed of officers seemed to despise the native cultures.

> William Jones (1746–94) translated *Shakuntala* into English.

Jailers and priests preached to prisoners. There was now communal cooking, which did not allow prisoners to cook their own food and thus maintain caste distinctions. Students in mission schools were gifted with the Bible (a system that persisted well after the 'Mutiny', as seen in articles and photographs from periodicals like the *Juvenile Missionary Herald*).

> There were nineteen missionary societies and 222 mission stations in India by 1851.

The Western system of medicine required that all patients were treated alike by the doctors and hospital administration—irrespective of questions of the 'veiled' woman and caste.

Perhaps the most visible marker, for the Indians, of the government's indifference to their beliefs was the great reforms that were initiated after 1830s. Led by Charles Grant and the rest of the 'Clapham Sect', and supported by Raja Rammohan Roy (1772–1833) and others, the government banned sati, encouraged widowed women to remarry and allocated separate funds for women's education in schools. This 'reformist' zeal was perceived as unacceptable interference in native traditions which, the Hindus argued, preceded even European civilization.

J.B. Hearsey wrote to the Deputy Adjutant-General, W.A.J. Mayhew at Barrackpore, in a report filed in late January 1857:

> Perhaps those Hindus who are opposed to the marriage of widows in Calcutta are using underhand means to thwart Government in abolishing the restraints lately removed by law for the marriage of widows, and conceive if they can make a party of the ignorant classes in the ranks of the army believe their religion or religious prejudices are eventually to be abolished by force, and by force they are all to be made Christians, and thus by shaking their faith in Government lose the confidence of their officers by inducing sepoys to commit offences (such as incendiarism) so difficult to put a stop to or prove, they will gain their object.

Hearsey was definitely worried about the effect these rumours might have on his native soldiers. The tone draws our attention to the potent elements mixed into the breeze in January 1857: religion, reform, soldiers—Hearsey is predicting that the lower ranks of the native troops would believe ill of the government because they would listen to the rumours. And because these concerned questions of faith and religion, the effect will be powerful and dangerous.

The rumour-breeze of conversion was also helped along in its course across native troops of the Company by the 1856 General Service Enlistment Act. The Act obligated the new recruits to the Bengal Army to serve overseas if so required by the government. This was a shock to the Hindu sepoys, who believed that crossing the seas would mean loss of caste.

> Initially Brahmins and high-caste Hindus constituted the main component of the native Army. Later, in order to break this monopoly, Charles Napier ensured that Sikhs and Muslims also enlisted.

The sepoys believed that the Company, which they had served faithfully, now expected loyalty at the cost of their faith and religion. They also believed that from such a condition of service to conversion was but a step, for conversion would mean a larger number of Christian soldiers who would not mind serving anywhere in the world.

> *The sepoys were paid one-third the salary of European troops. Most of the sepoys came from the Oudh region (often called 'the nursery of soldiers')—in fact in the Bengal Army, three-fifth of the men in sixty-three infantry regiments came from Oudh. Many of the sepoys were Brahmins, upper-caste Hindus and Muslims. They lived in harsh conditions—in poorly maintained barracks and with their uniforms (made of thick European cloth, boots and all) exceedingly uncomfortable in the Indian climate. Promotions were almost non-existent, and many would move up in the hierarchy when they had only a few years of service left. The highest-ranking native officer was still lower than a junior English one. His pay was not commensurate with the price of food grains and general costs of living (a sepoy in Bengal would be spending Rs 3–5 every month on food grains alone). Initially, the English officer had been more understanding of their sentiments and needs. As the Raj progressed, however, the number of such officers lessened and the regiments were officered by Englishmen who had no interest in the men. Changes made in their service conditions through Dalhousie's regime (1847–56) and the early decades of the nineteenth century left the sepoys increasingly discontented. They were now required to pay for their postage, for instance. Those found to be unfit for active service were re-employed on cantonment duty instead of receiving invalid pension and retiring. Therefore the cartridge issue was only the proverbial last straw, rather than the main cause—to the sepoy it was the climax of a series of measures taken to degrade and harass the native soldier.*

When the Company stopped using the Mughal emperor's name on the coins in 1835, it marked a major reversal of policy— one that did not find favour among the subjects of the subcontinent. All along, the Company had projected itself as the vassal of the Mughal emperor, a vassal that continued to recognize the supreme authority of Bahadur Shah Zafar and acted in his name. From the role of dependants and subsidiaries, the Company now sought to present itself as the ruler. Lord Dalhousie (1812–60), the Governor General immediately before 'Mutiny' Canning, was a brilliant, if ruthless, administrator. It was Dalhousie who decided that India was better off under British rule than at any other time in its history. Driven by such an idea of an empire where all subjects were happy under the British sun, Dalhousie proceeded to annex numerous princely kingdoms. Sattara, Jhansi and Nagpur were annexed through an ingenious mechanism—the Doctrine of Lapse. Many British officers welcomed the move, arguing, like Dalhousie, that British rule saved the people from their (native) despotic and incompetent rulers. Thus a letter in *Daily News*, 22 March 1856, said:

> The British government had no other alternative except either withdraw altogether from the country, leaving its inhabitants to a still worse fate, or to administer entirely the government of the country…

Thus, in this argument, the kings were deposed for the welfare of the natives, and not for any untoward imperial ambition.[2]

Annexation was not just a bad move politically, it was also a reflection of the Raj's lack of cultural understanding. Hindu

---

[2] Not all British officers supported annexation, however. Officers like W.H. Sleeman (who had been the British Resident in Oudh) and John Low warned that annexation would anger the natives, and disillusion them against the British.

society had long accepted the arrangement that if a man did not have a natural-born heir, he could adopt a son and successor. Dalhousie argued that a king without a natural heir could not adopt a successor—the kingdom would be taken over by the Company. A biological problem was to be resolved through political legislation!

The loss of kingdom was perhaps a political disaster for both the British and the subcontinent, as subsequent developments proved. But it was an even greater disaster in terms of the message it sent out and the speculations it gave rise to. The natives saw their kings—who, in typical feudal fashion, they saw as icons of divinity—insulted and their powers taken away. They also saw the British as directly altering the milieu in which they lived—the fidelity to the king, the caste system, and the power and glory of the Mughal emperor.

During these troubled times, Nana Sahib, the Raja of Bithur (near Cawnpore), may have conducted secret parleys with other local kings and princes. He is said to have travelled as far as Ambala to ascertain the groundswell of resentment against the British. A contemporary historian, John Kaye, firmly believed that Nana Sahib was involved in detailed preparations for revolt, thus suggesting that the Mutiny was not an impulsive outbreak. Kaye wrote in his account of 1857: 'There is nothing in my mind more clearly substantiated than the complicity of the Nana Sahib in wide-spread intrigues before the outbreak of the Mutiny.'

Clearly, the 1850s saw a subcontinent where the rumour breeze often left discontent and anxiety in areas it passed through. It was in such a period of tension and anxiety that a prophecy fed itself to this breeze. According to the prophecy, supposedly one hundred years old, the British would leave India exactly one hundred years after their government established itself in India. Dated from 1757 and Plassey, it meant that the British would be overthrown (or would leave, though there seemed little likelihood that they would just up and away as though the vacation was over) in or around 1857.

> *Two Other Prophecies*
>
> *1843: Henry Lawrence said that the British defences in Delhi would collapse if ever attacked.*
>
> *1851: Charles Napier said that the Army in India would rebel because their British officers were not good enough.*

The more visionary of the English officers and statesmen—and there were very few by this time—believed India was getting ready to explode. Lord Canning (1812–62), who was to experience this explosion first hand as Governor General of India in 1857–58, was one of them. Charles Napier (1782–1853), the Commander-in-Chief, believed that the Bengal Army was a cauldron of discontent—in fact, he even informed the then Governor General, Dalhousie, that a mutiny was imminent.

> **Lord Dalhousie** *himself was alert to the fact that natives heavily outnumbered Europeans in almost every town. He had, therefore, warned against the withdrawal or reduction of European troops. He wrote in a letter of 6 August 1855: 'a country, though tranquil and unwarlike in itself, is yet liable to such volcanic outbursts of popular violence as this now before us.' He was referring to the ongoing Santhal rebellion.*

Charles Metcalfe mentions that he always expected to wake up to find India lost. General John Bennet Hearsey, the Divisional Commander at Barrackpore, was also certain of the impending storm.

> **Canning:** Charles John, Viscount Canning was the Governor General of India, 1855–62, with the Mutiny years right in the middle. His term was extremely turbulent, starting with the war with Persia, the Oudh annexation problems of 1856, and finally the Mutiny. He supported Dalhousie's stand that sepoys would have to serve anywhere the government required them to—a major cause of anxiety before the Mutiny. Later, he became notorious for deploring the excesses of the British soldiers, and acquired the epithet of 'Clemency Canning' for his plea for a more sober response to the Mutiny. After the Mutiny he confiscated the lands belonging to the rebel taluqdars, he was made India's first Viceroy in 1858.

The breeze of discontent had gathered substantial strength by now. It needed, however, just that additional element to whip it into a dangerous storm. As it blew over the country in 1856 and early 1857, it found not one but two such elements. These became the twin epicentres, the two vortices of the wind that was now growing into a storm.

*

One was a political situation, the other a technological one. The first event was the annexation of, among various local kingdoms, Oudh. The second was the introduction of a new kind of rifle and cartridge.

> *The Major Annexations*
> **1849:** the Punjab
> **1849:** Sattara
> **1853:** Nagpur
> **1854:** Jhansi
> **1856:** Oudh

Dalhousie declared that Oudh (as the British called Awadh) was badly governed—the term used was actually 'misgovernment'—by Nawab Wajid Ali Shah (1822–87). The Company had offered to negotiate with Shah. They proposed that he keep the main palace and titles, and receive an annual pension of Rs 1,800,000 if he conceded the state, just so that the Company could take care of the people, who had allegedly been much abused by Shah. The Queen Mother would receive an additional Rs 100,000 annually if she could persuade her son (Wajid Ali Shah) to sign! Unfortunately, Wajid Ali Shah had too much pride to stoop to a commercial transaction of this kind. He refused. The British annexed Oudh.

Apparently, Wajid Ali Shah's main fault was that he loved poetry, religion and sensual pleasures a bit too much to be a good ruler (and we all know how subversive and irresponsible poetry can be!). The irony was Dalhousie himself knew that the charge was not entirely accurate, as he admitted privately.[3]

The Muslim populace in northern India was angered at the sheer gall of the man (Dalhousie) whom they had just years before praised for setting up the railways. The result was an interesting development: both Hindus and Muslims came together in defence of their princes deposed by what was now identifiable as a common foe: the Company. After the annexation of Oudh both Hindus and Muslims composed and sang songs in praise of Wajid Ali Shah (these were recorded and published by William Crooke in the periodical *Indian Antiquary* in 1911).

---

[3] This crucial confession appears in a collection of Dalhousie's private papers (Baird 1911, p. 344).

Wajid Ali Shah: *The last king of Oudh, exiled to Calcutta by the British in 1856. He was later arrested and imprisoned on suspicion of having incited the rebellion, though there is no evidence that he supported the mutineers. Begum Hazrat Mahal and their young son, Birjis Qadr, the British believed, were acting on behalf of Wajid Ali Shah—probably an unfounded assumption. He was a patron of music and the arts and was believed to lead a licentious lifestyle—a theme the British, with their fascination for the private life of Indians, were to emphasize. Songs mourning his departure from Oudh were composed. Here is a sample:*

The Departure of Wajid Ali Shah from Calcutta

O Sripati Maharaj (Ram), thou art the remover of calamity.
When will my Lord return to his country?
The first halt was Cawnpore: the second at Benares.
The third halt was at Calcutta, and the Queens fled to the hills.
Bullets were flying in the Alam Bagh: there were cannons in the Machchi-bhawan
Swords were drawn in the Bailey Guard: it was dark with arrows.
Outside mourned the sepoys: in the gateway mourned the Kotwal.
In the palace mourned the Queens, and let their long locks fall dishevelled.
The cannons were left in the magazine: the elephants were left in the stables.
The swift horses were left in the city: our friends forgot their sympathy.
The Queens wept in the Kaisar Bagh, and let their long locks fall.
Saith Raghunath Junwar: 'It was the pleasure (Ram) that we should be in exile.'

Dalhousie was thus an instrument in the unification of the subcontinent—a condition for which his successor and later countrymen and women would pay dearly during 1857–58.

> *1857 was not the first time the sepoys had revolted against their officers and administration.*
>
> *In 1806 in Vellore the sepoys had revolted because they were asked to wear a new kind of headdress. This headdress had a leather cockade. The rumour was that this cockade was made of cowhide or pigskin. In addition, the sepoys were asked to stop wearing caste marks and trim their beards—the former offensive to the Hindu sepoy and the latter to the Muslim one (as we can see, the debates about scarves and veils among non-white races in twentieth-century England, USA and Europe has a history). Fourteen British officers and over 100 British soldiers were killed.*
>
> *In 1824 a Barrackpore regiment revolted because they were asked to go to Burma, and crossing the seas was unacceptable to the Hindu sepoy. The 47th regiment was disbanded after this.*
>
> *After 1849's annexation of the Punjab, ninety-five men of the 66th battalion were tried for mutiny, and the battalion was disbanded.*
>
> *In 1852 the 38th Native Infantry refused to go to Burma, and objected to the order.*

This was the unusual, and memorable, feature of 1857: Hindus and Muslims alike recognized the *Mughal* emperor as the defender of their respective faiths (in fact Hindu sepoys also called themselves 'jihadis') and enthroned him as the 'Emperor of Hindustan'. This acknowledgement of a Muslim king as a common icon was, perhaps, a recognition of Zafar's own character. Zafar had been one of the most tolerant and accepting Mughal rulers since Akbar. He insisted on viewing the Dussehra procession and banned cow slaughter even for Idd because it would offend the Hindu subjects.

> The British Government paid Zafar an annual stipend of Rs 12 lakh in 1812, and raised it to Rs 15 lakh in 1833.

The second development had to do with arms. The older musket was to be replaced by the more sophisticated Enfield rifle. This rifle required that the cartridge—which now was a single unit consisting of the powder and the bullet—had to have its tip bitten off so that the charge would ignite. This cartridge was wrapped in greased paper. The central question was the content of this grease.

> The greased cartridges were first sent out to India in 1853. But this lot of cartridges was returned to England in 1855.

Originally the greasing material used was a combination of vegetable oil and wax. Later the manufacturers discovered that tallow from beef and pig fat was a cheaper option.

> *In 1853 the Commander-in-Chief in India, the distinctively named William Gomm, had suggested to the government that unless the components of the grease used were acceptable to the entire native army, it might be dangerous to use them. His prophetic advice was unwisely ignored by the Military Board.*

Now, when the manufacture of these cartridges began in India after 1855 the makers were not instructed on the composition of the material. However, none of the new cartridges had actually been issued. The sepoys heard of it through another means. The new rifles were tested in various musketry depots, and sepoys from select regiments had been sent to train with these. It was these trainees who first began to wonder about the cartridges they might have to use with the new rifles. The rumours about the cartridges spread far and wide, and news of the discontent did reach at least a few British officers. Some took the warning seriously and sought to remove the sepoys' doubts regarding the cartridges. George Anson, the Commander-in-Chief in India, had in fact ordered that the cartridges be issued ungreased—an order that came a bit too late in the day, well after the rumour and disaffection had entered the already-mentioned breeze blowing through India in 1857.

> *The cartridge question has never been satisfactorily solved. There may have been adequate grounds for suspicion regarding the grease used. One crucial bit of evidence is in Lord Canning's letter of 7 February 1857 in which he stated that the grievance regarding the grease may have been 'well founded'.*

Other British believed, later, that the Mutiny leaders used the cartridge issue as an excuse—an idea that was shared by some natives too.

Most of the officers, however, chose to laugh off the very idea of Mutiny by the faithful sepoys. They continued to believe that to the native the Englishman was '*mai-baap*'—an old ethos

> 'In the cartridge dispute a religious element was involved, which served their purpose; inasmuch as the mass of the people (who are necessarily ignorant) were deceived and really believed that they were fighting for religion.'
>
> —Hakim Ahsan Ullah at Zafar's trial

where the English officer represented the benevolent if stern protector and provider of the native. In fact, Colonel John Ewart at Cawnpore is said to have cried out 'My children, don't do this, this is not your way' when he faced his mutinous soldiers! (He was eventually killed at Satichaura). Unfortunately, the *mai-baap* role did not fit the mercenary, callous and incompetent English officer of the 1840s—that day was long gone.

> *George Anson (1797–1857):* Commander-in-Chief of India when the Mutiny broke out. From all accounts he was a pleasant-enough person, but quite unsuitable to the task of resolving the conflict. He was also not very happy with the Company troops. At Ambala, when faced with the news of sepoy dissatisfaction regarding the cartridges, Anson asked the Indian officers present to dispel the rumours. Even on hearing of the uprising, Anson did not leave Shimla for a few days. He left for Delhi from Ambala only on 24 May, an action that earned him the ire of several officers. It was Anson who asked William Hodson to raise his famous irregular cavalry, 'Hodson's Horse'. He died soon after arriving at Karnal, on 26 May, of cholera.

This was where the British erred very badly indeed, because rumours, like bad dreams, have a way becoming real. Stories of disaffection were rooted in fact, and 'rebellion' and 'mutiny' were fast becoming actualities. Mysterious fires broke out in barracks and bungalows. Flaming arrows were shot into the air and at British residences. Mainoddin Hassan Khan's narrative mentions that the Telegraph Office at Ranigunj and an Englishman's bungalow were burnt down in January 1857—thus providing clear evidence of a mutinous spirit in Delhi. But the most puzzling of all the troubling events involved the utterly innocuous chappatis.

Chappatis, the staple fare of the northern Indian meal, began to circulate across the country from sometime around January 1857, or perhaps even earlier. Parallel to the circulation of rumours (and the movement of disgruntled sepoys from disbanded regiments, who moved back across the Oudh region to their native villages), these chappatis were noticed even by the British officers.

> 'I consider that the distribution of the chappatis first began in Oudh.'
> —Hakim Ahsan Ullah, at Zafar's trial

Several officers recorded their appearances, and pondered over the possible meaning. Some suspected that they were perhaps a new messaging service or a code for insurrection. Others assumed, in a land where superstition reigned and weird rituals were commonplace, that these were meant to be propitiatory—to appease gods against the spread of that summer scourge, cholera. A specific number of chappatis arrived at villages. The receiving village was asked to make an additional number and send them onward. In this way, they traversed hundreds of miles, with each village contributing. An extraordinarily efficient relay and postal system designed by the natives as an indigenous counter to the telegraph installed by the British government, the chappatis seemed to have reached even remote villages in northern India. What is interesting is that sometimes the villages themselves did not know the reason for the circulation of chappatis. To this day the chappati movement remains a mystery—were they simple rituals of appeasement? Or were they coded messages for insurrection?

> 'They [chappatis] were circulated indiscriminately, without reference to either religion, among the peasantry of the country.'
> —Jat Mall, at Zafar's trial

> *In addition to chappatis there were two other mysterious objects at the centre of the rumour mill. One was lotus flowers, which also circulated through the country. The other was bone dust. It was believed that the British mixed bone dust (from cows and pigs, to offend both Hindus and Muslims) in the flour sold. This was surely speculation, for the British had nothing to do with the flour business, but the rumour served as a useful fuel for the Mutiny.*

What is certain is that the chappatis were not the only means—if they were indeed a form of messaging service—of communication and contact.

> A mysterious Hindu fakir was reported in Meerut in April 1857, one month before the Mutiny. He had been sighted in Ambala a few months earlier. At Meerut he is supposed to have stayed with the 20th Native Infantry. This fakir was never identified, and his exact role in subsequent events remains unknown.

Maulvis and itinerant fakirs, such as the above Meerut fakir, walked miles, talking to people about the Raj.[4] A mendicant was apprehended as far south as Hyderabad (Deccan), where he had been exhorting the soldiers to rebel. A maulvi preaching jihad was also arrested in Hyderabad. In fact John Kaye, writing his account of the Mutiny, was certain that the Hindu Dharma Sabha and the

---

[4] An official memorandum was filed on this mysterious fakir. See S.A.A. Rizvi and M.L. Bhargava (ed) *Freedom Struggle in Uttar Pradesh* (1957), vol. V. There was also an extensive network of native spies employed on both sides. The spy Angad, for example, earned high praise from Englishmen like Martin Gubbins.

'venerable maulvis' had functioned as 'veritable messengers of evil' who criss-crossed the country and spread sedition. Agents of deposed princes and former sepoys also added their bit. The fakirs and maulvis commanded attention—as they had for centuries, and people listened to what they said about the firanghis. One such man was Ahmedullah Shah, the respected Maulvi of Faizabad (described by Amelia [or Amy] Horne, as possessing a 'somewhat distinguished mien'), once considered by the British to be the most dangerous man in India.

> *Ahmedullah Shah:* Famous as the 'troublesome fakir', and 'the Maulvi of Faizabad', Ahmedullah Shah may have been one of the earliest conspirators against the British. He was arrested in Faizabad in February 1857 but was later released by the mutineers. He may have led an army at Chinhat, where he acquired the reputation of being invincible. In 1857 he wrote a tract, Fatteh Islam, which was an analysis of the Raj and a call for revolt. A reward of Rs 50,000 was announced for his capture. He was finally killed when trying to enter the fort of Pawayan.

He travelled extensively, as far as the North-West Provinces, and may have been a prime mover in the spread of anger against the Raj. In any case, the maulvi, the fakir and perhaps the chappatis and bone dust came together in a dramatic mix—and catalyzed the reaction that upgraded the breeze of discontent into the storm of fury that broke soon after.

The Raj had been united, ironically, in two contradictory ways: by the British by means of their technological marvels like the railway lines, steam ships and the telegraph, and by natives by means of their 'primitive' courier system of word-of-mouth, the itinerant preacher and the chappati. 1857 would see European (colonial) technology pitted against this non-modern system.

> **Canals:** *Canals may have played a role in rousing the natives' suspicion about the British. The British had dug canals in the Doab region, especially the western Jumna one. However, these lands became barren. The natives suspected that the canals may have something to do with it, and this being the doing of the British, they ought to be punished. Protests about canals were recorded in Saharanpur, Delhi and Meerut.*

It is significant enough for us to remember that no technology has ever been so dominant (even when controlled by the iron hand of colonialism) that indigenous systems were completely wiped out.

> **Dak:** *The postal system in the North-West Provinces, called dak, was a collection of devices and processes. It used horses, runners and a combination of horse and cart (the mail cart, in which John Nicholson was supposed to have travelled towards Delhi from Ambala). The term used to describe this system was 'the dak is running', which implied that all was well. If it was 'the dak is stopped' it meant that the mutineers had blocked the roads and prevented the mail from coming through. 'Dak houses' were rest houses for government servants.*

*

The weather had indeed changed irrevocably. The wind was bad, disturbing and uncomfortable. It had gathered into a gale-force state now. On the stage of the subcontinent, even as the actors went about their business, it gathered force and broke. Indeed the metaphors of the wind and stage are quite appropriate to understand

the gathering storm

1857. The wind swept along the Raj's stage, moving characters and scenes swiftly, dangerously. The effect on the stage, the largest and most extravagant imperial setting ever seen in human history, was extremely dramatic.

There had never been anything as magnificent, as bloody or as shocking as the drama of 1857 in Britain's imperial progress. There were the stage whispers of discontent, the rumbling rumours about cartridges and caste, the

> 'In the sky of India ... a small cloud may rise, at first no bigger than a man's hand but which... may at last threaten to surprise his audience, and overwhelm us with ruin.'
> —Lord Canning

horrific killings, the violent retribution, the significant aftermath. There were commoners as heroes, formidable kings and queens, stupid statesmen, soldiers of epic courage, an old poet-emperor. The trumpet being heard was not always the Company's triumphal announcement of its presence to the world. It, this time, heralded the arrival of the *native* on the stage of history.

India 1857: the stage the world watched with awe, horror, anger, surprise, and sometimes with sympathy. One hundred and fifty years later, at a distance safe enough to better understand the events but never safe enough to escape their intense trauma, we now become the audience to the drama.

Two
The Summer of Discontent

Signs of a Summer Storm

Chronology of Major Events: January–April 1857
Barrackpore, Berhampore

End-January: Encounter between sepoy and khalasi; first rumours of greased cartridges

End-February: Sepoys at Barrackpore refuse cartridges, some disturbance in Vizianagaram, Andhra (perhaps unrelated) End-March: Mangal Pandey's actions at Barrackpore

Early April: Mangal Pandey hanged

End-April: Cavalry at Meerut refuses cartridges

*

We associate the Mutiny with Meerut, May 1857. But, as we have seen, smaller disturbances had occurred through the 1800–50 period. These were symptoms that the Raj was not at peace. However, the crucial events that would come close to ending the empire began only in January 1857.

Scene one in this great drama is located near Calcutta, the enormously profitable section of the Company's trading zone. The weather seems to have turned, somehow, in some undefinable fashion.

> By 1790s India was contributing £ 500,000 annually to the British exchequer, and Bengal provided 60 per cent of the trade.

Dum Dum had a large arsenal at in the 1850s. On this small stage, in January 1857, slightly buffeted by untimely breezes, appear two members of the human race: a 'lower-caste' khalasi and a Brahmin sepoy of the 2nd Regiment, Native (Grenadier).[1] The thirsty labourer requests the sepoy for a drink of water from the receptacle the latter is carrying. The sepoy is aghast at the man's temerity—a lower caste hopes to drink water from the Brahmin's lota! When he expresses his outrage at the labourer's breaking of established laws and caste taboos, the labourer mocks him: 'You will soon lose your caste, as ere long you will have to bite cartridges covered with the fat of pigs and cows'.[2] The sepoy, at first puzzled by the mockery and then anxious at the deeper implications, rushed back to his barracks and yelled at his comrades that they were all at risk from the new cartridges. The barracks erupted in debates and counter-arguments. What is clear now, in retrospect, is that this was only the opening scene.

---

[1] Regimental khalasis were often involved in making the cartridges.

[2] A report on this incident was filed by J.A. Wright, Commander, Rifle Instruction Depot, Dum Dum, 22 January 1857. It is printed in George W. Forrest, *Selections from Letters, Despatches and State Papers*, SLDSP 1.

Berhampore and Barrackpore constitute the near-simultaneous second scenes of the drama. The 2nd Native Infantry at Barrackpore refused to use the new cartridges on 4 February. This was a serious military offence and a court of inquiry was duly ordered. The witnesses during this inquiry affirmed that they had heard rumours about beef and pork fat being used as tallow material. Chand Khan, a sepoy, said during the inquiry: 'I have no objection to the bullet or powder, it is only the paper which I have doubts about, which appears to be tough; and in burning it, it smells as if there was grease in it'. Bheekun Khan, another sepoy, declared: 'I suspect there is cow and pig grease in them from a bazaar report.' The sepoys had also heard that the Company was planning to convert them all into Christians. Two days later an officer of the 34th Native Infantry was informed by a sepoy that the barracks were awash with rumours of a plot. This sepoy had been asked by the others to attend a meeting where many masked sepoys swore to die for their faith. They also believed, according to this sepoy who passed on the information, that this could be achieved only by the murder of the firanghis who were instrumental in putting their faith in crisis.

> 'If we cannot drive the firanghis from our land, we shall rot in the hot hell.'
> —Maniram, Dewan of Assam

Major General John Bennet Hearsey, the Commanding Officer of the Division at Barrackpore, reported the findings of the court of inquiry to Calcutta. He also expressed a certain amount of anxiety at the rumours brought him by his officers—the disaffection in the barracks, the insubordination among the sepoys and their general insolence to British officers. A.S. Allen of the 34th Regiment, Native Infantry, had, for instance, prepared a statement, countersigned by S.G. Wheler. A sepoy had informed Allen that:

> He [the sepoy] had become cognisant of a plot amongst
> the men of the different regiments, four in number, at
> this station, that they were apprehensive of being forced
> to give up their caste and being made Christians ... they
> were determined to rise up against their officers, and
> commence by either plundering or burning down the
> bungalows at Barrackpore; they next proposed to proceed
> to Calcutta and attempt to seize Fort William...

J.B. Hearsey tried to assuage the fears of the sepoys. His son, unimaginatively also named John Hearsey, a Lieutenant in the same division, demonstrated to the sepoys the working of the new rifles. The sepoys were not, according to both son and father, convinced.

But the General was not one to admit defeat easily. On 9 February he addressed his troops, assuring them that the Company and the British government would do nothing to imperil any native's faith. Addressing them more as a benevolent patron than their commanding officer, the General assured them that those natives who had converted to Christianity had done so of their own accord—there was never any question of coercion. Despite this assurance, the men of the 34th remained unconvinced. At a later inquiry, which Hearsey reported to J.H. Birch, Secretary to the Government of India, Military Department, on 11 February 1857, he mentioned the fact, based on the evidence presented by Sepoy Ramsahai Lalla, that a meeting of the sepoys from various regiments had taken place on 5 February. Later General Hearsey informed Calcutta frankly that 'it will be quite impossible to allay them' [the sepoys' fears about the cartridges]. He also added a note that was to prove prophetic—that the native *officers* were useless in such conditions because they were afraid of their men.

On the split stage of Berhampore and Barrackpore, another scene was being played out. On 26 February the 19th Native

Infantry at Berhampore refused to use the new cartridges—they had by now become certain that this was the British government's plot to make them lose their caste/faith and then make them Christians. Furious at the insubordination—*technically*, this *is* mutiny, when the cadre refuses to obey officers' orders—the officers led by a man notoriously short on tact, W.L. St. Mitchell, marched the entire regiment to Barrackpore to be disbanded (this happened on 31 March 1857). A large British regiment had recently arrived from Burma, and the officers hoped to use their presence as a shield against similar future mutinies. However, the British did not calculate the effect these to-be-disbanded soldiers of the 19th would have on the Barrackpore troops, who saw their fellow-sepoys being treated badly for trying to keep their faith. The order to disband spelt ruin for the soldiers, most of whom had served the Company faithfully for years prior to this day. Court-martial would mean not only a lifetime of ignominy but also the loss of pension benefits. Barrackpore sympathies were clearly with the men of the 19th. They also saw something else—that the British officers in India took the help of their troops just returned from Burma. It was interpreted as a sign that the British in India were unable to face the native troops on their own.

Barrackpore now becomes the third scene. On 29th March a Brahmin sepoy emerged from the barracks of the 34th in his dhoti, instead of the customary uniform, and carrying his musket. He was, it appeared from subsequent investigation, instigated by his comrades in the barracks. However, he emerged to find that he was all alone on the field. Sepoy No. 1446, 5th Company, 34th Regiment, Native Infantry, Mangal Pandey, in service for just over seven years, began a litany against both the Europeans and his cowardly comrades. He ranted and raved about how the Europeans were destroying their religion, and how they (the natives) needed to fight back. The rest watched in sullen silence. Pandey abused his fellow troopers, whom he accused of instigating him and who now refused to come out into the open. A native officer rushed to summon one Sergeant General Hewson, who, quite cleverly, asked the jemadar to arrest Pandey. The jemadar pointed out that Pandey was carrying a musket, and he could get shot, and so, no, thank you, he was not willing to give up his life just yet. At this moment Lieutenant Baugh rode up, and Pandey, swinging his musket around, fired, hitting the horse and spilling Baugh to the ground. When Baugh charged Pandey, the latter slashed at him with his sword, and cut him badly. Hewson was knocked to the ground by somebody—the culprit was never identified, but was surely a sepoy. At this point things get a bit blurred. Another sepoy, Shaikh Paltu (or Paltu Khan), grabbed Pandey by the waist. The injured officer raced away. Stones, apparently thrown by sepoys who admired Pandey's actions but did not have the courage to join him, struck Paltu Khan. Colonel Wheler (whom we have already met as the officer who insisted on preaching to his men) ordered the sepoys to arrest Pandey—they refused to obey the order. The other sepoys threatened to shoot Paltu, and he backed off, just as General Hearsey and his son John arrived, riding hard. John seeing Pandey turning with his musket called out to his father, the General, 'Father, he is taking aim at you.' The hardy old General barked out in response: 'If I fall, John, rush upon him and put him to death.'

The General ordered the jemadar and the others to arrest Pandey. The jemadar, Issuree Pandey, refused. At this point Pandey turned the musket towards his chest. Grasping it between his toes, he pulled the trigger with his toe. The bullet grazed his chest and shoulders, and he fell to the ground.

> 'Damn his musket.'
> —General J.B. Hearsey, when warned that Mangal Pandey was levelling his gun at him

Among those who testified to Pandey's actions (other than the English) in the court of inquiry of 30 March 1857 were Shaikh Paltu, Ganesh Lalla, Mukta Parsad Pandey, Soba Sing, Atma Sing, and others.

Pandey himself went on trial a week later. The composition of the trial's officers is interesting. The president of the court for this trial was Subadar Major Jowahir Lall Tewary. All fourteen members were Indian, with a majority being Hindus (perhaps Brahmins, judging from their names) and just two of them Muslims.

The Trial of Mangal Pandey, 6 April 1857

Question: Have you anything to disclose, or do you wish to say anything?

Answer: No.

Q: Did you act on Sunday last by your own free will, or were you instructed by others?

A: Of my own will. I expected to die.

Q: Did you load your own musket to save your life.

A: No, I intended to take it.

Q: Did you intend to take the adjutant's life, or would you have shot anyone else?

A: I should have shot any one who came.

Q: Were you under the influence of any drugs?

A: Yes, I have been taking bhang and opium of late, but formerly never touched any drugs. I was not aware at the time of what I was doing.

The prisoner was asked frequently if he would give the names of any connected with the occurrence, and was given to understand that he had nothing to fear from his own regiment by disclosing anything, but he refused to state more than the above.

> *The prisoner being called on for his defence says—'I did not know who I wounded and who I did not; what more shall I say? I have nothing more to say.'*
> *The prisoner being asked, says: 'I have no evidence.'*
> *The defence is closed.*
> *The Court is closed.*
>
> *SENTENCE*
>
> *The Court sentence the prisoner, Mungul Pandy, sepoy, No. 1446, 5th Company, 34th Regiment, Native Infantry, to suffer death by being hanged by the neck until he be dead.*
>
> *Approved and confirmed.*
> *Barrackpore(Sd) J.B. Hearsey*
> *The 7th April 1857*

Mangal Pandey was hanged as a mutineer on 8 April 1857. He was twenty-six years old. Jemadar Issuree Pandey who refused to arrest Pandey was also tried and hanged on 21 April. On 4 April Canning decided that the cartridges would not be withdrawn.

Mangal Pandey would become a spectre that haunted British India in a very different way through 1857 and later. Hereafter the British would refer to native sepoys as 'pandies'. And years later V.D. Savarkar would revive Pandey as the first hero of the 'first war of Indian Independence'—but we are getting ahead of the narrative here.

Around this time—end February 1857—another sepoy disturbance was recorded. A letter from the Commanding Officer at Vizianagaram (in what is now Andhra Pradesh), dated 28 February, records how the 1st Regiment, Native Infantry, refused to march or shoulder arms when given orders. Cries of 'deen deen' (for the faith) were heard from the grounds. The letter states that there seemed to be a 'pre-concerted arrangement' and that the 'ill-feeling exhibited by the Corps' was not 'confined to particular individuals but generally shared by all.' It is possible, however, that this disaffection was unrelated to Barrackpore or other places, and was provoked solely by the fact that due to a shortage of carriages the sepoys' families were not allowed to travel with them on the march.

Signs and news of unrest bewildered the Englishmen and women, many of whom saw Mangal Pandey and Berhampore as isolated incidents, short-sightedly ignoring the fact that such incidents were occurring in far too many places, and far too quickly. The 48th Native Infantry at Lucknow showed signs of discontent, as did the 36th at Ambala (even as George Anson was visiting the place). A surgeon's house in Lucknow was burnt down on 16 April. The 34th was disbanded on 6 May. Tempers and temperatures were running high by now, and the disgraced soldiers from the 34th returned to Oudh just as Henry Lawrence arrived as the new Resident. For some strange reason Anson refused to believe that things were really bad in the Bengal army and elsewhere. With the idea that these things would blow over—after all this was India, where *Great* Britain was in power—Anson and his aides retreated to their summer capital, Simla. Effectively, this meant that by early May there was no central command in northern India.

On 1 May the 7th Oudh Irregular Infantry, Lucknow, refused to handle the cartridges, followed by the entire regiment on 2 May. On 3 May Henry Lawrence was informed that the possibility of mutiny by native troops was very real.

*

The 'Devil's Wind'

Chronology of Major Events, May–July 1857
Meerut, Delhi, Agra, Gwalior, Kanpur, Lucknow, Jhansi

10 May: Mutiny at Meerut

11 May: Mutineers reach Delhi

13 May: Zafar proclaimed Mughal emperor

20–23 May: Mutiny at Agra

30 May: Mutiny at Lucknow

5 June: Mutiny at Cawnpore, Jhansi

3–6 June Neill's massacres at Benares, Allahabad

6 June: Cawnpore siege (Wheeler and his people) begins

12 June: Fatehgarh survivors killed

14 June: Mutiny at Gwalior

8 June: Barnard wins at Badli-ki-Serai, first major victory for British

25 June: Nana Sahib's offer to Wheeler

27 June: Satichaura Ghat massacre, four men survive

30 June: Lucknow siege begins

1 July: Nana Sahib proclaimed peshwa

5 July: Birjis Qadr crowned king of Oudh

15 July: Bibighar massacre

16 July: Havelock defeats Nana Sahib at Cawnpore

31 July: Canning's Resolution

*

The scene now shifts, dramatically, to another place: Meerut. Meerut was under Brigadier Archdale Wilson (1803–74), a man who had spent forty years in India but was not exactly renowned for his soldierly qualities.

> 'Devil's Wind' was the name given to the events of 1857–58. It became the title of several accounts (including fiction). Patricia Wentworth had a novel with this title in 1912 followed by G.L. Verney (1956) and Manohar Malgonkar (1972). John Entract's *The Devil's Wind: A Centenary Account of the Mutiny* appeared in 1957.

Dissent was rife in Meerut. The native troops, it was said, had sworn on the Ganga and the Koran that they would not touch the polluting cartridges. When he heard of this, one of their European officers, a Captain H.C. Craigie, warned his superiors that things were deteriorating in the barracks. Craigie's message to his superior went:

> The men of my troop have requested in a body that the skirmishing tomorrow be countermanded, as there is commotion throughout the native troops about cartridges, and that the regiment will become *budnam* if they fire any cartridges ... <u>This is a serious matter, and we may have the whole regiment in mutiny in half an hour if this be not attended to</u>.

This crucial warning, prophetic in its nature and panic-stricken in tone (note the emphasis) was the herald of the Mutiny.

It was Craigie's superior, George Munro Carmichael-Smyth, who in an appalling display of bad planning, ordered a drill on

24 April. Carmichael-Smyth's other subordinates believed that this was a bad move, especially since Carmichael-Smyth knew that the sepoys had refused to take the cartridge.

> **George Munro Carmichael-Smyth:** *Commandant of the 3rd Light Cavalry at Meerut in 1857. He was disliked by his men, and proved to be tactless. He ordered the drill of 24 April, against the advice of his officers, all of whom knew the sepoys' anxiety about the cartridges. The troops were to operate the guns using the new cartridges—by <u>tearing them open rather than by biting them</u>. When the eighty-five men refused, he court-martialled them. Carmichael-Smyth may have precipitated the Mutiny at Meerut with his actions.*

During the subsequent inquiry the sepoys stated unambiguously that the cartridges would make them lose their faith and caste. After court martial for insubordination, the eighty-five men of the 3rd Light Cavalry were sentenced to imprisonment with hard labour for ten years. There was no remission for any of the men, even those with a record of good conduct and faithful service. The 3rd Light Cavalry's court martial may be said to have been the point at which the fission reaction really set in. On 9 May 1857 the 3rd Cavalry, the 11th and 20th Native Infantry, select battalions of other divisions from artillery and battery assembled on the parade ground. Also present, as a threat and as a safety mechanism, were about 1,700 European troops.

> **Carmichael-Smyth's Report to G.P. Whish, Major of Brigade at Meerut, 24 April 1857**
>
> *Yesterday I ordered a parade to take place this morning for the purpose of showing the men the new mode by which they might load their carbines without biting their cartridges, and late in the evening I received information ... that the men of the 1st troop would not receive the cartridges (which were the same that they had always used) ... This morning I explained to the men my reason for ordering the parade, and I first ordered the havildar-major to show them the new way of loading, which he did, and fired off his carbine. I then ordered the cartridges to be served out, but, with the exception of the men noted in the margin [Heera Sing, Pursaud Sing, Golam Nubbee Khan, Shaik Golam Mohammed, Dilawar Khan], they all refused to receive them, saying they would get a bad name if they took them, but that if all the regiments would take their cartridges, they would do so. I explained to them that they were not new cartridges, but the very same they had always been using, and once more called on them to receive the cartridges, saying, 'You see the havildar-major has used one'; but, with the exception of the men above-mentioned, they all still refused; after which I ordered the adjutant to dismiss the men, as they were too large a party to send to the guard. The party consisted of ninety men.*

What followed was a colossal political and military error of judgement. Under the impression that a thorough ritual humiliation and public punishment of the 3rd would make the rest of the native troops wary of insubordination, the court-martialled men were roughly stripped of their uniforms and their ankles shackled like common prisoners. During this procedure many of them called out to their comrades in other battalions to rebel against the British. Others even threatened the British officers on the field. Finally, after what seemed an age, the men were marched off to prison. Some of the witnessing native soldiers were deeply moved, and even the British officers present felt that the severity of the punishment was unwarranted. Major General W.H. Hewitt, commanding the Meerut division records: 'the majority of the prisoners seemed to feel acutely the degradation to which their folly and insubordination had brought them.' Even Anson, the Commander-in-Chief, normally not the most sagacious of men, believed that this public humiliation was uncalled for.

In sending them to prison as common criminals, Carmichael-Smyth and the others gave a focal point to the subsequent events on 10 May.

It must be remembered that in one earlier case at least, the prison had been the centre for a revolutionary movement: the Bastille prison and the French Revolution, a little over fifty years before Meerut. As in France, the native troops in Meerut initiated the 'rebellion' with a momentous act: the freeing of imprisoned men.

> Colonel John Finnis was perhaps the first Englishman to be shot during the Mutiny.

The 'Devil's Wind' had found its vortex.
The Mutiny had arrived.

*

Sunday, 10 May 1857, a blazing hot day in Meerut where the very roads of the town seemed to conceal flames underneath. The

British at church had, however, warmer news to report and discuss. Notices and posters had been pasted on the walls, calling upon all Muslims to rise up against the British government and defend their faith. It seemed a matter of some concern to H.H. Greathed, the Commissioner of Meerut. But other than these posters, there was nothing stirring in the town.

It was around six in the evening that Hugh Gough (1833–1909), an officer of the 3rd Light Cavalry noticed smoke rising from the Native Infantry lines and the noise of musket fire. Full of foreboding he raced out, jumped on to his horse and turned to the lines to investigate.

Native sepoys mixed with the people in the market place. The market was in uproar as insults (about the sepoys' cowardice in not rescuing their imprisoned comrades) and arguments (about what the sepoys wanted/intended to do) fanned the angered sepoys' passions. Some one cried out that British troops were headed their way. The atmosphere in the bazaar and barracks crackled, alive like electricity in the air.

Meerut exploded.

The infantry lines were soon up in flames as the sepoys, now openly disobeying the orders of those of their officers who had arrived, rushed to grab their weapons and headed for the jail. According to W.H. Hewitt's memo, dated 11 May 1857, to Colonel Chester, the Adjutant General of the Army at Simla, the mutineers not only freed the eighty-five imprisoned soldiers but also 1,200 other prisoners. Mrs Muter, who would also write a narrative of the Mutiny, waited patiently at the Church for service to begin. When told that there would be no service due to the disturbances, she waited for half an hour more, assuming it was just a small problem. Finally, driving home, when she saw two Europeans being chased by dozens of furious-looking Indians, she realized that it was not, as she had put it earlier, 'a slight disturbance'. Several British officers headed for their regiments, under the impression that they could talk to them and perhaps calm them down. When they reached the troops, they discovered that talking or listening was not on the agenda for the day—those of the officers who were fortunate, like Lieutenant Mackenzie, got away into the summer darkness. The others fought, but were killed.

> The rebels attacked visible symbols of British authority, and British presence, in every town—the government buildings, churches, tombs, the residences of British officers/civilians, banks, army cantonments.

Those British they met on the way were shot, a few escaped by hiding and the kindness of their servants. One pregnant woman was killed and mutilated, another was killed with her children, yet another (sick with smallpox) was burnt in her bed ... the catalogue was beginning to assume astronomical proportions. A medical officer who witnessed the events wrote: 'the work of indiscriminate European massacre began without regard to rank, age, sex, or employment, furious and merciless.' Native Christians were also sought out and killed. A native catechist, Joseph, whose account was recorded later[3], mentions how, when the mutineers caught him, they yelled 'he is a Christian, kill him.'

One message may have got out of Meerut before the telegraph lines were cut. Kate Moore's telegram of 10 May 1857, announcing the Mutiny at Meerut, went like this:

> The cavalry have risen setting fire to their own houses and several officers' houses, besides having killed and wounded all European officers they could find near the lines ... so passed the whole night of Sunday the 10th of May...

---

[3]In N.A. Chick, *Annals of the Indian Rebellion of 1857-58* (1859).

Elsewhere in the town, the British officers quickly discovered that they had no control over the sepoys. Most of them gave up the effort of pacifying their men—some were shot even as they talked to the men—and turned their efforts at protecting themselves and their families. Carmichael-Smyth was one of those who escaped. When they tried to contact Delhi they discovered the extent of the threat—the telegraph lines had been cut. Archdale Wilson ordered out the 60th Rifles who, the officers discovered, suddenly seemed to be able to work only in the slow mode. Asked to stop the 'mutineers'—they had acquired the name in a few hours—the 60th went out to the burning bungalows and nearby groves but did not think of pursuing the mutineers. This was another tactical error, but one which the officers could not have known at the time (Archdale Wilson and William Hewitt of the Meerut Division came in for scathing criticism for this lapse). The mutineers had no intention of staying in Meerut after what they had done. Their destination lay elsewhere.

The whole Meerut situation was over in two hours.

Some later commentators believe that the officers and British in Meerut did not try enough to stop things from getting out of hand. A few officers offered to ride to Delhi for help (since the telegraph wires had been cut), but permission was denied. Charles Rosser offered to chase the mutineers—permission was denied again. One Lieutenant Möller actually managed to arrest a mutineer, thus proving that they could have been stopped. It is a matter of speculation—if the rest had made a greater effort, and Wilson and the rest of the British possessed a bit more tact, would things have been so bad for the many who died at Meerut? Or, even more to the point, would it have prevented the *spread* of the Mutiny?

Even as the events occurred, commentators were trying to analyze causes and consequences. Thus a Minute filed by Mr Grant on 11 May 1857 declared that the men refused to bite the cartridges not because of disaffection but because of the 'unfeigned dread of losing caste'. He then analyzed the reasons for this dread:

> Sepoys are, in many respects, very much like little children and acts, which on the part of European soldiers would be proof of the blackest disloyalty, may have a very different significance when done by these credulous and inconsiderate, but generally not ill-disposed beings.

Grant thus attributed the Mutiny at Meerut to the sepoys being gullible to rumours and gossip rather than any conscious decision on their behalf. It was an interesting insight, with the old image of the child-like native (seen in British colonial writing from the early-eighteenth century, and even in the work of erudite statesmen like Edmund Burke).

> The official number of Europeans killed at Meerut was forty-one, including eight women and eight children. J.A.B. Palmer's 1966 study puts it at fifty.

Why and how the mutineers came to decide that Delhi was their destination is a matter of speculation. Delhi was, of course, the seat of the only surviving icon of the former Mughal power left between Khyber and the Irrawady. Muhammad Bahadur Shah, more popularly known as Bahadur Shah Zafar, the last of the great Mughals, descendant of Timur, Babur and Akbar, resided in the magnificent Lal Qila (Red Fort) at Delhi.

His powers greatly reduced, his income almost non-existent and his dignity as 'emperor' in shambles, Zafar, now eighty-two years old, had little left by way of ambition. His life was restricted to some poetry (both Mirza Asadullah Khan 'Ghalib' [1797–1869] and Zauq [1789–1854], the Mughal poet laureate, lived in Delhi at this time), the garden, and efforts at persuading the British to recognize Jawan Bakht (1841–84), his son from Begum Zeenat Mahal (1821–82), as the successor to the throne.

> *Muhammad Bahadur Shah II, aka Bahadur Shah 'Zafar' (1775–1862):* The eldest son of Akbar Shah II was sixty-two years old when he ascended the throne at Delhi. He was interested in Sufism, mysticism and calligraphy, was a lover of poetry and enjoyed cooking (he is believed to have invented a particular sweetmeat). He was troubled by family quarrels, and the British treatment of the great Mughals. He had very little power outside his palace, and subsisted on a pension from the British government, though the latter still proclaimed they were his vassals (a point they ignored when Zafar was prosecuted) in 1858. He died in exile in Rangoon. He is known today mainly as a poet.

> Bahadur Shah Zafar had a Sufi father and a Rajput princess mother. He refused to eat beef, and wore the caste mark and brahmanic thread when visiting Hindu temples.

Having acknowledged that the Mughal empire had been effectively and insidiously replaced by the British one, Zafar had withdrawn from politics.

> *Firoz Shah:* A cousin of Zafar. He became well known as a brave fighter and strategist. He was friends with Ahmedullah Shah, the Maulvi of Faizabad and Begum Hazrat Mahal. After the Mutiny collapsed he fled to Mecca where he is supposed to have died in poverty.

But Delhi was also important—and we cannot be sure that this had indeed occurred to the Meerut mutineers, for some historians believe it was a spontaneous decision—for other reasons. It had a huge quantity of ammunition. It lay between the Punjab, where a good deal of the British forces were concentrated, and the rest of India. If the British lost Delhi, their forces would be divided into two—the Punjab on one side, the rest of India on the other.

> **Begum Zeenat Mahal:** *The senior wife of Bahadur Shah Zafar, whom she wedded in 1840. She became Zafar's favourite queen (displacing Taj Mahal Begum). Her son from Zafar, Jawan Bakht, was the centre of the dispute with the British: she persuaded Zafar to declare him heir, and forced him to plead with the British to recognize Jawan Bakht. She may have struck a deal with William Hodson about the surrender at Humayun's Tomb. Exiled with Zafar to Burma, she died there.*

Therefore, Delhi. The city about which Charles Napier had once predicted: 'some day or other much mischief will be hatched within those walls.'

Napier was about to be proved right.

What is fascinating in its irony and tragic in its outcome is that news of the Meerut events *had* arrived in Delhi. When the message arrived at the home of Simon Fraser, the Commissioner, he was asleep, and his servant did not want to wake him. Fraser received the message only the next morning. By then it was too late. Another version of the story is that Fraser received a letter from the civil authorities at Meerut. But he was tired and put the message in his pocket without reading it. It was in his pocket even when the mutineers arrived.

History perhaps is made through such accidents.

On the morning of 11 May the Meerut mutineers arrived, looking less like Company soldiers (even though they were in uniform) than a bunch of mercenaries, at the Red Fort. They rode in and called out to Zafar: 'We pray for assistance in our fight for the faith!' Zafar, unaware of their actual demands (or ideas), but certain that this did not augur well for his own self, immediately called for Captain Douglas, the head of his bodyguard. Douglas asked the mutineers to disperse, for they were disturbing the king. Instead, the mutineers turned through Rajghat Gate and entered the city. Later a larger number of the Meerut mutineers arrived at the palace. Theophilus Metcalfe (1828–83), Joint Magistrate in Delhi, moved quickly. He asked for guns to be readied as he rode about checking sections of the city. The Europeans were already beginning to barricade areas. Metcalfe, inspecting the various gates to the palace, had a narrow escape. Rushing away unarmed on his horse he was hit by a stone thrown from a house. Knocked unconscious into a ditch, Metcalfe ceased, for the time being, to be an active participant in the events that were now tumbling along.

Meanwhile, Delhi was rapidly filling up with the dead bodies of Europeans—soldiers, merchants, missionaries and officers. Many escaped because of the continuing loyalty of their servants. Some died defending themselves.

Elsewhere in the city the full impact of the events was making itself felt. Captain Robert Tytler—whose wife Harriet would eventually write a memoir of her experiences—noticed a restlessness among his men as news of the Mutiny spread.

> The son of Robert and Harriet Tytler, born in the back of a cart outside Delhi, with the Europeans preparing for their assault on the capital of the Raj, was named, in honour of his timing, Stanley Delhiforce.

> ### English Supporters?
>
> *It was said that a few Englishmen converted to Islam and sided with the natives when the Mutiny broke out. One Englishman took the name Abdullah Beg and seems to have fought alongside the mutineers. Beg finds mention in Mainoddin Hassan Khan's narrative in* Two Native Narratives of the Mutiny *by Charles Theophilus Metcalfe. Another was a Sergeant Major Gordon, who, it appears, manned the guns at the Delhi walls. Later, Gordon surrendered to the British, but since there was no evidence that he actually fought, he was not prosecuted. Hugh Gough's* Old Memories *(1897) mentions Gordon. Five other Englishmen, including the Postmaster of Moradabad, Powell, had converted to Islam, but may not have participated in the battle. They were imprisoned by the mutineers, and escaped during the battle for Delhi.*

Officers in the mess hearing of the troubles quickly set about gathering those they could summon and trust. The Meerut mutineers fired at them as they tried to secure the Kashmir Gate, and when the British officers asked their accompanying men (the 38th) to fire, they only fired into the air, and eventually moved in to attack them alongside the mutineers. George Willoughby, helped by a few subordinates, was trying during this time to secure the magazine and prevent it from being seized by the mutineers (the treasury, defended for some time by Mr Galloway, had fallen). Willoughby decided on a last, desperate measure, in case he was unable to fend off the mutineers. He prepared a deadly chain of gunpowder across the area. When the mutineers came closer he ordered the magazine to be blown up, killing many of the attackers, himself and others in the process (one estimate put the number of dead at twenty-five sepoys and 100 onlookers). The rest of the officers tried to get away as bullets whistled past their heads and arrows and swords seemed to appear from nowhere to hack and cut. Some managed to get away to the nearby Metcalfe House, several died on the way. Others made for Karnal, almost everyone arriving haggard, bleeding, in torn clothes and in varied states of shock and incomprehension. What struck them most forcefully, as numerous documents reveal, was not the massacre or the bullets—it was the recognition that their own men had turned against them.

Brigadier Graves at Delhi Ridge kept looking out hopefully at the road from Meerut, expecting reinforcements. Unfortunately, Hewitt at Meerut had done nothing—this was to prove a costly error. The rest of the civilians and officers scrambled over the walls of the Kashmir Gate, fastening their sword belts together for the women to climb. Many died in the attempt, as the rebels kept up non-stop firing. Eventually those who managed the climb (and the jump/scramble down the other side) escaped into the countryside, to be later discovered by a European force from Meerut.

In the middle of the carnage, deeds of loyalty and courage stood out. In several cases the servants hid the British children, gave shelter to the men and women, and continued to treat them with enormous respect. They were supplied food and drink, and places to sleep, even though they knew that they ran the risk of certain death at the hands of the mutineers for harbouring Europeans and/or Christians.

And now appeared on the scene two unlikely heroes, the remarkable Eurasian signalers, William Brendish and J.W. Pilkington. When they discovered that the telegraph line had been cut, they swam the river to see what the problem was. Later, discovering that their superior, Charles Todd, had not returned from his inspection, they realized that things were horribly wrong.

Seeing that the lines to the north were unaffected, they sent out what turned out to be one of the most frightening bits of news the telegraph system in India had ever carried (though it was said that the electric telegraph had saved the empire—places like Lahore and Madras were informed of Meerut and Delhi within a few days of the uprising). The telegraph message, to Ambala, said: 'we must leave office. All the bungalows are being burnt down by sepoys from Meerut ... Mr Todd is dead I think ... We are off.' Later in the day, Pilkington sent another message out of Delhi: 'Cantonment in a state of siege ... Mutineers from Meerut ... cut off communication with Meerut ... Several officers killed and wounded ... Information will be forwarded.' The last did not happen: this was the last message out of Delhi for some time.

Pilkington did not sign this message, which reached Ambala, and then burnt across northern India.

And Delhi burned.

Another unlikely hero was a Dr Batson. He offered to take a message, requesting more European troops, to Meerut. Since he could speak the local language fluently, and could disguise himself as a fakir, he was confident of surviving. What did him in was that pride of the European race—his clear blue eyes! Caught by Muslim mutineers he survived because he was able to sing praises and prayers to the Prophet in the mutineers' language. He is an unlikely hero because after this incident, which smacks of both courage and naivete, Batson spent the next twenty-five days wandering around assorted villages and jungle! He, of course, never reached the message to its destination.

Many such stories survive from those febrile days in 1857. Survivors like Harriet Tytler, Fred Roberts, Edward Vibart, Mrs Peile and others published accounts of their trauma. Tytler and others eventually reached Karnal and safety on 12 May, driving part of the way on a *gharry* with a splintered wheel and often having to battle mutineers. But grisly events were unfolding within the palace of the last Mughal.

In the palace Simon Fraser and Captain Douglas had both been killed. And then, in what was to have profound consequences in the British retribution, fifty European and Eurasians were taken prisoner and shut away in a small dark room of the palace. Later they were taken out and shot or put to the sword in the palace premises.

> **Hakim Ahsanullah Khan:** *Zafar's confidante. It is believed he and Zeenat Mahal had been negotiating with the British. The rebels discovered this and attacked his house, but Zafar's intervention saved him. He was the man who persuaded Zafar not to lead the final assault. At the trial, however, Ahsanullah Khan testified against Zafar, and was therefore pardoned by the British.*

One of those who survived (by passing off as a Muslim) was a Eurasian, Mrs Aldwell, who testified at the trial of Zafar in 1858. She stated:

> Between eight and nine o'clock, viz. on Saturday, the 16th of May, the whole party of the Europeans, with exception of myself, three children, and an old native Mahomedan woman, who had been confined with us for giving food and water to some Christians, were taken out and murdered. .. they were taken out of my sight, and as I heard brought under the Pipul tree by the small reservoir in the courtyard, and there murdered with swords by the king's private servants. None of the sepoys took part in killing them...

John Chalmers writes:

The brutes oiled over and set fire to one lady, killed children at the breast; and 50 children who got into the palace of the king, who, the rascal, was put on the throne by us, and has received £ 12,000 a month of pension for years, were, after remaining there 5 days, stripped naked, paraded through the crowded streets of the largest city in India in that state, under a burning sun, and then killed with spears slowly and in cold blood—ladies and children who never knew what it was before to walk a mile.

Naturally, in such European accounts the suffering of their women and children was highlighted. Chalmers' description, with the excessive details, is a good example of how the Mutiny has been narrated in histories. Native 'offences' were described in grisly detail. Few European accounts of the corresponding brutality of British soldiery exist, though. References to women who threw their children into wells (Jhansi, Delhi), and jumped in after them, to prevent falling into the hands of advancing European forces, were made in passing. British brutality was represented as 'justice', as though the terminology lessened the intensity of violence.

It was a matter of dispute as to whether this massacre had been ordered by Zafar's son, Mirza Moghal (1828–57), by the palace guards or by the private servants of the king. Mirza Moghal would soon assume charge of the rebel action in Delhi.

> 'These Christians were put to death by Sidi Nasir, Allah Dad Wilayati, and the sowars of Gulab Shah, and certain khas-bardars of the king. They were killed with swords. Allah Dad Wilayati was in the service of the king.'
>
> —Hakim Ahsan Ullah, at Zafar's trial

Mainoddin Hassan Khan, who wrote one of the two main native narratives of the Mutiny (the other was Munshi Jiwan Lal), claims he pleaded with both Zafar and Hakim Ahsanullah Khan that the Europeans should not be killed, but both the authorities declared their helplessness at the mutineers' resolve.

> 'I heard in the city that the king did wish to save the Europeans, particularly the women and children, but that he was overruled by the violence of the soldiery, and had not the firmness to oppose them.'
> —Jat Mall, at Zafar's trial

From Mainoddin Hassan Khan's narrative

Ahsanullah Khan: 'The bagheelog [runaways] will never abandon the slaughter of Christians. If they are interfered with, yet worse things may happen. When satiated with the blood of Christians they will direct their attention to us and to our property. Let us take care of ourselves.' I [Mainoddin Hassan Khan] replied: 'Hakimjee, your judgment is not good. The massacre of innocent women and children is not a good work in the eyes of the Most High God. When this insurrection is suppressed, and the English power re-established, the saving of these lives will stand you in good stead. Even if you incline to the opinion that the English power is gone forever, these lives you have saved will redound to your glory and honour.' I told him it was my opinion that the insurrection would continue only a short while, and besought him to act on my advice. Hakim Ahsanullah remained silent as if lost in deep thought.

The 'Devil's Wind' Onward

All over northern India eruptions came thick and fast after 20 May 1857.[4] Fatehgarh, Aligarh, Bareilly, Rohtak, Moradabad, Nimuch, Shahjahanpur all saw native troops revolting, in some cases supported by civilians—a feature that changed the texture of the rebellion, lending it the colour and weave of a popular and not simply a military movement.

> 'It [the "mutiny"] burst on us at Gwalior like a thunderclap, and paralyzed us with horror.'
> —Mrs Coopland

One reason for the civilian unrest during this time was that in many cases the Englishmen simply abandoned stations and took their families to safe places, leaving the town to the mercy of mercenaries and soldiery. Others tried desperately to retain their men. They promised rewards, raised private regiments and even hired criminals to work for them. In any case, they did not expect the rebellion to last very long. Reporting on the events in an American newspaper, Karl Marx said: 'the rebels at Delhi are very likely to succumb without any prolonged resistance.' He was very wrong.

> The Commissioner of Jabbulpore printed his own banknotes to persuade his men to stay on at a higher wage.

---

[4]There is, as P.J.O. Taylor points out (1997), an inexplicable 'lull' in activities, from 11 May till about 25 May. For Taylor this seems to suggest that the original date set for the Mutiny was *31 May*, and that 10 May at Meerut might have been premature, when the sepoys were still unprepared. It is a point worth considering.

Our story must hereafter move between several places and events, all unfolding with startling rapidity and unbelievable ferocity in numerous cantonments, towns and villages in northern India. It is therefore less a sequence than a dissemination, a scattering of incidents. Cawnpore, Lucknow, Meerut, Gwalior, Agra now enter the stage. And some new dramatis personae.

The mutineers needed *one* success. And the British needed to deny them that very success. The cornerstone of the Mutiny's success or failure, and the Britishers' continuing stay in India or their exit was, of course, Delhi. When the mutineers managed to take over Delhi and drive out the British, it sent out a message: the Raj was vulnerable. For, if the British could be driven out of Delhi, they could be driven out from the rest of the subcontinent. Henry Lawrence, placed at Lucknow which would soon erupt, recognized this, and informed his superiors that 'tranquility cannot be much longer maintained [in India], unless Delhi be speedily captured.'

> *Henry Lawrence (1806–57): Brother of John Lawrence (1811–79), became better known as 'Lawrence of Lucknow', and was Commissioner of the troubled state of Oudh. He had appealed to Canning just a few days before that the native troops should be treated better. He was well loved by his troops, many of whom remained with him through the dangerous times. A man with a distinguished military career, Lawrence first became notorious for refusing help to the besieged Wheeler at Cawnpore (but he had sent eighty-four men before the siege began—and Wheeler sent them back), though his decision, based on the hopelessness of the situation, was probably correct. He was injured in the siege of the Residency, and died of his wounds.*

After 16 May, when it was clear to every observer that Delhi was Mughal again, the 'Devil's Wind' swept across the country with renewed vigour.

The telegram of 15 May 1857 from the Governor General to the North-Western Provinces stated quite simply: 'Proclaim martial law at once.'

On 17 May the 25th Bengal Native Infantry at Fort William, Calcutta, tried to obtain ammunition—apparently with the intention of looting the city and killing the Europeans. The 70 Bengal Native Infantry repulsed them and informed the European officers. The 25th was disbanded.

On 31 May some of the Lucknow populace decided to join the militants, but were dispersed by the police and the army. Others were caught and eventually hanged.

During all this, Commander-in-Chief Anson was making uncertain moves and did not do much for British morale. John Lawrence, Chief Commissioner of the Punjab, urged Anson to disband the Ambala native regiments because they were likely to join the mutineers. Brigadier Wilson, after much to-ing and fro-ing, however, secured Meerut from further damage, but may have unwittingly allowed Delhi to fall because he had not asked his troops to pursue the mutineers fleeing Meerut. Anson died on 27 May of cholera, and was succeeded by Henry Barnard. Barnard, marginally more decisive, headed for Delhi and Meerut, accompanied by British troops who were now keen on revenge (stories of the massacres of their countrymen and women had by now spread). In one of his last missives, dated 23 May 1857, Anson wrote to W.H. Hewitt in Ambala: 'It would be very desirable to push forward some reconnaissance to as near Delhi as possible ... They [the detachment of mutineers on the Meerut side of the river] should be captured, and no mercy must be shown to the mutineers.' The British response—brutal suppression—was already taking shape here.

> **Henry Barnard (1799–1857):** Assumed charge as Commander-in-Chief of India after Anson's death. He built up the forces outside Delhi, but did not have much opportunity for battle because he died of cholera on 5 July 1857.

As they progressed, the soldiers accompanying Barnard executed sepoys and natives and even fakirs. But why mendicants and fakirs? Their careers as couriers who passed mutinous messages were beginning to be visible. The magistrate of Patna, William Tayler, arrested all the leading Wahabi maulvis in town, and managed to check the insurrection, thereby suggesting the active role of the maulvis in the uprising.

British retribution was beginning to script its own horror story. Barnard's force executed natives in large numbers, often burning entire villages in their fury. A soldier mentions how they 'hanged *all* the villagers who had treated our fugitives very badly'. Vast swathes of land were left devoid of human population through mass executions. Trials were farces, since the natives' guilt had been established by the simple fact that they were *Indian*. Corpses lined the streets, as men were hanged from every available tree. In Ajnala (Amristar), in a clear act of betrayal, 282 Lahore sepoys who had surrendered were summarily executed, *even though they had been promised a fair trial*. Harriet Tytler mentions how her husband had seen the body of a Muslim baker. The reason? He had been late with the breakfast bread for several days. No inquiries into such acts were conducted. If the natives killed European civilians—and therefore perpetrated unpardonable excesses in waging war against unarmed innocents—the British did the same in hanging maulvis, fakirs and villagers.

All this was *before* Cawnpore.

Disturbances were reported all across Gujarat and

present-day Rajasthan. Records from various archives (in the local languages) are listed in P.M. Joshi's *Disturbances in Gujarat (1857–64)*. Maganlal, Rango Bapuji, Naikdas and other figures led smaller rebellions in Baroda and other places, though their stories have not found expression in the general histories of 1857. V.G. Khobrekar's 'Introduction' to the volume points out that the archival record disproves the old idea that Gujarat did not witness any insurrection.

Things were not exactly quiet further south. It is interesting to note that much of the plotting and attacks against the British were led by *Muslims*.

In central India, letters may have been written to Maharaja Tukoji Rao Holkar II, according to Henry Scholberg.

Hyderabad was a state described as 'always inflammable', and the Minutes of Consultation (3 September 1857) looking back at the months, believed that Hyderabad 'was sure to be deeply excited by the course which events had taken in the North West in the proclamation of a Mahommedan Government at Delhi.' In Hyderabad, where a new diwan, Salar Jung, had just assumed office, posters asking the Muslims to rise against the British appeared on city walls on 13 June. The placards and posters were particularly critical of the Nizam for not supporting the rebellion. Some of them even warned the Nizam and Salar Jung that they would be reduced to labourers soon. However, the Resident, Colonel Davidson did not heed the warnings. On 11 June the 1st Cavalry of the Hyderabad Contingent, travelling from Mominabad to Aurangabad, halted their march, saying they would not leave Hyderabad state, nor would they fight the rebels. British reprisals, by now a proven method, were immediate: two were blown from guns, seven shot, four cut down, dozens hanged, forty transported, 100 disbanded and sixty flogged. On 17 July, the Imam of the Mecca Masjid was heckled during his speech. Cries of 'deen deen' rent the air. Soon after, a crowd of about 500 Rohillas rushed towards the Residency. It was led by Turrebaz Khan (one more of the heroes who does not figure in histories of 1857) and Maulvi Ala-ud-din. They were forced to withdraw under heavy cannon firing from Major S.C. Briggs, the Residency Commander. Rewards of Rs 5,000 were announced for the capture of the two leaders. Turrebaz Khan was caught trying to flee the city, and was shot dead. His body was displayed in a public place. Ala-ud-din was caught in 1859 and sent to the Andamans where he died in 1884.

In Madras, there was considerable anxiety about the native troops. According to the Minutes of Consultation, dated 3 September 1857, the fall of Delhi was crucial. 'It was therefore necessary to consider what effect this prolonged struggle and the temporary existence of a Mohammadan Sovereign at Delhi, was likely to produce in this Presidency', it stated. Triplicane's Muslims seemed to be highly restive and on 29 June military posts were established in the area. In Chingleput, a Muslim worker of the court was implicated in 'seditious plotting'.

The Political Agent at Belgaum reported a specifically Muslim disaffection on 28 July. An emissary, Zanool-ab-deen, was caught with documents that claimed officers and native regiments around Belgaum had been 'gained' and the 'extermination' of the English was at hand (Minutes of Consultation, 3 September 1857, recorded in Madras Record Office, Judicial Department GO 1081). Stacks and godowns of grain were set on fire in Bellary in June.

Armed Rohillas crossed over from the Nizam of Hyderabad's territory into Kurnool and Cuddapah. Around 20 June, Muslims from Cuddapah were reported to have moved northwards, to join the mutineers from other parts. One Sheikh Peer Shah was arrested in Cuddapah in October 1857 for preaching sedition in the cantonment there. Peer Shah had apparently claimed that by

Moharram the English government would end and the Mughals would be restored.

Around the time of the Bakrid festival in mid-July, the Muslim population of Seringapatnam and Mysore appeared disturbed and European troops had to be sent there. On 10 July an unidentified green flag was seen in Masulipatam (now in Andhra Pradesh), accompanied by proclamations and calls to slaughter the British. Prayers for the success of Zafar's army were also pasted on walls.

At Shorapore, Bheem Rao, a tahsildar of Bellary, was supposed to have led the rebels.

At Parlakimidi, a feudal chief, Dundasena, led a band of men who burnt and robbed villages in the area. European troops eventually captured him and he was handed as a rebel, though his exact role in the 1857 rebellion is uncertain.

At Rajamundry eleven Muslims were arrested on the charge of plotting against the government.

In Yernagudem (in the Godavari area of Andhra) a private dispute between families threw up Karukonda Subba Reddi as a leader. Subba Reddi gathered some hill tribes and staged armed encounters with European troops. He was eventually caught. During his trial he stated that he had been inspired to rebel because he was sure of Nana Saheb's victory. He was hanged as a rebel.

Robberies were reported from Jaggiapet, Rudravaram and other places, where Rohillas had been seen.

Bengal sepoys and foreign emissaries were reported from various parts of the Madras Presidency.

People travelling across the country were apprehended on the suspicion of being rebels. For instance, a party of four men and two women were detained at Rajamundry in July 1857. They were deemed to be 'bad characters' (as the letter dated

18 July 1857, by A. Purvis, Magistrate of Rajamundry, puts it) for they had little money and one of their swords seemed 'lately ... sharpened'. The travellers themselves claimed to be pilgrims.

*

Outside Delhi, Henry Barnard encountered stiff resistance at Badli-ki-Serai, but managed to beat the rebels back. On 8 June 1857 Barnard established a camp on Delhi Ridge, a location from which further movements into the city would have to be made. This was the first major move toward recapturing Delhi.

Delhi was, expectedly, the centre of action. This was a city transformed in May–June 1857. Christians were sought out and murdered. The mutineers acknowledged the return of the Mughals with Zafar being restored to the throne (unfortunately, they omitted to ask him if he was willing, or able). Zafar's son Mirza Moghal had taken charge, apparently at the suggestion of Mainoddin Hassan Khan, and headed operations from the palace. Hassan Khan admits that this act implicated him in the Mutiny. But he also claims: 'I was actuated by no feeling of opposition to the English, against whom I knew the struggle was hopeless.' But at the moment, things were going fine indeed.

The bewildered Zafar, who by all accounts had no prior inkling of the Mutiny (though the trial of 1858 sought to establish precisely this fact of his involvement in the intrigues), was persuaded to hold a durbar—the first in years, to show the world that the Mughal empire was up and running again. Guns were fired to herald the return of the Mughals. A working constitution, the *Dasturul 'Amal*, was drawn up. After more persuasion Zafar finalized positions for his many sons and relations, and was forced to write letters to the rulers of Patiala, Bahadurgarh and other places, asking for forces to join his (Zafar's) army to fight the firanghis.

the summer of discontent

Mirza Abu Bakr, Zafar's grandson, was given the charge of the cavalry. According to Mainoddin Hassan Khan the force of mutineers in Delhi on 12th May was:

5	Regiments Native Infantry	2,000
1	"	350
1	Battery Artillery	180
Total		2,530

A Military and Civilian Management Committee was formed. Local grocers and traders were asked to give up large quantities of grains and even money (eventually the petitions of the traders would be produced as evidence in the trial of Zafar). The Meerut troops did not get along with either the Delhi populace or the troops assembled from Delhi. The 'Devil's Wind' brought to the Delhi summer chaos, lawlessness, plunder and death. It was the saddest summer of all, despite the brief flash of Mughal imperial glory. The poet Mirza Ghalib (who rewrote his memoirs after the British reclaimed Delhi) mourned the lawlessness of the city.

> 'In truth one cannot perceive of justice under other auspices than those of the British.'
> —Mirza Ghalib

Ghalib recognized that Zafar had no control over the mutineers. He wrote:

> As the moon is eclipsed, so the army overshadowed the King. An eclipse cannot obscure the crescent moon, but only the full moon, but only the full moon of the fourteenth night. The King was a waning moon, yet his light was eclipsed.

The old king was troubled at a very personal level—his palace began to take the appearance of the serais that the Mughals had built all over India, places of rest for weary travellers. The troops walked in and out of his palace, even rode through his beloved gardens and were shockingly disrespectful to him even though they recognized him as king. Munshi Jiwan Lal's account describes the insolence of the mutineers:

> Forgetful of the lofty tone of the morning's order, and of the high toned phraseology expressive of the King's dignity, they addressed him with such disrespectful terms, 'Arre, Badshah! Arre, Buddhe!' ('Arre' is a slang expression used by the common people to attract attention, but a most insolent form of address to use to a monarch or any superior). 'Listen,' cried one, catching him by the hand. 'Listen to me,' said another, touching the old King's beard. Angered at their behaviour, yet unable to prevent their insolence, he found relief alone in bewailing before his servants his misfortunes and his fate.

Zafar, it is now evident, was not in control of the events—a fact that the prosecution chose to ignore at his trial in January 1858. He kept threatening to leave for Mecca if this kind of disrespect continued, and wrote a letter to Mirza Moghal to this effect. He also had no ambition of retrieving the power of the Mughals. Further, he was uncertain of the exact nature of the British response to the events—what he knew was that they were not likely to take kindly to them. Other accounts, however, present a different picture. Among those who testified at Zafar's trial were natives like Munshi Mohan Lal, who stated that after the initial reluctance to be actively involved, Zafar altered his role and stance. Mohan Lal claimed that Zafar issued orders, was aware of all the movements of troops and rebels taking place in Delhi, and even called upon Hindus and Muslims to unite in this battle for their respective faiths.

Delhi itself was now crowded with mercenary sepoys and rebels. Feeding them, paying their salaries and organizing them was becoming a logistic nightmare. Traders and local businessmen resented the princes' extortion. The sepoys themselves did not always obey orders, and Mirza Moghal found it hard to command the kind of respect the Englishmen had been able to muster with ease.[5] The civilian population was increasingly unhappy.

Marauding and pillaging robbers outside the city, roaming the countryside, did not help matters. Mujahideen in large numbers were also arriving in Delhi, adding to the city's woes. Little did they realize that this was only a preview. When the British retook Delhi, the plunder would be even worse: it would be accompanied by massacre.

> 'Houses were abandoned and the apartments were like free tables of booty to be plundered at will.'
> —Ghalib

At this point Muhammad Bakht Khan, an Afghan who claimed royal lineage, arrived in Delhi with a large number of soldiers to support the rebels. He ingratiated himself with Zafar and managed to restore some order to the palace, much to the old king's relief.

Bakht Khan made tall claims about how he would defeat the British, even as the Europeans were beginning to assemble on Delhi Ridge. Zafar, by now cognizant of the competence (or lack of it) of Mirza Moghal, Abu Bakr and Bakht Khan, was not very sure that the rebels would beat back the advancing British troops whose guns were beginning to sound closer with each day.

The British began preparations on Delhi Ridge. These were hampered by some amount of jealousy, indecision (principally by Brigadier Archdale Wilson) and anxiety.

---

[5]That the Mutiny provided a chance to settle old quarrels among the zemindars and local rulers was reported by several natives. One such account from Cawnpore, for instance, records 'zemindars of neighbourhood fighting amongst themselves in payment of old quarrels.'

> **Muhammad Bakht Khan:** *In September 1857 when the British had collected outside Delhi to begin their attack, he offered his services to Zafar. Bakht Khan struck terror and restored some order in the army. He threatened even the princes—he warned, quite earnestly, that he would cut off the noses and ears of any prince who indulged in extortion. Later he went to Farrukhabad and from there joined Begum Hazrat Mahal in 1858.*

The 2nd Bengal Fusiliers and other troops were located on Delhi Ridge, unsure of the battles ahead. It was certain that without reinforcements a full-fledged attack on Delhi was out of the question. The 60th Rifles arrived, followed by the Sirmur Battalion led by Charles Reid with a large component of Gurkhas and finally William Hodson and his famous Hodson's Horse.

> **William Hodson (1821–58):** *He had acquired a reputation for being an utterly ruthless adventurer—he once rode from Ambala to Karnal to Meerut and back, a distance of 250 miles, in two days (21–23 May 1857)—and he had arrived at his destination, and his destiny. Was known to be a plunderer, and was under suspicion for fraudulent financial transactions. He created a company of irregulars, Hodson's Horse. His actions at Delhi would send him, marking his way, through the gateway of fame (or notoriety), a gateway that will forever be called Khooni Darwaza after Hodson passed through killing the three Mughal princes in cold blood. His letters were eventually published by his brother as* Twelve Years of a Soldier's Life in India *(1859). He was shot entering a house, apparently looking for loot, during the battle at Begum Kothi, Lucknow.*

*

The Mutiny spread across northern India and the North-Western Provinces. However, civilians and officials, converted Christians and even some maulvis refused to participate.

Landowners saw this chaos as an opportunity to reclaim their lands, and joined their former princes and rulers. In Chhota Nagpur, a zamindar named Bhola Singh tried to enlist the support of local landlords. Thakur Bishwanath Sahi and Pandey Ganpat Rai (a former diwan of the Chhota Nagpur estate) led the rebels. Sahi was described as 'one of the most influential zamindars in Chhota Nagpur'. The Rajas of course were happy to announce that they were back in power, stepping into the power vacuum created by the missing British forces and authority. Miscreants had a field day—moving from place to place to plunder and pillage. Months later this kind of plunder by the Gujjars would contribute to the fall of Delhi back into the hands of the British. In Sirsa—where, according to one twentieth-century historian (J.K. Gupta, 1986), the villagers were oppressed after the British takeover of the region in 1837—both Hindus and Muslims rose in rebellion, and by the first week of June the entire district of Sirsa was free of British rule.

Fatehgarh, a place on the Ganga near Cawnpore, was the site of a factory manufacturing gun carriages. It had a highly secure fort, with a 1,500-yard moat, and was situated in the middle of a ravine. One hundred and twenty civilians, mostly women and children seeking to escape the imminent attack by mutineers, went out from the fort towards Cawnpore by boat. An account of the events was later provided by Hingun, an ayah in the service of one J. Palmer, the deputy collector of Farruckabad, to G.W. Williams, investigating Cawnpore (*SLDSP* 3). Their escape ended when they were stopped at Bithur, Nana Sahib's stronghold. They were tied together and taken to Cawnpore on 11 June. On 12 June many of them were shot dead on Nana Sahib's brother, Bala Rao's orders. Hingun stated:

Early in the morning we reached the rebel camp at Jewhee Medaun. It was about 700 paces from the entrenchment, and firing was going on between the British and the rebels. The European gentlemen were made to sit in one row, their hands were all tied, and the ladies and children were placed in front of them. A resaldar and subadar, mounted on horseback, came and ordered the whole of the Europeans to be killed. The sowars of the 2nd Cavalry with some 300 sepoys commenced firing on them, and some poor children, who were not killed by the musketry, were cut in half, dividing them at the legs into two parts.

Witnesses have claimed that Nana Sahib was against killing the prisoners, but Bala Rao went ahead anyway. It was a preliminary moment to Satichaura and Bibighar. The Satichaura and Bibighar massacres have so imprinted themselves on human memory that this, the first major massacre at Cawnpore, is all but forgotten.

> *There may have been two survivors of the massacre of the Fatehgarh refugees. One was a five- or six-year-old girl who was found near the river. She was rescued and may even have been adopted by Nana Sahib (in 1859 Jung Bahadur of Nepal asked Bala Rao to return all European prisoners, and Bala mentioned a girl, who had been lately handed over to the English). A second survivor was possibly a woman, Miss Sutherland, who claimed a native trooper had rescued her. She published an account of her experiences in a periodical in the 1890s.*

In Gwalior the Englishmen and women had indeed heard of the 'troubles' at Dum Dum and Barrackpore but, as one survivor put it in retrospect, 'we soon ceased to be interested in the affair, thinking it only some trifling explosion about that bugbear, caste.'

The Scindia had to admit that he could no longer guarantee the safety of the Europeans in Gwalior. The Europeans decided that they would send the ladies to his fort. 'Fifteen or sixteen carriages dashing through [the streets], surrounded by hundreds of wild Mahratta horsemen, filled with English ladies and children', writes a commentator of the 'transfer'. Matters were not helped when they heard that Europeans had been massacred in adjacent Jhansi in early June. 'All save a very few believed that our Empire was in its last hour', noted a commentator.

The Gwalior Residency came under siege, and this was despite the Raja of Scindia's continuing loyalty to the British. Officers who tried to reason with the sepoys were summarily shot. The European women were, however, spared and the Raja managed to provide them safe passage to Agra. Mrs Coopland wrote of the escape from Gwalior: 'Some of the women had no shoes or stockings; and one tore off pieces of her dress to wrap round her bleeding feet.'

The Mathura treasury was shifted to Delhi by the mutineers there—the consequence of a delay in giving permission to the magistrate, Mark Thornhill, to move it to safety in Agra. Nearly half a million rupees fell into the hands of the mutineers as a result. An interesting sidelight to the mutineers' efforts was that the locals quarrelled over the leftover coins and attacked each other with swords in the now-burning premises of the treasury. Many died of sword wounds but also from falling masonry. Thornhill himself tried to return to Mathura in a bid to reinstate British authority and prevent further plunder by villagers from the neighbouring areas who had come together under the leadership of one Debi Singh. He returned to find his own house ransacked.

What is evident from the accounts is that there was large-scale plunder and arson in these areas—whole villages ransacked, mobs loitering everywhere, the police, the army and local authority missing. Thornhill in fact mentions in his 1884 autobiography, *Personal Adventures and Experiences of a Magistrate*, that the entire area seemed to look less like an ordered British-governed territory than a feudal kingdom! He was right.

It was a time of general chaos, as there was no central authority—either on the British side or on the mutineers' (who were by now scattered and affiliated with smaller Rajas and leaders). The countryside was devastated, Rajas roamed in cavalcades proclaiming their authority, villages created barricades and watch towers, the towns lit with small fires and appearing ghostly, with damaged buildings and forlorn streets. For the civilians there was little peace. It was the worst of times.

At Agra John Colvin, the Lieutenant Governor, delayed asking the Christians to take refuge in the fort, which was being barricaded against possible attacks by mutineers.

John Colvin (1807–57): Lieutenant Governor of the North-West Provinces in 1857. He attracted notoriety, like Canning, for proposing that mutineers who laid down arms would be allowed to go away free.

There were endless debates about how to deal with the events: should the British continue to behave normally, as though there was nothing tumultuous underway? Or should they retreat to the fort thereby sending out the message that the mighty empire builders were indeed running scared? Colvin informed his fellow officers in other towns that the North-Western Provinces would soon be back to normal—a prediction that turned out to be cruelly wrong. Some of his comrades in Agra, who seemed to understand the pulse of the native troops better, lacked his certainty, and many did voice their anxiety, only to be ignored and even berated for lacking in confidence. Lieutenant Governor John Colvin was about to discover that there was a difference between being brave and being rash. Bad news came in every day about natives firing at Europeans, mysterious fires in the city and other smaller events. On 13 May a small force set out from Gwalior, whose ruler was still on the side of the British, towards Agra.

> ### Colvin's Proclamation, 25 May 1857
>
> *Soldiers engaged in the late disturbances, who are desirous of going to their own homes, and who give up their arms at the nearest government civil or military post, shall be permitted to do so unmolested. Many faithful soldiers have been driven into resistance to government only because they were in the ranks and could not escape from them, and because they really thought their feelings of religion and honour injured by the measures of the government. This feeling was wholly a mistake; but it acted on men's minds. A proclamation of the governor general now issued is perfectly explicit, and will remove all doubts on these points. Every evil-minded instigator in the disturbance, and those guilty of heinous crimes and against private persons, shall be punished. All those who appear in arms against the government after this notification is known shall be treated as open enemies.*

It was only around July that Colvin accepted the inevitable and asked the women and children to move into the fort. With no Europeans, the cantonments fell to the mercy of the native troops and miscreants. Mob activity increased and the looting of bungalows made everyday news. More frightening was the news coming in of Christians being tracked down and killed in large numbers, with entire families being wiped out on occasion.

Conditions in the fort were in sharp contrast to the lives the Europeans had led thus far. Six thousand people, ranging from civilians to soldiers, filled the fort. Water was getting to be precious, stocks of food began to fall and people lived on lentils, rice, and cold meat. Rubbish and disgruntled faces could be seen everywhere. It was also unrelentingly hot. Expectedly, given the heat, filth and crowded conditions, cholera soon made its appearance and claimed several lives. In addition there were rumours of impending enemy attack. Under the deteriorating circumstances Colvin proved increasingly incapable of handling the situation, and Colonel Cotton finally took command of Agra.

> Mr Monckton of Sialkot twice escaped the mutineers by being carried out, wrapped in a white sheet, like a corpse being taken for burial.

Elsewhere in the north-west, the British began to gather more support, and even managed to raise levies and fresh recruits (in fact, to the tune of 34,000). John Lawrence, alert to the significance of Delhi, despatched six battalions of European artillery towards Delhi. Lord Canning, despite pressures from his countrymen and military advisers, refused to order martial law in Bengal, though he did ask for additional troops from Britain. Instead he issued a proclamation in which he emphasized that the British government would never interfere with the religious beliefs of the natives. Published in the widely circulated *Calcutta Gazette*, the proclamation said that subversive attempts were on to 'persuade Hindoos and Mussulmans that their religion is threatened secretly.' In fact, the proclamation went on to state, 'the British had invariably treated the religious feelings of all its subjects with careful respect.' Canning also did not sympathize with the opinion rapidly gaining ground, that harsh measures of punishment were mandated by the events. Canning was already on the way to acquiring that notorious epithet that would haunt him for the rest of his life: 'Clemency Canning'.[6]

Elsewhere, in early June, a hero of rather dubious distinction, James Neill, massacred suspected mutineers at Benares, and disbanded regiments and battalions. Neill's actions are a good instance of the extraordinary brutality of British soldiers in their quest for vengeance.

> ***James Neill (1810–57):*** *The man notorious for the brutality with which he executed mutineers, especially at Benares and Allahabad (the latter preceded the Cawnpore massacres, and therefore may have led to Nana Sahib's actions, rather than the other way round, as European historians try to suggest). He ordered the natives to lick the blood off the floor, before hanging them. George Campbell sickened by Neill's sanction of excessive brutality, declared: 'I can never forgive Neill for his very bloody work.' He had problems with Havelock when they arrived as the first relief of Lucknow. His torture of the captured mutineers, in his own words, is recorded in James Hewitt's* Eye-witnesses to the Indian Mutiny. *Neill was killed in the battle for Lucknow, 25/26 September 1857. He was hailed as the 'avenger' by Trevelyan in his 1865 work,* Cawnpore.

John Lawrence of the Punjab, like many others, wished for stern measures and a swift counter-strategy. By disbanding 36,000 men and confiscating about 70,000 stands of arms, prohibiting iron clubs and imposing restrictions on the movement of all chemicals useable in the manufacture of gunpowder, Lawrence

---

[6]It must also be noted that Queen Victoria was also very circumspect about retribution to be meted out to the mutineers. Alert to the racial aspects of the situation, Victoria supported Canning, and emphasized the need to steer clear of the natives' religion.

may have secured the Punjab. But he also recognized that he was holding the area by the proverbial skin of his teeth, especially because the news of rebel victories from other regions could energize the native troops in his territory—and he needed to act quickly with effective military and political strategies.

Factored into his strategy was, at this moment of crisis, the courage and dependability of one man—someone whose very presence, it was believed, would drive the mutineers away in panic, a man whose reputation as the toughest European in Asia preceded him everywhere, a man credited with having 'kept the border' safe from Afghani tribes. As the Mutiny's true extent and threat became fully visible, and the urgent necessity to retrieve Delhi became clear, it was to this formidable man that John Lawrence would turn. He was already a legend in his lifetime—notorious for being indifferent to his own suffering, free with inflicting it on natives and enemies—when he left Peshawar on 14 June with one final destination, Delhi, and one goal, the empire's safety. When the Raj was in shambles, its citizenry under threat and the country in chaos, John Nicholson was the man the British in the north looked to. He could not, must not, fail. He didn't.[7]

> 'The punishment for Mutiny is death.'
>
> —John Nicholson

Allahabad was in uproar, with massive arson and looting—the telegraph system was destroyed, the railway tracks ripped up, the market place looted. There were fears that the hardy and courageous tribesmen of the Sikh army, thus far staunch supporters of the British, might rebel. On 13 May when they heard that the Bengal sepoys planned to attack the Lahore Fort, Robert Montgomery,

---

[7] William Dalrymple's (2006) description of Nicholson as an 'imperial psychopath' is the best I have come across so far.

the Judicial Commissioner, and Brigadier Stuart Corbett disarmed the Indian garrison. This was perhaps fortuitous, for there may have existed a plot between the Lahore and Ferozepur troops. And Ferozepur, most frighteningly for the British, had the largest arsenal in northern India—its capture by the mutineers would have spelt doom for the entire North-West Provinces. The parade of 13 May at Ferozepur revealed to its brigadier, Peter Innes, a sense of the mutinous spirit. On that same evening the troops mutinied at Ferozepur. At Peshawar, Nicholson and others were expecting a mutiny any day, and even went to bed fully armed and dressed on the night of 21 May.

> *John Nicholson (1821–57): He had faced action in Afghanistan previously. Surrounded by the enemy, and ordered by his officer to surrender, Nicholson refused, arguing that if the English surrendered, their Hindu sepoys would be massacred. After his officer shouted at him, Nicholson flung his weapons down and burst into tears. Predictably, his sepoys were massacred. Reginald Wilberforce recounts how Nicholson once cleaved a man's head in two with one stroke of his sword, so hard that he almost divided the man in two, before turning away with the comment, 'Not a bad sliver, that.' He is said to have displayed the heads of executed criminals on his desk when he administered the Punjab before the Mutiny. His utter disregard for procedure ensured massive executions of suspected mutineers. Often, his heroic deeds have obscured the fact that he was extremely brutal in his treatment of natives. Admired by his Indian sepoys as 'Nikal Seyn', an incarnation of Vishnu, he was as free with flogging before the Mutiny as he was with executions during 1857. A Punjabi ballad narrating the bravery of Nicholson was also popular, with its English translation provided by David Ross in his 1882 book on the Punjab.*

> **Robert Montgomery:** *Judicial Commissioner of the Punjab and based at Lahore in 1857. On hearing of the Meerut incident, in the absence of the Chief Commissioner (John Lawrence), Montgomery ordered the disarmament of the native troops at Mian Meer. He may have averted a major uprising in the Lahore division, and therefore in the North-Western Provinces, with this quick action. In fact he was called 'the man who saved the Punjab' after this. In 1858 he took charge as the Chief Commissioner of Oudh, and later served as the Lieutenant Governor of the Punjab.*

Meanwhile, around 25 May, Nicholson proved why he was so crucial to the empire—he hunted down the mutineers, chasing them non-stop across the ravines and ridges. There were, of course, no prisoners to be brought back—they were simply executed. When he came back to HQ he had been on horseback ceaselessly for over twenty hours, across 70 miles of harsh terrain. His reputation for being invincible was being created.

In the first week of June, forty mutineers were blown from guns in parade grounds and maidans. The effect was gruesome and spectacular, and was calculated to have an effect of absolute horror on the natives. The British had begun to demonstrate that they were second to none when it came to brutality. But the more gory action was about to occur further south. Many others were shot. Sita Ram Pandey's account mentions, in a particularly poignant passage, how he was ordered to execute his own son, who had been arrested for mutiny. He was, after tearful pleadings, eventually excused from the task.

> The method of blowing from guns was last used in 1825. It was not, contrary to received wisdom, a British invention—it was a recognized punishment for mutiny for a long time, and the Mughals had used it too.

All incidents of British brutality were quietly, deliberately erased from European history books with just one incident: Cawnpore.

At Cawnpore, on the banks of the holy Ganga, Major General Hugh Wheeler (1789–1857) believed that things were relatively secure. There were, to be sure, moments of anxiety upon hearing the news from Meerut and Delhi, but confidence was back on high by early June. When it was pointed out to him that the native troops heavily outnumbered the Europeans, he continued to express faith in the former's loyalty. As in other cases, such confidence was possessed only by the commanding officer. Wheeler's compatriots residing in Cawnpore, who had been threatened, warned and advised to leave over the course of May, did not quite share his sense of security. His officers began hoarding stocks of food, strengthening the barracks (where, it had been decided, they would take refuge should the mutineers launch a strike) and making plans for organized evacuation. The barracks themselves were not very sturdy nor very capacious structures. A few outhouses and two main buildings stood a mile from the river. The officers noticed that it was also in open land, with absolutely no cover. These factors were to prove crucial in the days to come. On 21 May, women and children moved into the entrenchment.

Enter a figure, soon to be the most hunted man in British India, one whose exploits constitute the stuff that nightmares are made of (they certainly haunted the British imagination for decades afterwards[8]): Nana Sahib. The Company had decided that the pension collected by Baji Rao Peshwa II, need not be extended to his adopted son, Nana Sahib, a man who enjoyed European culture but did not enjoy the treatment Europeans in India gave him.

---

[8]Until 1878 a model of Nana Sahib existed in the chamber of horrors in London's famous Madame Tussaud's.

> ***Nana Sahib:*** *or Dhondu Pant. Achieved notoriety as the 'butcher of Cawnpore'. He was the adopted son and heir to the state of Bithur (Kanpur). Known to have been a connoisseur of the arts—his palace was full of Kashmiri carpets, he played Chopin on the piano, and supposedly could read and enjoy (even) Balzac. He is supposed to have made secret trips to various places in the north, trying to learn the exact conditions of the British and maybe even conspiring with native troops. In any case, he was initially undecided about joining the mutineers, and was perhaps threatened with the loss of what little territory he possessed. He may have ordered the massacre at Satichaura Ghat and later that of the women and children inside Bibighar. Nana Sahib and Rani Lakshmibai knew each other as children. He was never caught, and till his supposed death in the jungles of Nepal in 1859 or thereabouts, remained one of the most wanted men in India.*

Nana Sahib sent emissaries to the government in India, and even to England to restore his pension.

> ***Azimullah Khan:*** *Secretary and confidante to Nana Sahib. Might have been a key figure in the conspiracy of 1857. Was Nana Sahib's emissary to England to plead on behalf of Nana Sahib. He was supposed to have been a very handsome man, and may have met Dickens, Thackeray, Carlyle and Tennyson while in London. Apparently Azimullah won the hearts of several British ladies. Dozens of letters to him, written by infatuated Englishwomen and one Lucie Duff Gordon who described herself as Azimullah's 'English mother', were found in the palaces at Bithur. Fred Roberts in* Letters Written during the Indian Mutiny *(1924) mentions discovering these letters and expresses dismay and disgust at the stupidity and bad taste of the British women. Azimullah is supposed to have died of smallpox, years after the Mutiny.*

The British were unsympathetic and Nana Sahib incensed. It was at such a moment that the Mutiny erupted in Meerut. His confidante, Azimullah, made a tour of the regiments in the north, and Nana himself may have made clandestine visits to Lucknow and other places seeking to understand the pulse of the sepoys. It is more than likely that he met with the Begum of Oudh (Hazrat Mahal) and thought of mutually beneficial plans for evicting the British.

> ***Begum Hazrat Mahal (d. 1879):*** *The junior wife of the deposed Wajid Ali Shah of Oudh who apparently had upwards of sixty wives and concubines. She was said to have been extremely beautiful and very ambitious, especially on behalf of her ten-year-old son, Birjis Qadr. She wanted Oudh back, though mainly for her son. Hazrat Mahal was able to rally the rebels around her, and Oudh itself became a symbol of all that the British could do to the local rulers and kingdoms. Birjis Qadr was crowned in August 1857 by the rebels. When Delhi fell, Hazrat Mahal was defiant and continued to inspire the rebels to fight on. She did, however, enquire the terms of her surrender, when she was told she might be lucky to retain her life. She rejected Queen Victoria's Proclamation of 1 November 1858, saying it was patently false: the British would never honour their promises. She crossed over to Nepal where Jung Bahadur refused to help, but finally relented and let her stay on. She was one of the heroines of the Mutiny, even though Rani Lakshmibai seems to have cornered all the attention.*

Martin Gubbins was certainly suspicious of the Nana, having heard rumours that Nana Sahib had been secretly meeting conspirators from the troops. Like Henry Lawrence (the Commissioner of Lucknow and brother of John Lawrence), he believed that Wheeler would be foolish to trust the man whose antagonism to the British was well known. Lawrence wrote a note to Wheeler asking him to be mindful of the Nana. Lawrence sent Wheeler eighty-four men, just in case. The confident Wheeler, in an act of generosity that might well have precipitated Cawnpore, believed his position was safe as compared to Lawrence's at Lucknow, and sent them back.

> ***Azeezun (or Azizan):*** *A courtesan at Cawnpore, she may have been one of the key conspirators of the 1857 events. Nana Sahib and Azimullah Khan both knew her. G.W. Williams recorded testimonies (printed in SLDSP 3) by natives where her name comes up. One, 'Jankee Pershaud, Merchant', states: 'The day the flag was raised, she was on horseback in male attire decorated with medals, armed with a brace of pistols, and joined the crusade.' P.J.O. Taylor suggests that she was aware that the Cawnpore Mutiny was planned for 4 June 1857. There are references made to another courtesan or prostitute named 'Oula' in Nanuckchand's narrative about Cawnpore (SLDSP 3), who may also have played a significant role in the Cawnpore events. Saul David identifies her as Adla, Nana Sahib's favourite courtesan.*

Wheeler was confident for another reason: his wife was Indian, and a close relative of Nana Sahib. This, Wheeler assumed, was adequate guarantee that Nana Sahib would not move against him. He was wrong.

On 5 June 1857 all the dire predictions came true. The 2nd Cavalry at Cawnpore started the firing and the plunder, and were joined the next morning by the 53rd and the 56th. During the course of the events a petition was presented to Nana Sahib, requesting his support for the mutineers. Nana Sahib, assuming that this might just get him his kingdom, and seeing in it a chance to trouble the British who had refused to recognize him as king, agreed. For a brief time he even toyed with the idea of leading the mutineers to Delhi, but eventually changed his mind.

> ***Jwala Prasad:*** *One of Nana Sahib's military leaders, he started his career as a soldier under Baji Rao. He might have been the conduit of information and liaison with the other native troops, and was certainly one of the most influential leaders and strategists. The evidence recorded later by G.W. Williams at Cawnpore suggests he was one of the masterminds behind the Satichaura massacre. He was later hanged by the British.*

An attack on the Europeans seemed imminent and Wheeler finally accepted that they were heavily outnumbered. Mid-morning on 5 June, the first shots were fired at the barrack's entrenchments. Now, the entrenchments that stood between the Europeans and the Nana Sahib forces were hardly secure. Termed the 'fort of despair', its earthwork was loose, badly built and had walls just four feet high. The whole structure was also in the open, providing wide and sweeping access to the rebels *from every side* if they arrived in sufficient numbers. It was a terrible choice of location, especially if the Europeans had to defend. Wheeler would have been better off shifting to the magazine, with its huge arsenal. But Wheeler was not preparing for a long siege. He was under the impression that the mutineers would, after their first round of mutiny, head out to Delhi, as their comrades at Meerut had done. His choice of the barracks was also apparently governed by the fact that it was closer to the main road, and any relief force heading towards Cawnpore would find it easier to reach them. All of these proved to be costly errors.

If there was an eye for the storm of the Devil's Wind, that eye was Cawnpore. It would turn out to be one of the bloodiest episodes of the Mutiny.

Nana Sahib was organizing his men for a planned and effective attack against what he knew was a considerably weak enemy. In this he was assisted by a man who would, more than anybody else, evade the British through 1857–58 (only Nana Sahib himself proved more elusive—he was never caught)—Ramchandra Panduranga. For the British, and for Indian history, Ramchandra Panduranga, brilliant military strategist and guerrilla fighter, would become legendary as Tatya Tope. It is possible that Nana Sahib was organizing the army of rebels in order to not only finish off Wheeler and company, but also perhaps retrieve a large kingdom out of the chaos that was northern India. In this he may have been encouraged by the support he got. Local landlords, including Muslim ones (Nana Sahib was a Brahmin) like Mohammed Ali Khan (better known in history and documents as Nane Nawab) and soldiers agreed to help him. The Nana was so confident of his moves and his imminent victory that he actually sent a formal letter to Wheeler, informing him that an attack would be launched the next morning, 6 June! He had, according to the diary account of Nerput, a native (*SLDSP* 2), an 'opium Gomastha' at Cawnpore, established himself in the magazine on 5 June. Nana Sahib then released the prisoners (a total of about 400, according to Nerput), 'opened the armoury, and gave every prisoner any arms he wanted on condition of remaining with him.' The Nana was preparing his army, an irregular one, admittedly, but still an army.

It is possible that despite the odds against Wheeler, the disaster could have been averted if the relief force headed towards Cawnpore had not been delayed at Benares on 4 June and at Allahabad on the 6th. James Neill had prepared to leave Benares on the 4th but was stopped by its station commander, George Ponsonby, saying the native troops at Benares were about to mutiny. Neill did effective damage control at Benares, but for Cawnpore this proved fatal. Neill's large-scale massacres at Benares and Allahabad in early June may indeed have led to Cawnpore.

After the attack was launched, as promised by Nana Sahib, the entrenchment faced almost continuous firing, severely injuring many Englishmen and women, and killing several others. Accounts of the survivors (most notably the ones by Mowbray Thomson, *The Story of Cawnpore*, 1859; J.W. Shepherd, *A Personal Narrative of the Outbreak and Massacre at Cawnpore*, 1879) mention dozens of incidents of mutilation, painful deaths (limbs and parts shot off, so the victim lasted for days in some cases, eventually dying due to loss of blood), burying loved ones and the constant scream of bullets ringing in their ears. There was not enough space to bury all those who died, so bodies were dumped in a disused well in a compound. When the firing abated a bit, men crawled across to a well—the only source of water in that withering heat—to get the precious liquid. Many were, of course, injured or killed by sniper fire during this process. The armed resistance/defence of the Europeans was sporadic, with so many artillerymen and infantry personnel dead or injured. As the siege went on Wheeler was discovering that his position was precarious. Something drastic had to be done to prevent a total slow massacre of the people in the entrenchment.

By 7 June, Nerput's diary records, 'the rebels have murdered every Christian they could find.'

Wheeler's first step was predictable—he wrote asking for help. Wheeler's letter of 14 June 1857 has itself become a legend. Wheeler wrote: 'We have been besieged since the sixth by the Nana Sahib ... Our defence has been noble and wonderful, our loss heavy and cruel. We want aid, aid, aid!' Martin Gubbins, to whom the appeal was made, wanted to send out a relief force. His superior, Lawrence, refused because, as he said, he did not see any chance of success in a battle for Cawnpore.

> **Martin Gubbins (1812–63):** *The Finance Commissioner at Oudh. He had the reputation of being a difficult man, and did not get along too well with his fellow officers, especially with the Acting Chief Commissioner of Oudh, Coverley Jackson. After the Mutiny he was appointed a judge in the Agra Supreme Court.*

Nana Sahib rightly read Wheeler's situation as desperate—short on ammunition, medicine, food and water, saddled with dozens of injured and the dying, and women and children, and no European relief force in sight. Nana Sahib therefore suggested that the British surrender: faced with 4,000 native troops, Wheeler could only muster 250 fit men. Wheeler made one last desperate plea for help (again to Lawrence), once again a classic bit of prose capturing the agony of 1857, and quoted in almost every historical account of the Mutiny:

> British spirit alone remains, but it cannot last forever ... We have no instruments, no medicine, provisions for a few days at furthest, and at no possibility of getting any, as all communication with the town is cut off. We have been cruelly deserted, and left to our fate: we had not 220 soldiers of all arms, at first. The casualties have been numerous ... We have lost everything belonging to us, and I have not even a change of linen. Surely we are not to die like rats in a cage.

John Kaye records the content of Nana Sahib's offer of 25 June, sent through Mrs Greenway: 'All those who are in no way connected with the acts of Lord Dalhousie, and are willing to lay down their arms, shall receive a safe passage to Allahabad.' This message had no signature, and Wheeler therefore refused to accept it. The second time, it was the same message, but now carried Nana Sahib's signature.

> The identities of the messengers who carried out Nana Sahib's terms to Wheeler have been debated. Both were women. The first may have been Mrs Greenway, of a prominent business family in Cawnpore. The second was Mrs Jacobi, a Eurasian woman who was being held prisoner by Nana Sahib.

Wheeler was persuaded to accept, and he sent out a response that they were willing to surrender. He insisted that carriages be arranged for the injured, the women and children, that the British be allowed to carry their arms, and that they be given boats to travel to Allahabad (the roads were not considered safe, since the country was awash with rebels and robbers). The Nana agreed. The point of departure chosen for the boats with the beleaguered British was Satichaura Ghat, adjacent to a temple. Vultures, riding the 'Devil's Wind', darkened the skies as they scoured the grounds, picking at the numerous corpses scattered around.

On 27 June 1857 the decrepit-looking British trooped out of the entrenchment towards the boats. Wrapped in bandages made from shirts and skirts, many bleeding and limping, others distraught but everyone expressing simultaneously, relief and anxiety, the British made their weary way. Their route was lined with large crowds of peoples—according to the testimony of Khoda Bux before G.W. Williams (recorded in *SLDSP* 3), there were '10,000 or 12,000 people, consisting of rebel troopers, sepoys, Tillingas [Telugus], villagers.' Native troopers, recognizing their former officers, solicitously enquired about their health and their families. Some others, however, spat on the officers and abused them. When the English reached the Ghat, they discovered that they would have to wade out in knee-deep muddy water to the boats. The men began to help the women and children across. And then things went horribly wrong.

Accounts from the period differ in their interpretation of what actually happened. It is possible that the tension was very high and the British had fired because they had misunderstood sounds from small arms fire from the shores. They believed that the troopers accompanying them were firing. The boatmen, it was said, had secreted burning coals in the thatched roofs of the boat, which is why they caught fire so quickly once the firing started. The British immediately responded to what they thought was treachery by the men who had promised to see them off safely. Those carrying weapons opened fire. (This is the interpretation suggested by Michael Edwardes in *Battles of the Indian Mutiny*, 1963). The natives massed on the shores assumed that *they* were being shot at by the departing British, and returned the fire.

Mowbray Thomson's account states that the boatmen jumped off the boats when the British were climbing on, suggesting treachery and planning. The men tried to push the boats away, others fired back. Many fell, shot, into the waters. The boat roofs caught fire, and when additional native troops came down the ravine they bayoneted the women and children. In any case, it was a massacre, and no amount of 'they-did-it-first' argument will change that. According to certain British commentators the massacre was planned, for even the guns had been located and concealed in advance—thereby suggesting cold-blooded massacre.[9]

Once the firing stopped the native troops came down and ordered the men and women to form separate groups. Mowbray Thomson was one of the four men (the others were Henry Delafosse, Private Murphy and Private Sullivan) who survived, making their way on foot to Allahabad. One hundred and twenty-

---

[9] A memorandum by Lt Col Williams, Military Secretary to the Government, North-West Provinces, is emphatic on this point of a pre-planned massacre. The memo, along with a massive amount of invaluable evidence by natives at Cawnpore, is reprinted in *SLDSP* 3.

five women and children survived the massacre at Satichaura Ghat. They were taken prisoner. However, according to witnesses like John Fitchett (who deposed before G.W. Williams, and recorded in *SLDSP* 3) the women were not 'ill-treated or disgraced in any way.' They were

> Made to sit in the veranda morning or evening for fresh air; they did not like this, as people came to look at them. I heard them say 'that Europeans never thus treated their prisoners.'

Two Eurasian girls, Amelia Horne and Margaret Wheeler (Wheeler's youngest daughter, also called Ulrica) were supposedly taken away by the troops. These two women also pass into the chronicles of the Mutiny as heroines.

Miss Wheeler is said to have bravely battled the mutineers, then killed her Muslim captor and his entire family and finally thrown herself down a well—a story initiated by the statement of 'Marian Ayah' and recorded in N.A. Chick's Annals of the Indian Rebellion of 1857–58 *(1859) and by news reports in* Friend of India. *Another story is that she survived well into the twentieth century, living as a Muslim woman in Cawnpore. 'Miss Wheeler' became the subject of plays and pictures as an icon of British courage. A steel engraving,* Miss Wheeler defending herself against the Sepoys, *was reproduced in Charles Ball's* The History of the Indian Mutiny *(1858–59). Edward Leckey in his* Fictions Connected with the Indian Outbreak of 1857 Exposed *(1859), however, disputes Marian's account.*

This was the account given by Mr Shepherd, where he mentions the signs of a conspiracy and Miss Wheeler:

The report of three guns was heard from the Nana's camp, which was the signal (as previously arranged) for the mutineers to fire upon and kill all the English; and accordingly the work of destruction commenced. The boats' crews and others were ordered to get away; some of the boats were set on fire, and volley upon volley of musketry was fired upon the poor fugitives, numbers of whom were killed on the spot; some fell overboard, and attempted to escape by swimming, but were picked off by the bullets of the sepoys, who followed them on shore, and in breast-deep water... The boats were then seized upon both banks, the river not being very broad, and every man that survived was put to the sword. The women and chidren, most of whom were wounded, some with three or four bullet-shots in them, were spared and brought to the Nana's camp... One young lady, however, was seized upon (reported to be General Wheeler's daughter) and taken away by a trooper of the 2nd Light Cavalry to his home, where she at night, finding a favourable opportunity, secured the trooper's sword, and with it, after killing him and three others, threw herself into a well and was killed.

The captives were shifted to a small house, originally built by a British officer for his mistress, and therefore named Bibighar. Other European women who had been caught trying to escape from Fatehgarh and other places joined them later. There were, in total, about 200 women and children inside the Bibighar. The conditions were horrendous, and many women and children fell sick with cholera, and about twenty-five died in a week. What happened next is another example of how panic operates. But the events at Bibighar were almost certainly initiated because of another development.

Amelia (or Amy) Horne wrote two accounts; one was published in Chick's collection of 1859, and the other in 1913. The first account goes as follows. She emerged from the river at Satichaura, bruised and in a state of semi-nudity, having fallen into the river after the shooting and dragging herself along through the shrubbery. She was caught and taken to Bithur, where she was cared for by an African (whom she described as 'my sable benefactor'). In her later account she mentions Liaqat Ali, who offered her her life if she converted to Islam and agreed to go with a trooper (years later, when caught, Liaqat Ali persuaded the British to spare his life, based on his granting Amy Horne hers). The trooper was Mohammed Ismail Khan. It is possible she was raped (even C.B. Saunders, who was emphatic that no **Englishwoman** was dishonoured, mentions that some Eurasians may have been 'obliged to sacrifice their honour') even though she does not mention it. They moved to Lucknow, where she remained captive. Eventually she made a deal with Ismail Khan—if he let her go, she would try and ensure he was pardoned. She left captivity at Allahabad, and reached her uncle's house. Eventually she married William Bennett, producing an account, Ten Months in Captivity.

Liaqat Ali: A maulvi of Allahabad, and an extremely influential figure of the Mutiny. He liaised with people, and declared that the Mutiny was a jihad, a holy war against the Christians. He may have rescued Amy Horne. He took possession of Allahabad in June 1857, and was later proclaimed governor. He evaded arrest for nearly fifteen years and was finally arrested at Byculla Railway Station—with several gold ingots in the hollow of his cane. His claim to having saved Amy Horne may have saved his life—he was transported to the Andamans instead.

The man sent to recapture Cawnpore was Henry Havelock—soon to be a major hero, alongside Nicholson and Colin Campbell—who was of the opinion that there was no negotiation possible with mutineers.

> *Henry Havelock (1795–1857):* Lord Hardinge had once predicted: 'If India is ever in danger, the government have only to put Havelock in command of an army, and it will be saved.' Referred to as 'Holy' Havelock for his piety, he attained the unique reputation of winning every battle against the rebels, almost always with about 1,000 men. He was the man behind the famous march to Cawnpore in July 1857 and the first relief of Lucknow. He was knighted but didn't live long enough to enjoy it—he died of dysentery during the second relief of Lucknow.

The first forces heading for Cawnpore had reached Benares on 3 June, well *before* the first attack by Nana Sahib (on 5 June) and the crucial siege. And this is why the miscalculations, confusion and events that followed were so tragic.

Havelock was advancing rapidly towards Cawnpore, meeting up with James Neill on 11 June. Like Havelock, Neill was sworn to action and retribution for the Mutiny and mutineers. However, their progress was slow, hampered by assorted factors ranging from cholera to summary execution of mutineers. Neill sent Sydenham Renaud onward, ordering him to destroy any rebel strongholds or places of refuge. Renaud did exactly that—burning whole villages on his route, massacring natives by the hundreds. When Havelock's men marched, they did so on roads whose trees had mutineers hanging from their branches. 'We will save them [the women and children at Cawnpore], or every man will die in the attempt' declared Havelock. It was not to be.

Often ignored is this sequence: Neill's actions at Benares and Allahabad *preceded* Cawnpore, and to see Cawnpore as having provoked Neill's brutalities is to forget chronology. It is more than possible that it was Neill's horrific massacres that provoked Nana Sahib.

In the face of the approaching army Nana Sahib proclaimed himself Peshwa on 1 July.

Nana Sahib's Proclamation, 1 July 1857

Every man belonging to the Artillery, the Infantry and the Cavalry, who has joined us in the contest, a pension will be given for one generation, to his son, or his wife, or his mother or his sister, or his daughter. And whoever has been, or may be incapacitated by wounds, he will get a pension for his life according to custom; and those who are not incapacitated, and remain on duty, and those who get old in the service, will also receive pension according to custom.

Realizing that he had a more formidable foe facing him than the bunch of decrepit men and women he had fought in the entrenchment and killed at Satichaura, Nana Sahib panicked. His advisers, including Teeka Singh, Bala Rao, Tatya Tope and others, pointed out that the captives would be witnesses against him and the rebels. Somebody recommended that they should, therefore, be put to death. Orders were issued by person or persons unknown. When some of the sepoys protested that they could not, would not kill the memsahibs and children, the services of others were used. On 15 July five assassins, some of them butchers by profession, went in, and emerged a few hours later. The next morning the dead bodies from Bibighar, and some living ones (including at least three boys), were dumped into a disused well. Bibighar was about to pass into legend and Cawnpore was on the verge of becoming the most famous city in the British empire.

> **Hossaini Khanum:** *She was one of the slave girls in Nana Sahib's palace. According to witness depositions to G.W. Williams this woman, called simply 'the Begum' in the accounts, supervised the prisoners inside Bibighar. It is suspected that it was Hossaini who ordered the massacre of Bibighar, and, when the sepoys proved reluctant, fetched her lover Sarvur (or Sirdar) Khan, who was perhaps a Pathan. It is said he had to go back for fresh swords during the massacre. She was never found, and is one of the mystery figures of the Mutiny.*

Havelock's forces met the Nana's army at Maharajpur outside Cawnpore. Havelock's Highlanders, who had acquired a reputation for being fearless, advanced, having just marched 20 miles, across open ground into the face of heavy gunfire. Despite the massive firing they did not fall back. Stepping over the dead and dying, they pushed on relentlessly, and slowly Nana Sahib's army discovered that they might have to withdraw. 'Another charge ... wins the day', roared Havelock, and threw his men into the attack again. It is said that the relentless British charge despite their obvious losses and weaker numbers may have unnerved the rebels. Whatever be the reasons, Havelock took the day.

Nana Sahib escaped to Bithur, and Havelock's exhausted but triumphant men marched into Cawnpore on 17 July, joined soon after by Neill and his forces. They went through the streets, now eerily calm.

> 'Sacred to the Perpetual Memory of a great company of Christian people, chiefly Women and Children, who near this spot were cruelly murdered by the followers of the rebel Nana Dhundu Pant, of Bithur, and cast, the dying with the dead, into the well below, on the XVth day of July MDCCCLVII'
>
> —Inscription on the wall around the Bibighar well

Then the soldiers marched into Bibighar, and confronted walls imprinted with bloodied hands, matted hair and limbs strewn across the floor and blood everywhere. Reeling from the sight, they emerged from the buildings, and were intrigued by a series of tracks leading out of Bibighar, tracks that looked as though things had been dragged over the ground. The British soldiers following the tracks arrived at the well, and looked in.

Perhaps it would be correct to say that the fate of the rebels all over India was decided at this moment. Perhaps it is true that the desire for and the exact nature of the retribution was formulated in the minds of the British soldiers looking down that well. Perhaps the later Raj's aggressive imperialism and ruthlessness had its embryonic moment now. Perhaps it would be correct to say that out of the twisted, shadowy masses lying in that well came the shape of the future.

What the soldiers *saw* was dismembered bodies of dozens of women and children, but what they *perceived* was an India where every mutineer, maybe every native, would pay the price for Nana Sahib's actions. The sight was unforgettable, and the story of 'these most atrocious, fiendish murders', as one British soldier put it, unforgivable.

> 'This is a sight I wish I have never seen.'
> ——Major Bingham on Bibighar

James Neill swore an oath never before heard in British India: 'every stain of that innocent blood shall be cleared up and wiped out ... the task will be made as revolting to ... each miscreant's feelings as possible ... after properly cleaning his portion the culprit is to be immediately

> 'The Tragedy at Cawnpore excited an intense national hatred in the breasts of Englishmen in distant countries.'
> —John Kaye

hanged.' Those unfortunate enough to be caught were, to fulfil this oath, made to lick a portion of the floor clean, after which they had beef and pork stuffed down their throat (to make them lose their caste) and then hanged.

Englishmen and Europeans across the world responded with fury, and offered their sympathy and support for the British in India. News of native massacres of Europeans appeared in periodicals and newspapers in Britain regularly, and fanned the rage. The story of the brave Christian child who stood before the sepoys and declared, 'Oh, kill me! I am not afraid to die. I am prepared to die; but spare my father on whom so many lives and so much happiness depend', which appeared in a magazine for children (the *Juvenile Missionary Herald*, November 1857), moved the British. The nation called for sacrifices and justice. Thus the *Dublin University Magazine* reported in October 1857: 'The Tipperary Artillery Militia ... proffering their voluntary services to maintain the honour of England, and avenge the sufferings of her sons and daughters in the East ... Sure are we that there are multitudes ready to respond to the call of more men for India.'

There were no accounts of the British retribution for Bibighar. The English men, women and children who died in Cawnpore entered record and history books, and had epitaphs and glowing memorials dedicated to them.

The dead natives remained unnamed.

> On the site of the Bibigarh massacre the British erected the Memorial Well Gardens. No Indians were permitted to enter it. In 1947 it was renamed Nana Rao Park.

Lower cadres of the European soldiers took similar oaths. 'Neither man, woman or child of the beast's [Nana Sahib's] family [should be] left alive', screamed an officer in Calcutta. They were further angered by stories of Englishwomen being dishonoured by the mutineers, stories, it was established after due inquiry, that had no basis in fact, and Lady Canning personally wrote to Queen Victoria assuring her of this.[10] John Alexander Ewart found the head of an eighteen-year-old girl in the jungles near Satichaura. His wife had been killed and their small daughter missing. Shocked and furious he declared: 'I am no longer a Christian.' Trevelyan's *Cawnpore* wrote about this transformation of the British soldier:

> It seems strange if the Sahibs could not afford time to pay off an old score that had really been incurred. But the truth was that it mattered to them very little whom they killed, as long as they killed somebody. After the first outbreak of joy and welcome the inhabitants of Cawnpore began to be aware that the English were no longer the same men, if indeed they were men at all.

What was not known at the time to Neill and his men was that the men in charge of Bibighar were *not* the ones involved in the massacre—that had been executed by Sarvur Khan and four others (two Muslims and two Hindus)

> 'Our women were not dishonoured save that they were made to feel their servitude. They were taken out, two at a time, to grind corn for the Nana's household.'
> —John Kaye

---

[10] A 'Memorandum on Treatment of European Females' was submitted to Lord Canning in December 1857. The document is available in William Muir, *Records of the Intelligence Department of the Government of the North-West Provinces during the Mutiny of 1857* (1902). Lady Canning's letter is cited in Macmillan (1988). It was, however, a subject of public debates and literary writings during the period, as critics have pointed out (Sharpe 1991; Paxton 1999).

at the instigation of Hossaini Khanum, who perhaps wanted Nana Sahib implicated in the whole diabolical deed. What was also ignored was the amount of criticism levelled by Indians against Nana Sahib's actions (though considering Neill's actions at Allahabad *before* Cawnpore, it is doubtful if it would have made a difference). For the British every Indian was responsible for Cawnpore and Bibighar, and every Indian would pay.

> **William Muir:** *He was Secretary to the Government of the North-West Provinces. He edited the enormously significant* Reports of the Intelligence Department of the North-West Provinces, *which contains the memorandum and recorded evidence that disproved the theory that Englishwomen were dishonoured during the Mutiny.*

Bibighar became a rallying war cry for the British soldier, and was to resound throughout British India in the months to come.

> Bibighar claimed 191 victims, with seventy-three women and 124 children.

The effect was therefore, only to be expected. Mass executions were the order of the day everywhere. Trials were a mere formality, as many documents record. The fate of the mutineers had been decided well before they were caught. One magistrate even acquired the epithet 'Hanging' Power for executing over 100 men in three days.

It was with this series of incidents in the background that Henry Havelock was marching towards Lucknow, where a siege similar to the one at Cawnpore was underway at this very moment, the native troops there having mutinied on 30 May 1857, well before Bibighar and Nana Sahib.

In fact, sickened by the news of British retribution across northern India (especially places like Benares), Canning issued a Resolution on 31 July. The Resolution outlined a series of administrative steps for court martial and the dispensation of justice. Canning proposed that those mutineers who had been arrested unarmed and who were not guilty of violence should be tried through formal military tribunals. He also argued that they needed to treat those native troopers who had alibis for the atrocities differently.

The Canning Resolution caused an immediate uproar. The European population in India, having by now heard of Meerut and Satichaura, was furious with Canning for even suggesting these procedures. Most wanted swift action, and procedure be damned. Also, the English were against the native troops as a whole, and the question of discriminating between them did not, according to them, arise at all.

The horrific question that now hit the British after Bibighar was: would Lucknow prove to be another Cawnpore?

The man in command at Lucknow, the capital of Oudh, was Henry Lawrence, who had moved from Oudh only in the March of 1857. A strong believer, taskmaster and workaholic, Lawrence was assisted by Coverley Jackson and Martin Gubbins (the latter was to eventually write an angry if detailed account, *The Mutinies in Oudh*, 1858). Lawrence took note of two facts: that the annexation of Oudh had left the natives furious and saddened, and that the troops in Lucknow were very badly organized in terms of their distribution. All the European troops, a sum of less than 1,000 in the Oudh region, were concentrated in Lucknow, along with 7,000 native soldiers.

Minor incidents of unrest and arson recurred through May. News of British reversals and defeats from elsewhere had reached Lucknow, thereby calling into question the image of British invulnerability. The Europeans were no longer gods and were as a result often insulted in the streets or glared at insolently. Gubbins proposed that native regiments must be immediately disarmed and more European troops brought in to prevent further trouble. Lawrence was reluctant to do so, arguing that that might create an image of frightened Europeans. Instead he set about putting together provisions and guns at the Residency and a nearby broken-down fort called the Machi Bhawan. Lawrence, it was evident, was preparing for a siege rather than an offensive against the mutineers.

On 30 May during dinner, the British heard the sound of gunfire. Henry Lawrence, recognizing the arrival of the long-awaited Mutiny, took charge immediately and dashed off to the cantonments. Meanwhile the sepoys advanced upon the officers' mess and nearby buildings, and these were soon aflame.

The battle for Lucknow was on. As the backdrop, a curtain in gruesome detail for the British to see and shudder, was Cawnpore.

The next morning Lawrence managed to drive off a bunch of mutineers who had collected on the road at the race-course. A few were taken prisoner. But Lawrence had been lucky up to this point—a fairly large number of native troops, including the guard at his home, remained loyal. Things would have been very different otherwise. But in other sections of the city the native troops were on the campaign. Lieutenant Grant, of the 71st, was bayoneted in his hiding place under the bed (where his faithful subadar had secreted him), receiving fifteen slashes and stab wounds before he died. Many other such cases were reported as the mutineers swept through the city.

> 'Such a combination against us has never been known in the annals of its history.'
>
> —*A Lady's Diary of the Siege of Lucknow*

Lawrence decided to launch an attack on the mutineers on 31 May. Led by Martin Gubbins and Lawrence himself, the European forces and the faithful sepoys faced the rebels at Mudkipur. In the course of the encounter many of the native troops deserted Lawrence, but the latter managed to defeat them. Rioting, the natural consequence of the collapse of administration as we know it, began in earnest on 31 May. But, we also know that such rioting and plunder are not always spontaneous but are usually engineered. Such may have been the case here too. Later inquiries, says T.F. Wilson in his *The Defence of Lucknow* (1858), revealed the existence of a conspiracy, with Shurruf-ud-dawla, a noble of Wajid Ali Shah's court, as a possible instigator. Christians were sought out and their property looted. After a few days of such plunder, the city lapsed into an unexplained calm. Police patrols were a common sight, and natives were subject to closer scrutiny.

The entire Oudh region exploded in June.

The Faizabad regiments mutinied on 8 June. On the 9th: Dariabad, Secora, Salone and Sultanpur. On the 10th, Pershadipur. On the 11th, Gonda. In just a fortnight, Oudh was gone. In July, Kunwar Singh's intrigues with the troops at Dinapore resulted in a mutiny there. Then Dinapore's commander, George Lloyd, badly executed a move against the rebels. Despite their reverses the rebels, numbering over 2,000, escaped to Arrah.

The Arrah siege was an extraordinary moment in the battles of the Mutiny: sixty-six men held out against thousands of rebels for eight days before help arrived in the form of Vincent Eyre's force.

> **Vincent Eyre (1811-81):** *Eyre, nicknamed the 'Cabool Man' was already a hero before Arrah. In Afghanistan he had volunteered to be a hostage in exchange for his men's lives. On his way to Buxar, Eyre heard that Arrah was under siege. On his own, and in complete contravention of military law—he was not ordered to make this move—he proceeded to Arrah. Arrah was a centre of resistance—in fact, it was crucial if the British wanted to keep the entire Bihar state. He burnt down Kunwar Singh's palace. Eyre was also involved in the relief of Lucknow with Campbell, and the later retrieval of parts of Oudh.*

Kunwar Singh proved to be a wily fighter, escaping skirmishes with great agility. He would play a major role in the days to come. Other leaders also sprang up. Hare Krishna Singh—who, P. Kumar claims (1983) was the real leader in Bihar—recruited 3,000 soldiers to assist Kunwar Singh. Hare Krishna Singh was arrested in 1859, refused to hire a defence attorney at his trial, and was hanged at Jagdishpur.

> **Beni Madho:** *The Rana of Shankerpur and Kunwar Singh's son-in-law. He was Begum Hazrat Mahal's close ally. He was offered a free pardon but refused because Oudh was not to be returned, and he believed his first loyalty was towards Oudh. He was eventually killed in Nepal in a battle with Jung Bahadur's army. A poem written in his praise, and collected by William Crooke, ran as follows:*
>
> The Rana Beni Madhav was a very strong man.
> He wanted a fight and stood ready for it.
> The steel of the Baisas of Baiswara is hard.
> Now it fell to him to face the English.

Preparations at the Lucknow Residency meanwhile went on briskly: nobody among the British for a minute doubted that this was only a temporary lull. Lawrence prepared a chain of command too, just so that there would be no confusion in case of an emergency, or a death. The Residency slowly filled up, as refugees from nearby Sitapur (which had its quota of the Mutiny on 3 June) arrived on 4 June. The women went about doing their bit, as the men inspected fortifications and ammunition. Diarists like Katharine Bartrum provide details of the conditions of the siege. As rumours of an imminent attack by the mutineers, now gathering in and around the Residency came in, Lawrence wrote to the Commissioner at Benares on 16 June: 'the rebels and mutineers are said to be closing in on us.' He was right.

> **Katharine Bartrum:** *Was doubly unfortunate during the siege of Lucknow. Her husband, Dr William Bartrum, had been killed, and she lost her child soon after. She kept a detailed diary of the days in the Lucknow Residency, published as* A Widow's Reminiscences of the Siege of Lucknow *(1858):*
>
> *July 31: My own little babe is taken ill with cholera...*
> *August 1: Last night Dr Wells told me my child was dying; he was so ill he would take no notice of me...*
> *August 2: A day of intense misery, for I was taken ill myself; there was no one to nurse my child and I was almost too weak to hold him...*
> *August 3: Mrs Clark's infant died today...*
> *August 8: Another has been taken away: poor Mrs Kaye has lost her child...*

The heat was awful, adding to the Residency's misery. The rains appeared to be advancing with the monsoons finally hitting Lucknow on 22 June, just ahead of the bigger storm. On 30 June a small force—about 600 men—left Lucknow to meet the rebels at Chinhat. The expedition, led by Lawrence personally, was an unqualified disaster. When they stopped they discovered that the rations had been forgotten. They were tired, hungry, ran short of water, and lost men without gaining even a tactical advantage. One of the men to fall was a fine officer, Colonel Case, whose wife, Adelaide Case, would write an important account of the incidents at Lucknow (*Day by Day at Lucknow*, 1858). The others were massacred systematically until Lawrence, appalled at his error, ordered a retreat. The whole encounter lasted exactly an hour.

Lawrence may well have precipitated the longest siege of the Mutiny with his proactive move against the rebels at Chinhat. Pursuing the retreating European soldiers, the rebels, recognizing their upper hand, and who had previously stayed far beyond, now came right up to the Residency. By nightfall on 30 June, they had surrounded the Residency, now occupied by the grievously wounded men and officers who had retreated and required medical attention. The first relief would arrive only months later, towards the end of September, and the second, which accomplished the evacuation, only in November when Colin Campbell's forces reached Lucknow.

> ***Colin Campbell (1792–1863):*** *The Commander-in-Chief of India, Campbell became one of the heroes of the Mutiny. He led the second relief of Lucknow which finally saved the besieged men and women in the Residency.*

After the siege was launched, the officers and Lawrence decided that it was easier to defend one position. They therefore shifted supplies from Machi Bhawan and blew it up, all the while under fire from the rebels.

Inside the Residency men and women set about making things as safe and easy as possible, not a very easy thing to do, considering the dwindling supplies and number of injured and children. People had lost even their clothes—one officer is said to have made a covering with the cloth from the billiard table—and went about in rags. Accounts from the period capture the horrors of the siege, the conditions inside the Residency, the valour of men and women and the selfishness and generosity of the people inside. Soon after the siege began Lawrence was hit by a shell. He never recovered and died forty-eight hours later on 4 July. Most of the people inside cooperated in trying to improve conditions. John Inglis writes: 'All have descended together into the mine, all have together handled the shovel for the interment of the putrid bullock, and all accoutred with musket and bayonet have relieved each other on sentry [duty]'.

Dr William Brydon: *Seems to have been the luckiest man in British India. He was the sole survivor of the disastrous Afghan campaign (1842), where 16,000 British and native troops were killed. His miraculous survival—riding injured on horseback after he had thrown his last weapon, the broken handle of his sword, at the pursuing Afghans—was so astounding that it became the subject of a painting,* **Remnants of an Army** *by Elizabeth Thompson (Lady Butler). As though this was not enough, Dr Brydon was trapped inside the Residency at Lucknow during the siege, was wounded—the musket ball hit him in the back and went right through his body—and survived.*

There were other problems. Brigadier John Inglis reported: 'an occasional spy did indeed come in with the object of inducing our sepoys and servants to desert.' The British officers had to keep an eye on the native troopers inside and the rebels outside. The belief that their native troops might be communicating with the rebels caused great anxiety, and often resulted in excessive suspicion.

Havelock was urged to proceed on the Trunk Road, but his telegram of 24 July 1857 was fairly simple: 'I must first relieve Lucknow.'

On 20 September good news finally reached the Residency—Havelock was expected to reach Lucknow in a few days. Havelock advanced with 1,200 British troops, 300 Sikhs and some dozen guns. He issued an order that there was to be no looting, that 'all British soldiers that plunder' were to be 'hang[ed] ... in their uniform.' Havelock was not very sanguine about being able to, first, arrive safely in Lucknow considering the Oudh country with its rebels and, second, that he would be able to relieve Lucknow. Enroute he battled rebels and locals at Unao, lost men to cholera, defeated rebel forces at Bashiratganj and finally returned to Cawnpore, unable to continue under such conditions. The reason for this return was Neill—who sent an urgent message that he was threatened by a rebel army of at least 4,000 men.

On 15 August, accompanied by about 400 men, Havelock moved against a rebel force of over 4,000 men at Bithur, leaving Neill with a 100 to defend Cawnpore.

Meanwhile in a surprising turn of events James Outram (1803–63) was appointed the head of the Dinapore and Cawnpore divisions. Outram, a distinguished soldier, however, informed Havelock that the right to relieve Lucknow remained Havelock's. On 19 September Havelock set out to cross the Ganga, and crossed into Oudh in pouring rain. Within sight of Lucknow, they encountered rebel troops stretching for over 2 miles at Alambagh, but managed to overcome them. Nearing the Residency there was confusion and debate about the best approach, considering that many routes that provided safety and cover were flooded after the rains. Captain F.C. Maude commanding the guns provided covering fire as they crossed the crucial bridge under heavy fire, into Lucknow. And then disaster struck.

With a clash of egos between Havelock and Outram the command was always in some doubt. The decision to take the street leading to the Residency was taken in a moment of confrontation between the two.

The soldiers paid the price. Rebels lined the rooftops and houses along the street. Neill was shot through the head and killed as the relief force moved under incessant firing. But at last, after heavy casualties, they arrived in sight of the Residency. On 25 September the soldiers of the relief force were welcomed with tears of joy and unspeakable sorrow by the hollow-cheeked tensed people in the Residency.

> 'Let us go then, in God's name!'
> —James Outram, on the relief of Lucknow

It was a major achievement by any stretch of imagination.

*

By August 1857 the rebels' movements and actions had more or less run its course. They did not have a coherent strategy in place even though local rulers were trying to band together. British troops, and native troops still loyal to them, were making advances in the Oudh region, and making sorties into the countryside, winning small and big battles. The communication system greatly helped in the troops' movements. Indeed the bulk of the documentation that shows us the progress of the British counter-attack consists of telegrams (most of these compiled in George W. Forrest's *Selections from Letters, Despatches and State Papers*).

The rebels retained control in most of the places that they had mutinied in. However, these places were also the sites of rioting and arson. The administration had broken down, though the local chiefs did try and ensure that the town continued to function normally. Raids by roaming communities of robbers, poor organization and general incompetence made things of everyday administration exceptionally difficult. Delhi was a good example of the confusion. While Zafar was nominally in charge, he may not have, perhaps, been aware of several happenings within the city. For example, the dozens of petitions submitted to him demonstrate the collapse of any system in tax-collection and law and order. Random arrests of uncooperative civilians were common, adding to the discontent in the city.

Some rulers and citizens offered support to the British.[11]

> *From the Hindoo and Mohomedan inhabitants of Madras; and to the Right Honourable Lord Harris, Governor of Fort Saint George, dated 2 July 1857.*
>
> *We want words strong enough to convey the feelings which are inspired by the frightful atrocities that have been committed. Their crimes admit no palliation ... We thus assure your Lordship in Council of our loyalty towards and deep sympathy for the British Government and with the relatives and friends of all who have fallen victim to those blood-thirsty and misguided men ... We beg to express our conviction that the overthrow of the British power in India would be the greatest calamity that could fall upon the natives...*

---

[11] These statements of loyalty were collected in the anonymously edited *The Mutinies and the People* (1859).

Thus the restoration of Zafar to the throne did not necessarily provide a leadership or a political structure. Mirza Moghal and Abu Bakr were too inexperienced to be effective. Zafar was past the point of caring, though he seems to have been annoyed at the ways of the rebels in Delhi—often ordering compensation for traders and prohibiting extortion.

> *Mainoddin Hassan Khan:* One of the two natives whose detailed accounts of the Mutiny were published by Charles Theophilus Metcalfe in Two Native Narratives of the Mutiny (1898), Hassan Khan was a thanedar at Pahargunj Police Station in Delhi. He mentions the circulation of chappatis. After the Mutiny broke out he claims he went to the palace and begged the king that the Europeans' lives be spared (Zafar responded by saying that the rebels were not obeying his orders). He helped Metcalfe escape, placed himself on the sick list and only attended to the king—because he did not want to be accused of being a British sympathizer, but also did not want to risk battling the British, whom he had served for so long.

The rebels in Delhi also received oaths of loyalty from local chiefs and Rajas. These chiefs did not however bargain for extra expenses in return for their loyalty—they were asked to supply horses, grains, money and other items to the Delhi administration, as support for the rebel cause and in the name of the Mughal emperor. Indeed, they may have extended their support in a bid to *augment* their incomes—which had been curtailed by the Company. The soldiers too were unhappy. Their salaries had not been paid, and they petitioned Mirza Moghal and Zafar repeatedly for the same. Many of the rebels may well have mutinied for financial reasons. Their pay in the Company army was meagre. They may have hoped for better pay under their native kings once the British had been overthrown. Nana Sahib encouraged this view among the sepoys and in one of his Proclamations he did announce a higher pay. Bishwanath Sahi in Chhota Nagpur promised rebel sepoys badshahi pay.

Instead of higher pay and better incomes, what the rebel sepoys and rajas got was extortion and no pay. There was, according to witnesses, an altercation in Delhi over the amount of pay as early as 28 May. The infighting stopped only after the arrival of Bakht Khan. The soldiers in Delhi were doubly affected—Gujjars roaming outside the city walls stole guns and foodgrains. It is more than possible that this last may have contributed to the collapse of Delhi and the Mutiny itself.

Civilians and some of the local rajas quickly tired of the rebels—they now wanted peace and some order. And this, they realized, could happen only if the British came and took back Delhi. The 'Devil's Wind' had more or less run its course, and like all winds, lost its intensity.

It was time for things to change, or rather, change back.

Change is often violent.

Three
The Retreat of the Native

From August 1857 the rebel armies suffered reverses, as the British forces regrouped and found a new determination—helped, in great measure by Cawnpore—and won skirmishes and battles in several places. As G.O. Trevelyan put it in *Cawnpore*: 'embattled in their national order, and burning with more than their national lust of combat, on they came, the unconquerable British Infantry.' Slowly but methodically, the British recaptured lost territories and cities. Battles by European forces in various sectors had one unique distinction after July 1857—they took no prisoners.

Retribution was to be swift, brutal and memorable: the natives would never forget the mass hangings, the blowing from guns, the depopulation of whole villages by a British soldiery that had acquired a viciousness unparalleled in its history.

The Raj and its Retribution

Chronology of Major Events, August–December 1857
Delhi, Agra, Lucknow, Cawnpore

13 August	Havelock returns to Cawnpore
14 August	John Nicholson arrives at Delhi Ridge

24 August	Nicholson defeats Nimuch rebels at Najafgarh
14 September	Battle for Delhi begins
20 September	Delhi cleared of rebels
21 September	Zafar surrenders
22 September	Zafar's sons/grandson shot dead by Hodson
25 September	First relief of Lucknow by Havelock and Outram
10 October	Greathed's column defeats rebels at Agra
17 November	Second relief of Lucknow by Campbell
26/27 November	Tatya Tope defeats Windham at Cawnpore
6 December	Campbell defeats Tope, takes Cawnpore

News about more European troops heading towards Delhi was filtering in. We have already glimpsed one such troop movement: racing down from the north at a pace—sometimes covering 40–50 miles in eighteen hours—that matched the temperament of the man in command. Hardly stopping for rest was the compact Punjab Moveable Column, led by the fiery-eyed, unsmiling, bearded man who would remain in the saddle in the blazing sun while his exhausted men slept in the shade, John Nicholson. He drove them on, knowing the urgency of capturing Delhi. At Amritsar, having been on the road unstoppingly, the officers were having their dinner and hoping for a night's rest, at the least. And then Nicholson announced, very quietly: 'Gentlemen, I do not want you to hurry your dinner, but the column marches in half an hour.'

> ***Delhi Field Force:*** *The name taken by the British Forces accumulating on Delhi Ridge in July 1857. It was first headed by Henry Barnard, and later by Archdale Wilson. It was put together as early as 17 May with 500 carts, 2,000 camels, 2,000 coolies and 2 million pounds of grain. According to a letter from Archdale Wilson of 24 July 1857, they had only 2,200 Europeans and 1,500 Punjabis, and required more reinforcements if they needed to attack Delhi.*

Nicholson's destination was the seat of power, Delhi. His advance was marked by mass executions of mutineers and ferocious skirmishes. Northern India trembled at the ferocity with which Nicholson decimated natives. To the British he was a hero. To the natives he was to prove the devil incarnate, and a devil apoplectic with fury at that. Nicholson had no patience with the business of court martial, the procedural formalities that the British, even in the moment of crisis, could not abandon. His was a far simpler way—the gun and sword, his aim was simple too, the defence of the empire. He left his signature at every town: the gallows, installed as soon as Nicholson arrived at any place. Nicholson reached Delhi Ridge on 14 August 1857. Fred Roberts records Nicholson's arrival in these terms in his account: 'by the grace of God ... like a king coming into his own'. William Hodson, who would play a prominent part in the Delhi events to come, wrote of Nicholson's arrival: 'the camp is all alive at the notion of something decisive taking place.' His arrival clearly had an energizing effect. European morale shot up immediately: perhaps the empire was not lost as long Nicholson was still fighting.

> William Hodson, of Hodson's Horse, was a student at Rugby under Thomas Arnold, the famous humanist-educationist and father of the great Victorian critic and poet, Mathew Arnold.

On 16 August news arrived that a batch of mutineers had left the city and was making its way northward. Archdale Wilson sent Hodson to tackle them. Hodson met the rebels outside Rohtak. Since his own army was ill-equipped to engage with the rebels in a town battle, Hodson embarked upon a brilliant strategy to draw them out into the open. He began to withdraw his men. The rebels assumed they were retreating, and raced out after them to finish them off. This was precisely what Hodson had hoped for.

Once he reached open ground, he raced back, and charged the rebel troops, now out in the open and the refuge of the town far behind them. In their retreat, the rebels lost fifty men.

> Charles Griffiths in his account of the siege of Delhi describes how rebel sepoys apparently played British tunes like 'The British Grenadiers' and 'God Save the Queen' on their bands, even as they fired at the Europeans!

By the last week of August the ammunition supplies of the rebels in Delhi were running low and their situation was getting desperate. However, this did not prevent them from making sorties against the gathered Europeans—after all they kept assuring Zafar that the firanghis could and would be driven back. But right now it was Nicholson's time.

John Nicholson leading, with his personal green flag held high by his massive Pathan bodyguard, an army of 1,600 infantry and 450 cavalry met Muhammad Bakht Khan's forces numbering about 6,000 at Najafgarh town. Nicholson continued on foot after his horse was shot. The British fought fiercely, clambering up the walls of the town in what might well have been a rehearsal for Delhi. Bakht Khan realized that the British forces were determined and therefore certain to win. What he then did may have altered the psychology of the mutineers all over northern India. Instead of continuing the battle, or at least making strategic moves, Khan withdrew. Now, Bakht Khan was the man who had taken command of the Delhi forces. It was Khan who had assured Zafar that they could win against the British. And now this confident soldier had retreated before the enemy. It seemed to the mutineers inside Delhi that the retreat augured ill for them all. John Nicholson, with less than half the numbers of his opponent, had defeated Bakht Khan.

It also proved to the rebel forces the extent of British tenacity.

However, the British had their own problems, mainly with their guns. Their guns misfired at an alarming rate, a situation that made the forthcoming assault on Delhi a difficult task. It was only much later they discovered that their gun lascars, whose sympathies were with the rebels, had tampered with the guns. The officers in charge did not always agree on strategy, and their ego clashes and prejudices often resulted in administrative chaos. Brigadier Wilson found it impossible to rein in the enthusiasm of William Hodson (who was, by all accounts, a loose cannon, to use an appropriate metaphor), or the crusade-like zeal of Nicholson. Nicholson himself held Wilson in contempt for being weak and indecisive.

> At one point Nicholson suggested that if Delhi had to be won the indecisive Wilson would have to be superseded.

Despite the problems all agreed that the priority was the capture of Delhi. Richard Barter in his *Siege of Delhi* (published in 1984) recorded detailed descriptions of the planning for battle and the battle itself. Siege batteries were laid near Mori Bastion, between the Kabul and Kashmir Gates, and the Water Bastion. The city had a twenty-four-foot-high wall running 7 miles around the city with a twenty-five-foot-wide ditch around it. The Gates were protected by at least forty large guns. The city itself held roughly 150,000 people. Their biggest advantage, as the news conveyed by the spies suggested was, paradoxically, their enemy. The British had about twenty-two light field-guns.

The princes leading the armies had no experience of war, nor of leading troops. Strategies were often contradictory, as were orders since the princes themselves did not agree on what had to be done. The first flush of the Mutiny had waned—Mirza Moghal and the rest discovered that while they took the city with relative ease, it was a wholly different business to retain it.

But what was also unsettling for the mutineers inside was that they were losing civilian support. The soldiers had to be paid, and the treasury was not equipped for this. The princes raised money from local merchants, who naturally resented it and began burying their wealth. Looting by mutineers was common, and lawlessness reigned. The civilians inside longed for the return of order—and it was abundantly clear that the mutineers could not achieve this.

> On a reconnaissance mission, Nicholson stood up on the city walls, in full view of the enemy. Apparently he was recognized as *the* 'Nikal Seyn' by the rebel sepoys, who were so much in awe of the hero that they did not even fire at him.

On the Ridge the ground rules were emphasized for all the men of the British troops: no prisoners to be taken, no women and children to be harmed and no plunder (this last was, of course, not obeyed, as we shall see). In comparison with the numbers of rebels inside Delhi, the attacking force was pathetically small: 5,000 men.

The battle that would decide the fate of the empire was about to commence.

*

On 13 September breaches were opened up in the two Bastions, preparing the way for the artillery charge. The British had five columns for the attack. Three were led by Nicholson himself and made for the Kashmir Gate. Major Reid led the fourth one to capture a suburb, Kishanganj, just outside the walls, and then mount an attack on the eastern Kabul Gate. The fifth was led by Brigadier Longfield as a reserve. Hope Grant led the cavalry defending the Ridge against a possible attack.

The ditch surrounding the walls had to be crossed with ladders, under heavy rebel fire. Nicholson led the 60th Rifles, and with sustained assault, captured the first breach. The British entered the city of Delhi near the Kashmir Gate—surely a turn in the tide in the bloody course of 1857. Meanwhile a small party of British and native troops placed bags of gunpowder under the Gate, and blew it open. George Campbell—a capable officer who Nicholson thought should supersede Wilson—led his men through the Gate. Two thousand men of the British attacking forces had by now entered the city.

Nicholson was now heading for the Kabul Gate. Major Reid, unfortunately, was unable to seize Kishanganj, and was himself severely injured. Things were not helped by conflicting commands from Richard Lawrence (who was to succeed Reid) and Captain Muter. In any case the Reid column was stuck. Some of the finest officers were dead, and the unit split up in the confusion and smoke. The enemy did not appear to be yielding an inch—after all they were fighting the battle for their very lives, and Delhi—and a massacre seemed more than likely. William Jones too found himself without support at the Kabul Gate. Nicholson, annoyed that they were losing the advantage gained, ordered Campbell to move to the Jama Masjid. He himself realigned his column and moved towards Lahore Gate. The column moved through the death-trap like Burn Bastion, with its narrow lanes and heavy rebel fire from the houses on both sides. Things were beginning to look really bad as each British attack on the Lahore Gate was repulsed.

To take that route was certain suicide, and the British recognized the impossibility of their situation. It may be a battle that would save the empire, but it was also a battle that would end their lives. At this point, trapped in a no-win situation and considering retreat, they noticed a well-known green flag, weaving through the smoke and sniper fire. A bear-like man, impatient with the failure, contemptuous of the possibility (perhaps, certainty) of death, indifferent to the impending massacre, was heading out to Lahore Gate. John Nicholson, never one to care for his personal safety, and perhaps actively seeking a glorious death, had one goal: Delhi. At all and any cost. His officers pleaded with him that the task was impossible and they could not charge. Nicholson rejected their pleas and arguments. Waving his sword high in the air he stepped out into the lane, in full view of every single sniper, shouting at his men to charge with him. The Gate had to be taken if Delhi was to be taken.

The bullet hit him just under the left arm. 'You are hit, sir', someone cried out to him. 'Yes, yes,' Nicholson is said to have responded irritably. Predictably, he refused assistance, and had to be persuaded to a shelter near Kabul Gate. Others wounded from other such charges were being carted away by the dozen. The dead, of course, lay there.

Captain Barter now took charge of the 75th. Holding on to the ground they had gained itself seemed difficult, to make another charge, impossible, even though Nicholson had demonstrated that it could be done. Campbell could not take the Masjid, which was heavily fortified with sandbags and all. He stayed put, awaiting reinforcements or further orders, a situation complicated by the fact that Nicholson was injured. Fred Roberts recorded his horror at what the loss of Nicholson meant: 'Other men had daily died around me ... but I never felt as I felt then. To lose Nicholson seemed, at that moment, to lose everything.'

By now British casualties had reached 1,000 (including sixty officers) and mounting, and Brigadier Wilson contemplated retreat. On hearing of this the injured but still fierce Nicholson is reported to have roared in his tent: 'Thank God I have strength yet to shoot that man, if necessary.' Nicholson, lying there dying, was certain that Delhi could be taken, if they were willing to charge. Another officer—also one who was not fond of Wilson—Baird Smith agreed with Nicholson. And hearing of his compatriot's courage, decided that the advance would continue. It is more than likely that Nicholson demonstrated the necessity for persistence, even at high costs. And it paid dividends. The British would not now withdraw.

British troops advanced, inch by bloody inch, into Delhi. Every house was a trap, every wall a cover, and every window a sniper-

> 'I am dying, there is no chance for me.'
> —John Nicholson, lying injured.

sight. Street fighting, never the best option for the troops, was the only order of the day. Indeed, Delhi was captured precisely through such street fighting. Hope Grant, leading the Cavalry Brigade, was full of praise for the native cavalry, saying: 'nothing could be steadier, nothing could be more soldier-like than their bearing.'[1]

And as they cleared street after street of snipers and rebels, Wilson encountered an unexpected, even absurd problem: his men discovered great stores of liquor everywhere. The effect can be imagined: drunken soldiers would not obey orders and made a perfect nuisance of themselves. Far from being orderly Company

---

[1] It is fascinating to note how every single memo, report and letter of the attack on Delhi written by senior or commanding officers, recorded the names of officers who had offered what they call 'assistance and support', in addition to 'nominal rolls of killed, wounded, missing.' In a sense it was a roll call of honourable conduct in war. Even in the thick of battle, the British obsession with documentation and archiving was not abandoned. For examples of such roll calls see *SLDSP* 1.

soldiery, they functioned—to use the term loosely—like village idiots. Things got so bad that Wilson ordered liquor hauls to be destroyed. They also looted the houses on the lanes they passed through, and many soldiers accumulated a fortune in the process. Thus, after the mutineers had raided Delhi's citizenry, the new powers exploited them and extorted money, and now the British soldiers looted them. Numerous accounts of this large-scale looting of Delhi exist.[2]

> 'Many a time has Delhi been the theatre of war and bloodshed, but never more so than during the Sepoy Rebellion.'
> —Bholanauth Chunder (1869)

There did not seem to be much to choose from: native pillager or foreign plunderer.

The soldiers shot, bayoneted or hanged natives encountered in the streets—suspecting many to be rebels. There was little attempt to cross-check their participation in the rebellion. These executions were random and instant. Mirza Ghalib mourned the situation in Delhi in a verse written as part of a letter:

> Every grain of dust in Delhi
> Thirsts for Muslims' blood.
> Even if we were together
> We could only weep over our lives.

On 16 September the British troops, not very sober, it appears, resumed operations. The rebels abandoned Kishanganj, leaving behind them a large arsenal of over 170 guns. The British were now shelling the palace itself. The Burn Bastion fell on 17th, and

---

[2] William Ireland, *A History of the Siege of Delhi* (1861), Richard Barter, *The Siege of Delhi* (1984), Fred Roberts, *Forty One Years in India* (1897) and Charles Griffiths, *The Siege of Delhi* (1910).

Jones, dividing his forces into two, sent one to the Jama Masjid and led the other to the Ajmer Gate. The Masjid eventually fell (after the Mutiny it was reopened for prayers only in 1862).

One more interesting turn was, however, still to come. The mutineers in the palace persuaded Zafar, all of eighty-two years, that he must himself lead the final charge against the enemy. But Zafar had had no experience of battle, except those feuds with his many cousins and family relations inside his palace. He saw himself as a poet rather than a warrior, (and hurling quatrains and couplets at the enemy has never won a battle yet). His advisers pointed out to him that he would be assured of ever-lasting fame if he died fighting the enemy. Zafar appears to have been swayed by the arguments—after all he was the descendent of Timur and Babur, great warriors before whom vast armies had retreated and proud kings surrendered. When it became known that the old king himself would lead the last sally, nearly 70,000 men collected outside the palace, ready to join Zafar on this, their last defence of Delhi and the Mughal empire. But the glorious final assault never took place. Hakim Ahsanullah Khan, to whom Zafar always deferred, argued against such an action. He suggested to the old king, that leading the rebel force would create the impression that he, Zafar, was the man behind the mutineers. On the other hand, if he did not, it was possible to make out a case that Zafar had acted under pressure from the mutineers and that he had never *willingly* sided with them. Zafar found the suggestion extremely attractive. He therefore fled with his family to the tomb of his ancestor, Humayun, on the Mathura road. There he waited, in great trepidation, for the British to arrive and decide his fate.

It took six days of fierce fighting to finally capture Delhi. The soldiers and artillery blew open the palace. The Union Jack flew once again from the ramparts on 20 September. The soldiers danced victory jigs in the Jama Masjid and victory fires were lit everywhere. Delhi was open for (Company) business again.

154 the great uprising

> At least 3,850 men from the British forces—including 2,140 Europeans—were killed in the battle for Delhi.

One person had to be informed of the triumph. John Nicholson lay in terrible agony, waiting for death, in his tent. He had declared he wanted Delhi to be taken before he died, and, as he put it, his wish was granted. Neville Chamberlain went to see him, carrying the news that Delhi was British territory again. The indomitable Nicholson mustered up enough strength to fire a celebratory shot from his pistol, much to the amazement of his troops.

Three days later, on 23 September, Nicholson died, mourned by his faithful troopers, who had called themselves 'Nikal Seynis'. A report published years later in *Fraser's Magazine* in February 1859 expressed its feelings about the reconquest of Delhi thus: 'Delhi is ours; but at what a cost in officers and men! And Nicholson is dead.' It was the one terrible feature of the British retaking of Delhi for most British men and women. Others like Karl Marx expressed the opinion that the retaking of Delhi did not necessarily mean the Mutiny was over—for parts of India were still held by the rebels, and the native proportion of troops far outnumbered the Europeans everywhere.

And then a long period of massacres began inside Delhi.

A reversal of Satichaura Ghat was on within the city, as the soldiers butchered the natives in the streets. In the Kucha Chelan area alone nearly 1,500 natives were killed. Animals gnawed the bodies lying in the streets and the stench was unbearable. Muslims in particular were sought out and killed. Mirza Ghalib records: 'In the entire city of Delhi it is impossible to find one thousand Muslims.' Even women were shot—though this may have been because the rebel sepoys often disguised themselves as women as they tried to escape. Some of the natives hid in cellars to escape the British. There was no food, and many fled into the countryside where the Gujjars plundered them. Theophilus Metcalfe even hanged them from the beams of his own house. There were gallows all over the city as the soldiers sought out possible mutineers and hanged them. Yet, in many cases, they did not bother to check whether those they hanged were really mutineers.

> 'Delhi is no more a city, but a camp, a cantonment. No Fort, no city, no bazars, no watercourses...'
> —Ghalib

Once again the Raj's brutal retribution proved astounding: civilians starved to death, if they were not hanged or bayoneted. According to Mrs Saunders, wife of the Commissioner, 'every native that could be found was killed by the soldiers, women and children were spared.'

> Queen Victoria 'bought' Zafar's crown and two throne chairs from Robert Tytler, but did not apparently pay him the promised amount of £ 500 according to Harriet Tytler's memoirs.

Delhi had been plundered before—Nadir Shah was its best-known plunderer—but this was on an unimaginable scale.

Delhi was rapidly becoming a mass grave.

One estimate cited by Francis Robinson put the number of dead at 30,000.

> Pork and beef were stuffed down the throats of natives so as to make them outcastes before they were executed.

Commentators from the time were horrified at the brutality of their men. Edward Vibart wrote in a letter that he hoped he would never see such horrors again in his life—and he was referring to British savagery. John Lawrence, aghast at the barbarity, pleaded for a transfer of administrative power to the Punjab government—a move that was taken seriously and implemented only in February 1858, and too late for Delhi.

> Captured natives were given what was called a 'Cawnpore dinner'—six inches of steel bayonet.

Out at Humayun's tomb the situation was fraught. The British wanted the king and his family captured. The man entrusted with this job was William Hodson, who may have negotiated with Zeenat Mahal. Hodson went to Humayun's tomb with fifty soldiers and sent in emissaries: would the king surrender voluntarily, he enquired? Mirza Ilahi Baksh, a kinsman of Zafar, persuaded the tired and very frightened old king that he should surrender. The government had assured him his life, informed Hodson. He reaffirmed the guarantee, and a few hours later, Zafar and Zeenat Mahal emerged from the tomb. The journey back was perhaps the saddest and cruelest any Mughal emperor had ever undertaken in their citadel, Delhi. Thousands lined the road, and walked behind the royal couple, as the procession made its way to the Fort. In a cruel irony, Zafar, now really 'the Shadow King' described by Maud Diver in her account of British India, returned to that icon of Mughal glory, the Red Fort, a prisoner. Later he was shifted to Zeenat Mahal's haveli in Lal Kuan.

Some of the Britishers were unhappy that the king had been captured and brought back alive—they felt that granting the leader of the rebels his life went against the very grain of justice.

The next day Hodson was back, this time to capture the princes, who they believed had ordered the massacre of women and children in the king's palace in May 1857. The three princes, Mirza Moghal, Khizr Sultan and Abu Bakr (the last was about twenty years old) emerged in silence, carefully watched by Hodson and his men. The streets were, expectedly, lined by natives again. The procession made its way slowly. As it neared the city walls, something happened that has never been satisfactorily explained. Hodson's account was that when the princes neared an archway near the walls, a massive gathering of natives pressed closer in (another officer's account states that it was only a small crowd). Hodson's interpretation was that the mob would have tried to rescue the princes.

Hodson's actions were calculatedly horrific and humiliating.

He went up to the princes and asked them to get down from the cart in which they were riding. He asked them to strip naked, an unpardonable offence to the princes (or to anybody). He then shot all three of them dead in full view of the crowd. The spot and archway would hereafter acquire the name Khooni Darwaza. Later, the unrepentant and brazen plunderer that he was, Hodson took away their swords and rings. A painting of Hodson shooting the princes (in the painting the princes are clothed) exists in the Swatantrata Sangram Sangrahalaya inside the Red Fort.

No enquiry was ever ordered into Hodson's conduct. But then victors do not examine their own actions.

> Twenty-one princes of the royal Mughals were hanged after the Mutiny.

The plunder of Delhi stopped only when Edward Greathed's column marched out of Delhi in pursuit of mutineers who were racing away in all directions into the countryside. Richard Barter records that this march was done *over* dead bodies—the smell was so bad he had to use eau de cologne (which he had looted from a shop!) to get through. Greathed, however, had another destination too—Agra, where the fort was under siege, and women and children were living (mostly dying) in appalling conditions.

Agra fort, towards which Greathed was racing, covering, it is said, about 50 miles in twenty-six hours, was a house of horrors.

The people there expected to die any day—either of disease or at the hands of mutineers. Even though the British residents inside had heard of the capture of Delhi, their faith was not fully restored. This was partly because the natives at Agra could not believe that the capital had been taken by the firanghis and continued to behave as though the rebels were winning.

However, by the time Greathed arrived, many of the retreating Delhi mutineers had dispersed to their villages. There was just one ambush, which was quickly taken care of. As can be imagined the conquest of Delhi had given the British soldiers enormous confidence, and these skirmishes were dealt with swiftly as the Raj rode back.

On 11 August part of the Lucknow Residency had collapsed, killing half a dozen men. Outram, Inglis and other officers found things slipping out of control even as they expected more attacks in the future, with the rebels having had time to regroup. Without delay the senior officers therefore set about repairing fortifications in the Residency.

If Delhi was being systematically plundered and converted into a graveyard, Lucknow fared no better. After Outram and Havelock's relief had entered the city, similar acts of arson and plunder took place.

British soldiery's looting of Indian towns—which attracts only passing attention in European narratives on 1857—ruined natives for life. If, that is, they had been spared their life, only to starve to death as there was no food. In most cases, these narratives focus only on the hardships endured by 'delicate' women inside the Residencies. The Lucknow siege narrative is a case in point.

> **James Outram:** *A well-known hunter. As Resident in Lucknow he had recommended annexation. After his invasion of Persia he had persuaded the Shah into accepting British terms. He was with Havelock at the first relief of Lucknow, and with Campbell at the second in November. He was later Chief Commissioner at Oudh.*

Our knowledge of the 140 days of the Residency siege relies largely on detailed diaries maintained by the women inside. According to one source (Richard Collier, 1963), there are at least twenty-seven diaries, most of them unpublished. There were many more, but they were lost in the wreck of the ship in which the survivors had been given a (free) passage to England, according to Mrs Adelaide Case (1858).

And indeed they did capture the British imagination. When published, the diaries stirred Britain like nothing else did. The British were proud of their women, the endurance with which they survived

> 'I knew if we survived you would like to live our siege life over in imagination.'
> —Anonymous [Mrs Harris?] *A Lady's Diary of the Siege of Lucknow* (1858)

in the terrible conditions of the siege. Victorian Britain found its new icon of womanhood: the tender, passive and vulnerable woman transformed into a caring, responsible and courageous one.

'I have seen ladies going out, at the risk of being shot, to pick up sticks [firewood]', wrote Julia Inglis. The women nursed the sick, cared for the children and even found sources for entertainment. Adelaide Case mentions how exceptionally kind Julia Inglis was—always carrying old clothes or something to drink to the sick. Maria Germon refers to the 'large number of clothes' she had to wash every day. She admits: it was 'labour that I never could have been equal to, especially in this country.' The conditions inside were in sharp contrast to their normal lives, where a multitude of native servants did every job around the house. Food stocks were diminishing alarmingly and rationing had started. Julia Inglis wrote, quoting another source:

> Nothing was thrown away. The full ration at first starting were a pound of meat and a pound of flour per man; this was reduced to twelve ounces, then to six, and after General Havelock's arrival to four ounces. Women got three-quarters rations, children half. Except for hospital comforts, and here and there private stores, there was little else procurable in the garrison—no bread, butter, milk, vegetables, wine, beer, or tobacco.

Some recorded the numerous deaths they saw, of their friends and family, during the days (Katharine Bartrum's record of deaths we have already had a chance to peruse in Chapter Two). In the midst of such suffering they also had to endure rumours—of what the condition of the rebellion was and of what the sepoys intended to do to them. Some, like Julia Inglis, often assisted the men with military tasks. And yet, according to the *Times* correspondent, W.H. Russell, protocol was maintained, about visiting and speaking while they were being shelled![3]

The British government, what was left of it, was also actively seeking the help of local rulers who may not have openly sided with the mutineers. The Governor General's telegram of 12 September 1857 requested Outram to negotiate for help with Raja Man Singh. The telegram asked Outram to assure Man Singh

---

[3] Alison Blunt, in a brilliant essay (2000), shows how the women inside the Residency maintained their imperial class status even in domestic duties during the siege. Class, apparently, survives sieges too.

that 'if he continues to give to the Governor General effective proof of his fidelity and goodwill, his position in Oudh will be at least as good as it was before the British Government assumed administration of the country.'

Evacuation, the only means of ensuring safety for those inside the Residency, was impossible until the neighbouring countryside was cleared of rebel presence. It was with this aim in mind that a second relief force, led by Colin Campbell (the new Commander-in-Chief of India who had arrived from Britain on 13 August 1857) was making its way on the Grand Trunk road from Calcutta towards Lucknow. It is said he feared another Satichaura Ghat at Lucknow, because Havelock had informed him that the Residency food stocks would last only till 10 November, after which they might have to surrender. They reached Cawnpore on 3 November, leaving it on 9 November, arriving at Lucknow's Alam Bagh soon after.

Campbell needed to be guided into the Residency through ambush-prone Lucknow streets. For this purpose, somebody had to provide him with a plan of the route and an idea of the rebel positions. A message had to be got across to him. It was a situation fraught with risk, for leaving the Residency for the open, rebel-filled country and traversing miles to meet Campbell was unthinkable.

> The second relief of Lucknow consisted of 4,700 men, forty-nine guns and mortars. They were preparing to face battle from 30,000 rebels.

Thomas Kavanagh, an Irish assistant Field Engineer, offered to take the message to Campbell. He painted his face black, disguised himself in native clothes, and accompanied by a native spy, Kanauji Lal, left the Residency on 9 November 1857. Finally, wading through muddy swamps and crawling across the land, they met up with Campbell's army. Kavanagh's actions earned him a Victoria Cross, and he went on to write a memoir about his experiences.

> From Thomas Kavanagh's How I Won the Victoria Cross
>
> *By three o'clock [in the morning] we arrived at a grove of mango trees, situated on a plain, in which a man was singing at the top of his voice. I thought he was a villager, but he got alarmed at hearing us approach, and astonished us too by calling out a guard of twenty-five sepoys ... Kanoujee Lal here lost heart for the first time, and threw away a letter entrusted to him ... I kept mine safe in my turban. We satisfied the guard that we were poor men travelling to Umroula ... after walking for half-an-hour we got into a jheel or swamp ... we had to wade through it for two hours up [sic] our waists in water, and through weeds ... I was nearly exhausted on getting out of the water, having made great exertions to force our way through the weeds, and to prevent the colour [Kavanagh had blacked his face before setting out] being washed off my face. It was nearly gone from my hands...We had not gone far when we heard the English challenge, 'who comes there?' with a native accent. We had reached a British cavalry outpost; my eyes filled with joyful tears ... My reception by Sir Colin Campbell and his staff was cordial to the utmost degree ...*

The message he carried was a set of suggestions for Campbell's approach into Lucknow. On 14 November Campbell finally began his march, what came to be known as the second relief of Lucknow.

Campbell marched through, and encountered fierce resistance at Sikandar Bagh. After the battle at the Bagh, where the Sikhs and Scottish Highlanders distinguished themselves, the rooms were piled high with bodies (about 2,000 had been killed—and at least one sniper was a woman). Campbell cleared other similar resistances (the Kaiser Bagh, the Moti Mahal) on the way and headed out to the Residency. The army split into two, as they circled the city with plans of entering it from two sides. The progress was moderately quick and the fighting intense. Outram won the Chakar Kothi. The Begum Kothi saw savage fighting before being captured. One of those to fall here was the notorious William Hodson, shot when he was trying to plunder a room. Campbell secured the city, going through the buildings and the various Baghs methodically. Lucknow was of course reduced to ruins—one of the things that the Mutiny did was to make cities mirror images of each other: every city a heap of rubble with dead bodies in the street and looted shops—as the British soldiery made merry with the loot.

He was greeted by Havelock, Inglis and a visibly relieved Outram. But the bigger problem remained: how to evacuate the Residency, now filled with over 1,000 sick and injured men, and about 500 women and children.

The process of evacuation was organized reasonably smoothly. The women put on whatever clothing they had left, secreting their money, jewels and mementos into them. On 19 November the first lot of women left the Residency (a famous painting, titled *The Flight from Lucknow*, by Abraham Solomon, depicts cowering English women, a loyal ayah and others leaving for safety). At this moment of respite, and triumph, Havelock contracted cholera, and died on 23 November. On 27 November, the indefatigable Colin Campbell left for Cawnpore (the troops were, strangely, also accompanied by women and children, and the sick, which slowed the march). On the defence, successful evacuation and rescue of Lucknow a General Order issued by the Commander-in-Chief read:

There does not stand recorded in the annals of war an achievement more truly heroic than the defence of the Residency at Lucknow...

> Campbell seems to have made a habit of marching with troops in far lesser number than his enemy. He headed for Cawnpore with 3,000 men, and nearly 1,500 dependent women, children, and injured!

The British troops in Cawnpore, led by Charles Windham, were taking a severe beating, and were likely to be overwhelmed any day. The forces of Tatya Tope and Nana Sahib proved too much for Windham. On 29 November Campbell's army first encountered Tatya Tope's troops—such encounters with Tope, a brilliant military strategist, would last another year and a half—just outside Cawnpore. Campbell managed to get to the entrenchments and ensured that the women and children were escorted out, enroute to Allahabad and Calcutta.

Free of the pressure of safeguarding the women and children, Campbell threw himself into counter operations. On 6 December he attacked Tope's troops, and won a crucial victory, one of a series to follow, December 1857 to June 1858. He captured Cawnpore and Fatehgarh in the space of a couple of months, and was then asked to turn to the rest of the Oudh region.

> 'Every eye in India is upon Oude, as it was upon Delhi: Oude is not only the rallying point of the sepoys, the place to which they all look ... but it also represents a dynasty.'
> —Lord Canning to Colin Campbell

Colin Campbell was sure that 'the subjugation of the province [Oudh] will follow the fall of Lucknow as surely as the conquest of France would follow the capture of Paris.' The gallant defence of the Residency, the actions of Henry Lawrence and the work of Havelock had turned Lucknow into an icon of British courage. All British eyes were upon Lucknow and the troops marching to save it. In fact, Lucknow was the rallying point for the mutineers too. After Delhi, Oudh was the only region with this degree of importance as Rudrangshu Mukherjee has demonstrated (1984). Lucknow and Oudh were therefore high on the priority list—to be retaken (for the British) and to be retained after gaining the Residency (for the mutineers).

One of the signs of the empire's return was, as can be imagined, executions. Villagers were questioned (if they were lucky) in a bid to capture the rebels. Those suspected of sheltering the rebels were flogged. Others were hanged.

Many rebels, however, escaped Campbell and the British forces. What was clear now was that the British armies had begun to win all battles, and not only street ones. The empire was beginning to return.

But the path of return was lined with native corpses, ruined villages and starving towns.

The Empire Strikes Back

Chronology of Major Events, January–June 1858
Delhi, Lucknow, Gwalior, Jhansi

2 January	Campbell defeats Nawab of Farrukhabad
27 January	Zafar's trial begins in Delhi
2 March	Campbell relieves Lucknow
9 March	Zafar found guilty
21 March	Lucknow captured
1 April	Ross defeats Tope at Betwa
3 April	Ross takes Jhansi, Rani Lakshmibai escapes
7 May	Ross defeats Tope and Rani Lakshmibai at Kunch

166 the great uprising

22 May	Ross defeats Rao Sahib and Rani Lakshmibai at Culpee
15 June	Maulvi of Faizabad killed
17 June	Rani Lakshmibai killed
2 August	Power transferred from EIC to crown of England
1 November	Queen Victoria's Proclamation

Delhi, **Lucknow**, Cawnpore, Agra were back under British control. Other sectors remained in the hands of the mutineers. Ahmedullah Shah, the Maulvi of Faizabad, once believed to be the most dangerous man in British India, was collecting troops, despite being shaken by the collapse of Delhi. He also perhaps guessed, along with the Nana, Kunwar Singh and Tope, that it was a lost cause.

> ***Kunwar Singh (d. 1858):*** *The Raja of Jagdishpur. He travelled extensively with the rebels, even though he was considerably older than the rest of them. He was known for great personal courage. He worked with Tatya Tope. He defeated Windham at Cawnpore in November 1857. He was injured while crossing the Ganga at Sheopore Ghat, hit in the hand by shrapnel. He is reputed to have cut off his hand and offered it to the Ganga. He died of the injury after a few days. People have argued that a few more of Kunwar Singh's calibre would have certainly meant the defeat of the British in 1857–58.*

Campbell's forces were on winning spree. They had been supplemented with better troops, and this added to their confidence. In February 1858 Campbell began the march to retrieve Oudh. First destination: Lucknow, which was finally cleared of rebels by 21 March.

Brigadier Walpole was asked to capture Bareilly but Khan Bahadur Khan held out with admirable tenacity. Begum Hazrat Mahal (the wife of the deposed king of Oudh, and the mother of Birjis Qadr, the heir to the throne, according to her) continued to resist from Oudh.

Khan Bahadur Khan had been proclaimed the Viceroy of Bareilly and had entrenched himself well. Walpole, from all accounts, was a hopeless soldier. His army met a taluqdar's troops at Ruiya[4], and was roundly defeated, adding to the remaining rebels' confidence that the tide could still be turned. Campbell, meanwhile met Khan's troops outside Bareilly, and, in sharp contrast to Walpole, won decisively. He then proceeded to tackle the Maulvi of Faizabad.

> There was a reward of Rs 50,000 on Ahmedullah Shah's head—adding to his status of being the most dangerous and elusive man in British India.

Ahmedullah Shah, the Maulvi, found support in Hazrat Mahal and Firoz Shah, the Mughal prince. He made guerilla attacks on Outram's forces, and remained elusive, always managing to escape even when his army was decimated. The maulvi never fell into British hands—adding to their sorrow, for Nana Sahib also remained free—but was shot dead by a nobleman when trying to enter the fort at Pawayan. In a sense the maulvi's death ended the rebellion in the Oudh belt. There was no leader, and very little organization left among the rebels. Campbell and Hope Grant went through the region, pacifying and persuading those chieftains and taluqdars

---

[4]Many taluqdars joined the rebels towards the later stages of the Mutiny. As a punishment the government confiscated their lands after the reconquests of Oudh and neighbouring regions.

who, having experienced annexation, were understandably reluctant. Individual forays and skirmishes continued, but they were of little consequence as the British restored their vice-like grip on the region.

The chronicle of the empire's return was being written in other places. The mutinies in Mhow, Indore and Agra had resulted in loss of control through 1857–58. Months of battles and sieges later, the rebels were evicted (in more ways than one) from these places.

The big battle remaining was Jhansi.

Jhansi had acquired a formidable reputation through the events that unfolded there during 1857. The state's main authority centred around Rani Lakshmibai, the widow of Gangadhar Rao, the Raja of Jhansi. Dalhousie, in keeping with his fascinating policy of acquiring territory, had rejected the Raja's choice of adopted heir, and annexed Jhansi, leaving the Rani to survive on a pension. After the Meerut events, the Political Agent, Alexander Skene, conceded her request to raise a personal bodyguard.

Jhansi had seen a massacre, one that anticipated Cawnpore by a few weeks. When the Mutiny erupted on 5/6 June 1857, the Europeans and other Christians had taken shelter in a fort. Seeing their situation was hopeless, they had surrendered. On 8 June the rebel leaders had offered terms—they would be spared their lives if they surrendered the fort. After the surrender fifty-six Christians (European and Eurasian) were taken to the nearby Jokhan Bagh and hacked to death. Skene was one of those killed, an incident that formed the subject of Christina Rossetti's poem.

In the Round Tower at Jhansi (1879)
Christina Rossetti

Hundred, a thousand to one; even so;
Not a hope in the world remained:
The swarming howling wretches below
Gained and gained and gained.
Skene looked at his pale young wife:—
'Is the time come?'—'The time is come!'—
Young, strong, and so full of life:
The agony struck them dumb.
Close his arm about her now,
Close her cheek to his,
Close the pistol to her brow –
God forgive them this!
'Will it hurt much?'—'No, mine own:
I wish I could bear the pang for both.'
'I wish I could bear the pang alone:
Courage, dear, I am not loth.'
Kiss and kiss: 'It is not pain
Thus to kiss and die.
One kiss more.'—'And yet one again.'—
'Good-bye.'—'Good-bye.'

Native and European depositions on the massacre survive, and were collected and reprinted (*SLDSP* 4). After the massacre the British suspected that the Rani had either encouraged the mutineers or refused to help the Europeans. The Rani, fearing attacks from the rebels, asked the Commissioner of Sagar Division, W.C. Erskine, for help. Erskine asked her to hold on to the administration until a new officer arrived. During this time, armies from two adjacent states attacked Jhansi, and no British troops arrived in response to the Rani's requests for help. The Rani's situation was complicated by her army's situation. Her troops threatened to leave her service and demanded their pay arrears if she did not agree to fight the British. However, there is also a suggestion that she may have been secretly conspiring with the mutineers and Nana Sahib and, according to some, had supported the massacre of the Europeans.

> *Rani Lakshmibai (1828–58):* One of the heroines and best-known names of the Mutiny, she, as a child, knew Tatya Tope and Nana Sahib. And, unusually for a girl-child of the period, she learnt to ride, use the sword and shoot. She was known to be extremely devout. Initially she was wary of siding with the mutineers. She escaped from Jhansi with her (and Gangadhar Rao's) adopted son, Damodar Rao, tied to her back. Subhadra Kumari Chauhan's famous poem immortalized her.

It is possible that Rani Lakshmibai was not in favour of battling the British—which would entail the risk of losing Jhansi. But her situation was desperate—she could not hold out against the neighbouring armies because no British relief was forthcoming. She then took a momentous decision: she sought to forge an alliance with the rebels so that the invading armies could be driven out. By default, therefore, the British assumed that she had joined the rebels. When the British troops under Hugh Rose (1801–85) appeared outside Jhansi on 21 March 1858, having had major battles with the armies of the Raja of Banpur and others on its journey, the Rani prepared to fight this new invader. Her subjects were on her side, even though they perhaps guessed that the battle was likely to destroy Jhansi. The statement of Sahibood-deen, the khansamah of Major Skene (recorded in *SLDSP* 4), noted this popular support for the mutineers: 'All the people of the town were with the sepoys.'

The Rani's motivational pleas, prayers and proclamations were enthusiastically received (except by the wealthy, who had to think of their property—quite a few managed to send their wealth to Gwalior). 'We fight for independence', declared the Rani.

The battle began with Rose's siege of the fort. Just when the wall had been breached Tatya Tope's troops appeared, to the great relief of the Rani. But Rose managed to push Tope's forces back, and returned to focus on Jhansi.

On 3 April 1858 Rose's forces managed to scale the walls and enter Jhansi. It was Delhi and Lucknow all over again. There was furious street-fighting as sniper fire rained down on the British. Natives executed in large numbers, families ruined by plundering British soldiers, excessive violence ... this blood-soaked script of the returning Raj is now well known.[5]

It was the departure from the script, of course, that created the legend of Jhansi.

Seeing the invading army stream across the streets, Jhansi's women threw their children and themselves down wells. It was a reflection of the nature of the Raj's return: the British soldiery's savagery had now become a dubious legend, and Jhansi's women did not wait to experience it. Death over disgrace: the 'upright' British soldier had offered a choice to Jhansi. They took the first.

In the European annals of 1857 the suffering and sacrifices of their women have been emblazoned. There is no mention of the suffering of Jhansi's many women.

Rani Lakshmibai escaped with her son, Damodar Rao, tied to her back—an action that immortalized her—and joined forces with Tatya Tope.

---

[5]Apparently 5,000 people were killed in Jhansi, a fact noted by a contemporary traveller, Vishnubhatt Godse in his Marathi travelogue *Majha Pravas* (first published in 1907, written around 1884–5).

Rose was incensed at her escape, though even he had to admit that Jhansi's people fought bravely. In a letter of 30 April 1858 he notes that 'the women [inside the fort] were seen working in the batteries and carrying ammunition.'

In the first week of May he arrived at Kunch, in a summer heat so intense that several of his men died of sunstroke and dehydration. In a report dated 2 June 1858 Rose described his army's condition in detail:

> This prostration of more than half a body of men by sun, after two hours' mere marching, and a similar amount of sun-sickness ... on the march to Mutha, give a correct estimate of the sanitary state of my Force before Culpee ... So many hours' sun laid low so many men. I had, weakened by every sort of difficulty, to conquer the greatest stake in the campaign, against the greatest odds; half of my troops sickly; every man of them ailing, to say nothing of a very numerous and daily increasing sick-list...

At Culpee, Tope and Rani Lakshmibai were joined by the Raja of Banda. In the resulting battle the rebels lost, despite the fact that Rose's army was so ill and weak. The Rani, again, escaped, as did Tope—he was indeed to become the Mutiny's greatest escape artist, evading the British well into 1859. Tope and Lakshmibai marched to Gwalior, where Scindia had declined to openly side with the mutineers, but whose loyalty remained suspect for the British. Scindia fought the rebels at Morar where his army suddenly threw in their lot with the rebel forces and Scindia himself was forced to flee to Agra.

On 21 April 1858 Kunwar Singh was severely injured when crossing the Ganga. Despite this mortal wound he managed to defeat Captain Le Grand's forces near Jagdishpur. But his wounds were far too severe, and he died soon after.

On 6 June 1858 Hugh Rose met Rani Lakshmibai's forces at Culpee, in what she knew was the most decisive battle of her life.

The odds were clearly against her. She was first unseated from her horse through a sabre cut, and then a soldier fired at her.

> 'She [Rani Lakshmibai] possessed the genius, the daring, the despair necessary for the conception of great deeds.'
> —G.B. Malleson on the Rani

Sitting leaning against a rock, she fired her pistol at her assailant. Enraged, he slashed at her, without realizing that it was the Rani herself he was attacking. Before dying she distributed her jewels (then worth a crore of rupees, apparently) to her faithful sepoys.

Poem on Rani Lakshmibai in William Crooke's collection
The Mutiny—1857

Sung by Rameswar Dayal Misra of Kotara, District Itawa.
Recorded by Raghunandan, Teacher of the School at Kotara.

Well fought the brave one; O, the Rani of Jhansi.
The guns were placed in the towers, the heavenly (magic) balls were fired.
O, the Rani of Jhansi, well fought the brave one.
All the soldiers were fed with sweets; she herself had treacle and rice.
O, the Rani of Jhansi, well fought the brave one.
Leaving Morcha, she fled to the army; where she searched and found no water.
O, the Rani of Jhansi, well fought the brave one.

> At the time of her death Rani Lakshmibai had a reward of Rs 100,000 on her head.

Her death on the field, dressed in a man's clothes, holding the horse's bit between her teeth and using her sword with both hands according to one account, made her a legend as the warrior-queen of the Mutiny. There was, of course, no other.

Hugh Rose praised her for her 'bravery, cleverness and perseverance', and compared her to Joan of Arc, and declared that she was the only man among the Indian mutineers. In his account of 13 October 1858 he wrote:

> One of the most important result [of the battle at Kalpi] was the death of the Ranee of Jhansi; who, although a lady, was the bravest and best of Military leader of the Rebels.

Song on Jhansi

Fell the trees, commanded the Rani of Jhansi,
Lest the Feringis hang our soldiers on them.
So that the coward English may not be able to shout:
'Hang! Hang them in the trees!'
So that in the hot sun they may have no shade.

Interest in Rani Lakshmi Bai has continued, in India and in the West, evidenced by biographical accounts appearing even today in respected journals like *Military History* (Pamela Toler's essay on the Rani appeared in this journal in 2006).

> 'The mutineers ... cremated the said Rani's body with sandal wood.'
> —Bhawani Prasad, 18 June 1858

Tatya Tope fled, leading the British forces on a merry chase across Rajputana, Nagpur, Bhopal—according to legend he never stopped for more than a day at any place. Some details of Tope's mode of functioning are available in an unusual document in Marathi, Pandurang Mahipat Belsare's *Atmahakikat*, written around 1900. (Belsare, along with his friend, had set out on an adventure tour of India in 1857, and had even worked for some time as Tope's accountants.) Tatya Tope was finally betrayed to the British by Man Singh, the Raja of Narwar—he was caught when asleep. On 14 April 1859 Tatya Tope, the last of the rebels, was hanged.

The search for Nana Sahib went for years. Documents published later reveal an elaborate network of spies set up to track the 'butcher of Cawnpore'. Descriptions of him were circulated by the British officers, and anybody resembling the descriptions quickly arrested—he was said to have been sighted in Gujarat and as far down as present-day Karnataka.[6]

Others believe he died in Nepal in 1859. In any case he evaded arrest, although he did try for amnesty, claiming he had never ordered the killing of the British. However, he did state in one of his last letters to the British government, with no decrease in menace nor a trace of regret, his ardent desire: 'We will meet, and then I will shed your blood and it will flow knee deep. I am prepared to die.'

> 'I believe that it was never actually ascertained that Nana Saheb died after wandering about in the Nepaul jungles, and I believe at various times men have been arrested as Nana Saheb.'
>
> —E.V. Mackay, Superintendent. of Police, Kathiawad, 16 Feb. 1894

---

[6] See Maharashtra State Archives, *Bulletin of the Department of Archives*, No. 9 and 10: *The Legend of Nana Saheb*.

On 1 November 1858 the Queen's Proclamation was delivered to the people of India. The Company era had ended in August when the power was transferred to the Crown. The Proclamation had another dimension to it: it announced an amnesty—'unconditional pardon, amnesty, and oblivion of all offences', in the Proclamation's terms—to all those rebels who were willing to return to their homes. However, there was to be no amnesty for those who had murdered Europeans or actively abetted the rebels. As the Proclamation put it:

> Our clemency will be extended to all offenders, save and except those who have been, or shall be, convicted of having directly taken part in the murder of British subjects. With regard to such the demands of justice forbid the exercise of mercy.

The amnesty was to last until 1 January 1859.[7]

The Proclamation did not mention plunder by British soldiers.

One of the harshest critics of this Proclamation and amnesty was Begum Hazrat Mahal. Hazrat Mahal entered Nepal in 1858, accompanied by her young son, Birjis Qadr (he was ten or eleven years old), but the ruler, Jung Bahadur, declined to help. His letter about not supporting the rebels pleased the British, and he was rewarded with the return of the lands he had lost to them. Hazrat Mahal argued that Britain would never forgive the rebels and that it would be foolish to trust the Proclamation.

---

[7]The Proclamation is available in A. Berriedale Keith, *Speeches and Documents on Indian Policy, 1750–1921* (1922), vol. I.

> ### Proclamation by the Begum of Oudh
>
> *At this time certain weak-minded, foolish people, have spread a report that the English have forgiven the faults and crimes of the people of Hindoostan. This appears very astonishing, for it is the unvarying custom of the English never to forgive a fault, be it great or small ... In the proclamation it is written, that all contracts and agreements entered into by the Company will be accepted by the Queen. Let the people carefully observe this artifice. The Company has seized on the whole of Hindoostan, and if this arrangement be accepted, what is there new in it? ... If the Queen has assumed the government, why does her majesty not restore our country to us when our people wish it? ... In this proclamation it is written, that when peace is restored, public works, such as roads and canals, will be made in order to improve the condition of the people. It is worthy of a little reflection, that they have promised no better employment for Hindostanees than making roads and digging canals.*

As clinching evidence she pointed to the numerous occasions when Britain had reneged on its treaties and promises. But what swung the balance in favour of the amnesty was that the rebels were tired of battles. They received little support from the rulers, and the civilians, who had been subject to extortion and harassment, had no sympathy for them. The latter wanted stability and peace, and this the rebels could not provide.

Begum Hazrat Mahal died in Nepal. Firoz Shah died in Mecca. Azimullah Khan was never caught, and is believed to have died of smallpox. Liaqat Ali was caught after decades in Bombay, and transported to the Andamans.

The violent 1857 Mutiny was put down with even greater violence. Its spirit produced the greatest non-violent revolution in human history.

The Mutiny was over.

The great uprising had begun.

Four
The Raj Rises Again

The Mutiny was clearly over by the end of 1857 itself, though scattered fighting, including the great Jhansi battles, carried on into 1858. The epilogue scripted for the Mutiny by the British was terrifying, cruel and unimaginably inhuman. The British had set out to reconquer territories taken by mutineers from July 1857. But they also set out to *demonstrate*, whenever they retook territories, that the Raj was back in power. In order to do so, in order to show the rise (again) of the Raj, it used the worst form of spectacle: mass executions and display of hanged native bodies. Allahabad, Benares, Delhi, Lucknow had streets, market places and roadsides lined by hanging bodies.

The idea was to instill terror through this gory spectacle. One Deputy Advocate General, F.A.V. Thurburn, even used the word 'display' to describe the hanging bodies (in connection with Allahabad and Neill's actions there). This was the grisly spectacle before curtain fall.

*

the raj rises again

This chapter has four parts. The first presents a cross-section of the reactions and responses to the events of 1857–58. The second deals a crucial event that is omitted in most accounts of 1857: the trial of the last Mughal emperor, Bahadur Shah Zafar. The third surveys, briefly, the changes effected after the Raj returned to the subcontinent. The fourth and final section presents some of the most prominent interpretations of the Mutiny.

Reactions and Responses

One characteristic feature of the Mutiny is that it is almost impossible to see the justness of either side, considering that both natives and British forces indulged in inhuman violence on a massive scale. Histories of the period, written predominantly from the European perspective easily mask the violence of the Europeans. Native works, being in the vernacular and local languages, are almost never used, and hence there is little to counter the established image of the 'cruel' native sepoy and the innocent European woman.

The events of 1857–58-India attracted, as can be imagined, strong responses. Considering the monumental nature of the events—sepoys shooting their officers, mutiny by entire regiments, massacre of women and children, the Raj on the run, epic valour, the looting of cities and the trial of an emperor for criminal conspiracy—the responses could not have been neutral or sober.

When the news of the Mutiny and the actions of the sepoys first reached British and European ears the instinctive reaction was disbelief and anger. How could the sepoys, nurtured by the Company and its officers, turn against their benevolent patrons? How could they, trained to use guns by European officers, aim their guns supplied by their European officers, against Europeans? Moreover, how could they divert the anger at their officers towards the women and children?

The first reactions of European officers and civilians were

predictable: control the spread of the dissension and mutiny at all costs. Any and every counter-measure was justified if it could help prevent the Mutiny from spreading across the entire subcontinent. Many officers therefore recommended harsh treatment of those mutineers who were caught. 'Let us propose a Bill for the flaying alive, impalement, or burning of the murderers of the women and children at Delhi', John Nicholson had written. They did not need a Bill.

> 'The slightest mawkish mentality [in the treatment of arrested mutineers] would be fatal.'
> —Robert Dunlop

Many called for swift retribution. Newspapers like *The Englishman* and the *Lahore Chronicle* carried angry letters from Europeans, demanding that the government not spare a single mutineer.

> 'Horrors such as men have seldom perpetrated in cold blood, outrages on women and children, atrocities and cruelties devilish in their kind—murder, treachery, rapine, mutiny—have been the expression of their rebellion.'
> —Blackwood's Edinburgh Magazine *(December 1857)*

One blamed the Mughal dynasty, while recommending: 'Leave not an Emir, or prince alive, or any belonging to them.'

Most of the Englishmen and women were puzzled at the violence and what they felt was an inexplicable native hatred of the British. They believed that the British had done nothing but good—the *mai-baap* role of guardian and provider—and the native's response was a betrayal of this relationship and trust. Mrs [R.M.] Coopland, who had noted that the sepoys were allowed to follow their own religious rituals, was so angered by the betrayal that she proposed a complete decimation of the Mughal dynasty and its city, Delhi.

Since they had betrayed their masters and benefactors, argued many Europeans, no native sepoy (or native civilian, for that matter) could ever be trusted again. But some expressed gratitude that 'so large a portion of the Indian army remained, throughout that troubled period, true to its alien masters', as an essayist put it in *Blackwood's Edinburgh Magazine* of 1861.

> 'Delhi ought to be razed to the ground, and on its ruins a church or monument should be erected, inscribed with a list of all the victims of the mutinies.'
> —Mrs [R.M.] Coopland

However, many British officers and statesmen were aware of the consequences of extreme British retribution. There were officers and British civilians, like Lord Canning, who were frankly appalled at the ferocity of British vengeance. Montgomery Martin, for instance, in a letter to the *Times* on 19 November 1857, declared that he could not walk on the Delhi streets any more. The reason?

On the roads were bodies of dozens of women who had had their throats slit. These were not acts of British vengeance, but the *consequence* of British actions in Delhi. The women had been killed by their husbands for fear that they would fall into the hands of British soldiery.

There is no greater evidence of the monster the British soldier had come to represent—the natives were willing to kill their family members rather than let them fall into British hands.

A British officer could not deal with the visible signs of British brutality.

The aim of such extreme brutality was not the mere suppression of the mutinous spirit, but rather to strike terror into the

> 'I protest against meeting atrocities by atrocities.'
> —Benjamin Disraeli

native population as a whole. It was saying, effectively: 'see what happens when you strike at the Raj.' The tactic worked for, as Mahatma Gandhi pointed out, the northern states remained rather quiet after 1857.

Canning believed that the mass executions of captured mutineers and civilians suspected of conspiracy did not solve the problem. Instead, he argued, it exacerbated tensions. He is reported to have said to an officer pleading for the fiercest vengeance possible on the sepoys that they must not mistake 'violence for vigour'. He mournfully informed his monarch, Queen Victoria, about the attitudes of his fellow Britons: 'not one man in ten seems to think that the hanging and shooting of forty thousand or fifty thousand men can be otherwise than practicable and right.' Canning was unique in the sense that he was not swayed by the reports of native atrocities coming in. Neither was he sitting back quietly while the Raj burnt. He took all the necessary steps to see that the Mutiny did not destroy the Raj—he ordered the disarming of native troops, imprisonment, and gave more powers to civil and military authorities to hold trials. But he refused to authorize vengeful strikes or validate violent reprisals that would be clearly and irreducibly racial in tone. He declared: 'I will never allow an angry or indiscriminate act or word to proceed from the Government of India as long as I am responsible for it.' Canning's resolution to take the legal route of trial rather than a vindictive genocide against the Indians may have, ultimately, helped the Raj—for it enabled a return to normalcy.

Canning came to be hated by many for his clemency and moderation, while others saw his actions and approach as visionary and sensible. Queen Victoria herself supported his stance, while those like Lord Ellenborough were furious

> 'I will not govern in anger.'
> —Lord Canning

at what they saw as his leniency towards the mutineers. One letter in the *Lahore Chronicle* of 13 June 1857 termed Canning's motto of clemency 'misplaced' because he was being merciful towards those who had not demonstrated any mercy. Martin Tupper, known as the 'English poet of the Rebellion', responded to pleas of clemency with the following opening lines in 'Liberavimus Animam' (published, curiously, in the humour magazine, *Punch*, on 12 September 1857):

> Who pules about mercy?
> The agonized wail of babies hewn piecemeal yet sickens
>   the air,
> And echoes still shudder that caught on the gale
> The mother's—the maiden's wild scream of despair.

Charles Dickens, the great novelist, was shocked at the sepoys' brutality (he had nothing to say about British retribution) and declared in a letter: 'I wish I were the Commander-in-Chief of India ... I should do my utmost to exterminate the Race upon whom the stain of cruelties rested.'

> 'No statesman is entitled to more generous consideration from the Government, the Parliament, and the people of England than Lord Canning.'
> —The *Times*, 10 May 1857

The British in India at the time of the Mutiny were inevitably praised as 'heroes'. As public recognition, about 50,700 Britons in India, both military and civilian, were awarded the Indian Mutiny Medal. Accounts of the suffering of the women transformed them into heroines and martyrs, adding an extra dimension to the idea of Victorian/English womanhood. Several British poets composed poems on the Mutiny. Many were struck by the unprecedented valour of ordinary civilians. 'Who saw the heroes of the Indian

Mutiny in the Company's lazy officials?', asked a report in *Blackwood's Edinburgh Magazine* in 1863.

Alfred Lord Tennyson's 'The Defence of Lucknow' is a good example of this kind of response. In the poem Tennyson emphasized the helplessness and the undaunted courage of the English. The refrain throughout this poem was: 'And ever upon the topmost roof our banner of England blew'.

From The Defence of Lucknow (1879)
Alfred, Lord Tennyson

Banner of England, not for a season, O banner of Britain, hast thou
Floated in conquering battle or flapt to the battle-cry!
Never with mightier glory than when we had rear'd thee on high
Flying at top of the roofs in the ghastly siege of Lucknow—
Shot thro' the staff or the halyard, but ever we raised thee anew,
And ever upon the topmost roof our banner of England blew.

Frail were the works that defended the hold that we held with our lives—
Women and children among us, God help them, our children and wives!
Hold it we might—and for fifteen days or for twenty at most.
'Never surrender, I charge you, but every man die at his post!'

Fire from ten thousand at once of the rebels that girdled us round—
Death at the glimpse of a finger from over the breadth of a street,
Death from the heights of the mosque and the palace, and death in the ground!

Praise to our Indian brothers, and let the dark face have his due!
Thanks to the kindly dark faces who fought with us, faithful and few,
Fought with the bravest among us, and drove them, and smote them, and slew,
That ever upon the topmost roof our banner in India blew.

Heat like the mouth of a hell, or a deluge of cataract skies,
Stench of old offal decaying, and infinite torment of flies.
Thoughts of the breezes of May blowing over an English field,
Cholera, scurvy, and fever, the wound that would not be heal'd,
Lopping away of the limb by the pitiful-pitiless knife,—
Torture and trouble in vain,—for it never could save us a life.
Valour of delicate women who tended the hospital bed,
Horror of women in travail among the dying and dead,
Grief for our perishing children, and never a moment for grief,
Toil and ineffable weariness, faltering hopes of relief,
Havelock baffled, or beaten, or butcher'd for all that we knew—
Then day and night, day and night, coming down on the still-shatter'd walls
Millions of musket-bullets, and thousands of cannon-balls—
But ever upon the topmost roof our banner of England blew.

Kissing the war-harden'd hand of the Highlander wet with their tears!
Dance to the pibroch!—saved! we are saved!— is it you? is it you?
Saved by the valour of Havelock, saved by the blessing of Heaven!
'Hold it for fifteen days!' we have held it for eighty-seven!
And ever aloft on the palace roof the old banner of England blew.

The poem is interesting because, in addition to the courage of the British, it also highlights the fidelity of Indians.

> *Memorials erected to the dead Europeans quickly assumed the status of holy spots, but were very varied in their tone and form. The doors of the Memorial Hall, Madras, were to be kept perpetually closed. They were also intended as a symbol of the British triumph over the natives. Thus the Mutiny Memorial on Delhi Ridge was built to be one and a half feet higher than the Asoka Pillar! The marble stone for Nicholson's grave may have come from Zafar's palace. A tablet marked the place where he was shot, and a garden (with his statue) named after him. But the key memorials were, of course, for Cawnpore and the great Lucknow siege. The Cawnpore Memorial Church's steeple was a vantage point from where visitors were shown the exact sites of the tragedy. A memorial was also constructed at the infamous well. The ruined Lucknow Residency was preserved as a ruin memorial. St. James Church in Delhi—where many Englishmen and women were killed around 11 May 1857— has memorial plaques to them. The wall at Arrah house, in which sixty people held out against thousands of rebels, was also converted into an icon of British courage with a memorial tablet placed by Lord Curzon himself. The Delhi landscape became iconic of British courage and resilience. But there were no memorials of native resistance in the same city.*

The natives, in sharp contrast, were demonized. The sepoy was now called a 'pandy', after Mangal Pandey. Nana Sahib became the epitome of all that was wicked in the native, especially after Trevelyan's *Cawnpore*, in which he described Nana Sahib as a 'world noted malefactor'. Henry Kingsley's 1869 novel *Stretton* described him as a man with 'the lust of blood on him' (a descriptive that applies equally well to James Neill, John Nicholson, William Hodson and other British officers in 1857). Though there was some grudging praise of native leaders like Rani Lakshmibai, they were by and large classified as evil.

Places like Cawnpore and Lucknow became sites of tourist attraction, a kind of martyr tourism.[1] The British traveller made visits to pay homage to the sites of massacre of his or her compatriots, and the sites of their courage.

Other British responses tried to examine the causes for the Mutiny. Did the Indians have a legitimate grouse against the Raj? Did both Hindus and Muslims feel equally angry with the British?

Benjamin Disraeli, the future Prime Minister, believed that the sepoys had legitimate cause for being unhappy with the Company. Disraeli was also one of the few statesmen who believed that the sepoys may have had 'adequate causes' to mutiny. He also believed that the annexation policy was a major mistake, and the native fury was perhaps justified. Disraeli wrote about the prevalence of adoption as a system:

> 'The principle of the law of adoption', he says, 'is not the prerogative of princes and principalities in India, it applies to every man in Hindostan who has landed property, and who professes the Hindoo religion.'

It was this widely established system that the British were destroying.

Some others proposed that the Mutiny should teach the British a valuable lesson. It should teach them that a foreign government may not always understand the needs of the people, and the natives may have taken what the British considered 'reform' for interference. Thus J.W. Sherer wrote in an account of the Mutiny, dated 13 January 1859:

---

[1] See Manu Goswami's essay (1996) on the theme.

> I trust experience may teach us to amend those parts of our administration which may be oppressive or distasteful to the people, so that they may accept our rule not only as inevitable, but also as that with which they are best satisfied

Sherer and many others, with the benefit of hindsight, were able to admit that things may not have been exactly wonderful under the Raj.

Benjamin Disraeli (1804–81): *Disraeli was in the opposition in the English Parliament when the Mutiny broke out. In fact he accused the Government of India of being both indifferent (to the natives' problems) and incompetent (in handling the situation). He believed it was a military mutiny. His comments were recorded and reprinted by Charles Ball in his account of the events. Later Disraeli as Prime Minister would be instrumental in declaring Victoria the Empress of India. Despite being a politician he was erudite and wrote fiction set in the industrial contexts of nineteenth-century England.*

Many agreed that force alone could never hold the empire. A commentator wrote in the influential *Edinburgh Review* of October 1857, by which time Delhi had already been reclaimed:

> We cannot permanently hold India by force alone. We may break down a native power; we may crush the rebellion of an army, although it carries the arms we have provided ... But we cannot do this in defiance of the active wishes of the great mass of the people. If not the thousands merely, but the millions were now against us, we should be soon swept into the sea.

In a sense this was prophetic: it was indeed the united native millions that would finally prove too much for the British.

There were harsh critics, who pointed to the incompetence of the officers in the Army. They argued that the earlier officers related better to the sepoys, cared for them and understood them better. The quality of officers had deteriorated, producing a breed of purely mercenary and incompetent men who did not care to establish trust among the natives.

It was a strong belief among the British that religious disaffection may have triggered the Mutiny. At the trial of Zafar, the prosecuting officer, F.J. Harriott, declared:

> There is no dread of an open avowed missionary in India. It is not the rightful conversion to Christianity, that either sepoys or natives are alarmed at. If it be done by the efforts of persuasion, of teaching, or of example,—the only means by which it can be done,—it offends no caste prejudice, excites no fanatical opposition.

This was in sharp contrast to other opinions, which blamed the sepoys' disaffection on the proselytizing by officers.[2] Evangelicals argued that the only way to ensure such mutinies would never occur again was to Christianize India.[3] Thus one commentator declared in an essay in the *Dublin University Magazine* in 1858, after the power had shifted to the Crown of England: 'Sooner or later

---

[2] For example, the comments in an essay in *Blackwood's Edinburgh Magazine*, (December 1857).

[3] Sherring, *Indian Church during the Great Rebellion* (1859). However, there was also opposition to the evangelical movement. For instance, people like Thomas Twining (1807); John Scott (1808) and Scott Waring (1809) were often critical of the missionary project of civilizing the natives—some even suggested that this might cause England to lose India.

caste must break up, and heathenism must yield to the unseen but all-penetrating leaven of Christianity.'

The Socialist leader Ernest Jones, who went on to write a long poem, 'The Revolt of Hindustan', claimed it was a national revolution and that it was provoked by Britain's capitalist exploitation of India. John Kaye and John Bruce Norton, two contemporary commentators, argue that the Brahmins were afraid of losing their authority because of the general reforms of Indian society, and that their resentment against being usurped in the power hierarchy by the British might have fuelled the rebellion. Norton wrote:

> Their [upper castes'] importance is lost, they no longer fatten on the revenues of the country, or thrive by the oppression of the masses; a task, which so far as it is permitted at all, we have ourselves monopolized.

John Kaye agrees with this analysis of the Mutiny's causes:

> They [Brahmins] saw that, as new provinces were one after another brought under British rule, the new light must diffuse itself more and more, until there could scarcely be a place for Hindooism to lurk unmolested.

This interpretation was shared by others as seen in this letter from the *Englishman* of 11 June 1857:

> This rise has not originated with the Sepoys; doubtless the cowardly prating, cunning Bengalee and Oriah Brahmins have put up men, whom they hate and fear, in order to try and creep, under their defence into the lucrative posts should the British Government in India be overthrown.

The historian Charles Ball attributed the revolt to maulvis rather than Brahmins. Several saw Dalhousie's policy of annexation as generating a legitimate grouse among the Indians. One commentator writing in the *Edinburgh Review* of October 1857 argued that the outbreak did not occur because of any 'resentment of a misgoverned people'. Rather, he argued, it was because the princes and chiefs of India had been badly treated, and it was they who provoked the mutiny.

While land reforms such as those by Lord Cornwallis were intended to be beneficial in the long run, the Indians may have seen them as detrimental to their way of life. The introduction of railways, English education and Western laws was a Europeanization—something the Indians may have resented, argued some British commentators. That is, British government policies themselves may have failed, as people like Fred Roberts (who spent practically his entire life in India) believed. Disraeli suggested that Indians were not yet ready for large-scale social reform, or even for responsible government.

*

European and American responses were more balanced. Of the commentators writing out of Europe, perhaps the most important was Karl Marx. Marx argued that England had created the rebellion with its own policies. As early as 1853 Marx had written critically of British rule in India: 'There cannot, however, remain any doubt but that the misery inflicted by the British on Hindostan is of an essentially different and infinitely more intensive kind than all Hindostan had to suffer before.' Marx was also sure that the Indians would not reap the economic benefits of the changes effected by the British. The empire was not meant to serve or benefit its subjects—it was meant to generate profits for the capitalists back in England.

the great uprising

> 'The profound hypocrisy and inherent barbarism of bourgeois civilization lies unveiled before our eyes, turning from its home, where it assumes respectable forms, to the colonies, where it goes naked.'
> —Karl Marx

When it came to atrocities—the hallmark of the Mutiny—Marx was certain that the natives alone could not be held responsible for the violence—it was the product of Britain's own actions in India.

Marx also argued that it would be wrong to say that all cruelties were only on the part of the native sepoys. He pointed out that the letters written by Englishmen and women were full of 'malignity'. The British army, he argued, was more brutal than any other in the world—an opinion that is significant because we live in an age where enemy armies are accused of brutality, even as one's own indulges in the same kind of inexcusable behaviour.

> 'However infamous the conduct of the sepoys, it is only the reflex, in a concentrated form, of England's own conduct in India, not only during the epoch of the foundation of her Eastern Empire, but even during the last ten years of a long-settled rule.'
> —Karl Marx

Like Marx, Frederick Engels was critical of the actions of British soldiers. He wrote:

> 'The sack of Lucknow in 1858 will remain an everlasting disgrace to the British military service.'
> —Karl Marx

The cruelty of the retribution dealt out by the British troops, goaded on by exaggerated and false reports of the atrocities attributed to the natives ... have not created any particular fondness for the victors.

Marx was also particularly appalled at the hypocrisy of the British when it came questions of post-battle looting. Describing the looting of Lucknow, he asked: would the British have forgiven any other army for such plunder?

> *The British soldiers were allowed three days of free looting. After this, in Delhi, the city and its treasures were treated officially as 'prize'. Official digging tickets were given to designated Prize Agents, reports Christopher Hibbert. Then officers and soldiers accompanied by coolies and guides (and in some cases by their wives) went on treasure hunts through Delhi. The systematic plunder was stopped only in December 1857. Property worth Rs 10,000 (and we are talking of this kind of money in 1857) was dug out from the Sriramji temple according to Surendra Nath Sen. The copper gilt domes of Moti Masjid, the Diwan-i-Khas and the Musamman Burj were auctioned. Fatehpuri mosque was sold, and Zeenatul Masjid used as a bakery. Jama Masjid was turned into a barrack. Most structures within the Red Fort were flattened, the Diwan-i-Aam transformed into a hospital. All houses, bazaars, mosques within 448 yards of the Fort walls were razed. The railway line was laid through the northern walls of the old Mughal palace. The Imperial Library, with invaluable manuscripts—including a rich collection of illuminating works dating back to Babar's time—was destroyed and materials dispersed into private and public libraries in Britain and Europe.*

A contemporary Russian commentator, Nikolai Dobrolyubov in *The Indian National Uprising of 1857* (1858) argued that despite its claim to being more humanitarian, British rule in India was just as despotic. He wrote:

> Though rejecting the absurd arbitrary character and ruthlessness of Asiatic despotism, the English Company

did not at the same time want to deprive itself of its advantages...

He accused the British of being impractical, of not really seeing whether their ideas of improvement and reform suited the Indians: 'The structure of the civil service and specially of the judicial system in India also shows how absurdly the European civilization was applied to the needs of the people.' The rural community was ruined, he argued, because of the British collector and their agents, who exploited the poor ryots.

The Sultan of Turkey sent a contribution of £ 1,000 to the London Fund for the relief of the sufferers of the Indian Mutiny. Through 1857 several native princes, sepoys and landlords pledged their loyalty to the British. British magazines proudly mentioned these letters. Letters of fidelity were also sent by groups of people in the Madras Presidency area, from Bezwada, Nellore, Dowleshwaram, Fort St. George and other places, and were reprinted in the *Fort St. George Gazette* through 1857. Many of these letters—what the British called 'Loyal Addresses' in their work—praised the Raj for having ended the tyranny of the feudal lords.

Those native troopers who stood by the British were rewarded. A list of such awards was later collected and published in the 1859 volume, *The Mutinies and the People* (written, it is now proved, by Sambhu Chandra Mukherjee). The gallant native troopers of the siege of Lucknow were given the Order of Merit, with 'three years of additional service' and offered promotions (*SLDSP* 3). Administrative reports of Madras Presidency for the years describe sepoys under General Whitlock who 'vied with the Europeans, and most unmistakably proved their loyalty in the eagerness with which they attacked the mutinous sepoys of Bengal' at the battle of Banda. Rajas who stayed loyal and provided material support to the British were well rewarded. Raja Sarup Singh of Jind, who paid a congratulatory visit to Archibald Wilson after the re-conquest/fall of Delhi, was rewarded for his loyalty with a large increase of territory yielding more than a lakh (of rupees), thirteen villages assessed at Rs 138,000 in one pargana, and a house in Delhi valued at Rs 6,000. He was also, most crucially, given a *sanad* granting the power and right of adoption should he not produce an heir. The Nizam of Hyderabad was given presents worth £ 10,000 and his diwan, Salar Jung, got gifts worth £ 3000.

> Hindus were allowed to return to Delhi in June 1858, and Muslims in August 1859. The Muslim population did not reach 1857 numbers until 1900. Ghalib's elegiac poetry, mourning the destruction of Delhi, inaugurated a new form of poetry, the Shahr-e-Ashub.

American responses condemned the massacre of women and children by the natives. However, commentators in *New York Daily News*, *Harper's*, the *United States Democratic Review* and the *North American Review* often pointed to British policy as a culprit. Mark Twain, for instance, saw the annexation policy as a key element in the rise of native discontent. One of the first reports on the Mutiny in the *New York Daily Times* of 6 July 1857 expressed its bewilderment that the insurrection should have originated at Barrackpore, near Calcutta, in the immediate vicinity of the capital of India, 'where the results of European civilization and enterprise are more apparent than in any other part of Hindostan.'

Many American commentators argued that despite the natives' anger at conversions and propagation of Christianity, Britain must continue the work. The reason, they argued, was simple. Christianity was the only solution to the uprisings. As a commentator put it in the *New York Daily Times* of 6 July 1857: 'as long as it humours the superstitions and prejudices that benight the

Hindoo mind, so long will its power in India be jeopardized by the mutinies and rebellions of the natives.' 'Christian religion', declared an essayist in *St. Louis Christian Advocate* of 1 October 1857, 'is not in the least reponsible for the mutiny.' Another proposed that any country conquered by the sword would eventually rise against the conqueror. Yet another added a crucial insight. The British were dependent upon an army recruited from a conquered race in order to 'hold in subjection' their own conquered countrymen! Several of the American commentators called for tolerance and sobriety on the part of the British. Charles Creighton Hazewell wrote in the *Atlantic Monthly* in 1857:

> It is earnestly to be hoped that the officers in command of the British force will not yield to the savage suggestions and incitements of the English press, with regard to the fate of Delhi.

Most Americans would have agreed with this conclusion from their compatriot:

> There cannot be two masters of the Indian Empire. The Briton must rule it politically and religiously, or he must be overrun by the treacherous and rebellious Indian. Every instance of servile respect for the caste superstition of the Hindoo subject, can only be attributed by him to fear in his Christian conqueror. It emboldens him for rebellion.

Commentators from other countries, while in general agreement about the Mutiny, registered their horror at the extreme violence of British retribution. Many saw Britain's policies in India as the prime cause of disaffection. Nicholas Dirks notes that Max Muller, the prominent German Indologist, for instance, located caste as the key question of the revolt. The British, Muller said, saw caste as incompatible with and unacceptable to military discipline, and this was the crux of the matter. Such incompatible notions of society were the basic flaws in the imperial façade.

American and European commentators did support the punishment of the mutineers, but felt that the punishment could extend to the entire native population—a feature of the British retributive system where entire villages were burnt on suspicion (unproven) of habouring mutineers.

One French commentator went so far as to declare that if the British did not stop their massacres of the natives the rest of the world 'will have to intervene to see that the Indians are not slaughtered.' Others argued that the British administration had converted India into an 'immense prison'. These responses address the other dimensions of the Mutiny, specifically, British brutality that matched, or in some cases exceeded, the native one.

Indians were divided about what 1857 stood for. Was it a full-fledged revolt against foreign rule? Or was it a localized rebellion by the native military?

> 'It was provoked by a fierce spirit of social reaction.'
> —M.N. Roy (1922)

Romesh Dutt, writing his massive history of India in 1897, saw it as a civil insurrection rather than a military one, but driven by political reasons. Syed Ahmad Khan in his detailed study of the Mutiny (1873) did not consider it a popular movement or uprising, though there was substantial civilian participation. Khan argued that there was a deep-seated resentment among the Indians well before 1857 and the cartridge question. Interestingly, he also believed that the annexation of Oudh could not have provided the impetus for such an insurrection. Khan pointed out that the men who mutineed had nothing to lose (unlike the princes or nobility). He also rejected the idea that the Mutiny was a national rebellion against foreign rule. The revolt was, for Khan, the result of a misunderstanding on the part of the Indians. They began to believe that every single law prepared by the British government was a means of degrading their culture and faith. Khan writes: 'They misapprehended every act, and whatever law was passed was misconstrued by men who had no share in the framing of it, and hence no means of judging its spirit.' To this ignorance on the part of the people about the government's policies, we can track the origins of the Mutiny, wrote Khan.

Among the Indian responses the most enduring one has been Veer Savarkar's. Savarkar coined the phrase, 'the first war of Indian Independence' to describe the events of 1857. Savarkar's 1909 book of this title was also instrumental in retrieving Mangal Pandey as the first Indian martyr of 1857. Savarkar argued that it was necessary for Indian nationalism to see 1857 as a foundational moment and event. He proposed that the heroism of Indian soldiers in refusing the cartridges and facing up to the British forces was an enduring part of national history. It was not for personal gain or pride but rather for the greater good of the community that the rebels fought the British, argued Savarkar. Savarkar thus gave the Mutiny the physiognomy of a grand *national* and *nationalist* rebellion.

Mahatma Gandhi's acceptance of the Mutiny as a war of independence is also tinged with disapproval of the violence on both sides. He wrote about the Mutiny in *Indian Opinion*, dated 9 July 1903 (*Collected Works*, Vol. 3):

> An appeal was made to the worst superstitions of the people of India, religion was greatly brought into play, and all that could be done by the evil-minded was done to unsettle peoples' minds, and to make them hostile to British rule. It was at that time of stress and trouble that the great mass of the Indian people remained absolutely firm and unshaken in their loyalty.

Later, in a talk delivered to the Seva Dal workers in August 1931, and published in *Young India* (*Collected Works*, Vol. 53), by which time his precepts on violence were in place, Gandhi referred to it as 'a war of independence fought with violent weapons'. Gandhi referred to Malleson's history of the Mutiny and went on:

> You will see that though the greased cartridges may have been an immediate cause, it was just a spark in a Magazine that was ready. The U.P., the storm centre of 1857, has for generations remained under a paralysis as perhaps no other province. For people have retained vivid memories of man turned beast, and masses who simply watched were mown down like corn stalks in a field.

Gandhi was concerned, quite rightly, about the effect of brutality on either side—the colonized who rebelled and the colonizer who sought to retain power by stamping out rebellion.

Years later Jawaharlal Nehru also described 1857 as the 'first war of Indian independence'. Netaji Subhas Chandra Bose believed that it was a crucial moment in Indian nationalism. He argued in his 1942 essay 'Free India and Its Problems' that the revolt failed 'due to defects in strategy and in diplomacy, on the part of the Indian leaders'.

India's official historian of 1857, S.B. Chaudhuri, characterized it as a civilian revolt, and suggested that it was a battle by natives against their foreign ruler. Other commentators have drawn attention to the multiple and complex ways in which civilian and military movements and alliances were supported by tribal and peasant rebellions during 1857, all of which contributed to the unrest of the time.

K.S. Singh shows how tribals actively contributed to

> 'It was nothing more than the last spasm of a dying feudalism.'
> —M.N. Roy (1922)

the rebellion.[4] Gautam Bhadra looks at ordinary figures of the rebellion, in an interesting and welcome departure from traditional interpretations of 1857 which focus only on leaders like Nana Sahib or Rani Lakshmibai.[5]

The safest, and perhaps most conservative, interpretation of 1857 would be that it was a popular uprising against foreign rule, planned in some places but, as it progressed through cantonments and regiments in northern India, spontaneous in others.[6] The civilian support of the military and the local chieftains suggests a mixture of the popular and military elements in the rebellion. That 1857 had a large *popular* base is clear from the number of folk songs and ballads on the subject.[7] A contemporary commentator, J.W. Sherer, in the preface to his *Havelock's March on Cawnpore*, noted that 1857 may have been a 'purely military mutiny' but 'the people seemed to side with the Sepoys', suggesting a popular base.

But there was also a degree of conspiracy here, as we shall see in the concluding section.

The Trial of the Last Mughal

Often dismissed in a few lines in histories of the Mutiny, the trial of Bahadur Shah Zafar, the last Mughal emperor, has seldom been examined in great detail, even in our own age where trials of dictators for their 'crimes against humanity' are commonplace. Let us first clear the grounds: what was the trial about? What were the charges? How did it proceed? And what did it achieve?

---

[4] Singh, 'Tribals in 1857' (1998).

[5] Bhadra, 'Four Rebels of 1857' (1985).

[6] The argument made by Rudrangshu Mukherjee, *Awadh in Revolt* (1984).

[7] See Badri Narayan (1998) on this theme of popular songs and works on 1857.

In order to emphasize their complete return to authority and the equally complete end of the Mughals, the trial of the Mughal emperor was held *in his own palace*. The monarch was reduced to a common conspirator and criminal in the Lal Qila's Diwan-i-Khas (the Hall of Special Audience). The treatment meted out to Zafar was, as we know from our times, a victor's routine behaviour: gloating and arrogant, malicious and unfair. It was calculated to reduce the scion of one of the wealthiest and most powerful dynasties in the world into an object of scorn, a felon and a common criminal.

And yet there is supreme irony in the event: neither the appointed commission nor the British government had any right to try Zafar—they were still, technically, his vassals.[8]

> *The President of European Military Commission that tried Zafar was Lt Col Dawes. The members included Major Palmer, Major Redmond, Major Sawyers and Captain Rothney. The prosecutor for the government was F.J. Harriott, the Deputy Judge-Advocate General. James Murphy's services were hired as interpreter because a vast amount of evidence was in Persian.*

The trial opened on 27 January 1858. It went on for twenty-one days, morning till about 4 p.m. every day. Zafar remained indifferent to the trial, occasionally even falling asleep. On some days, he would wake up to ask a question of a witness.

On the first day the charges against Zafar were read out. They were as follows:

1st — For that he, being a Pensioner of the British Government in India, did, at Delhi, at various times

---

[8]Indeed, as F.W. Buckler argued, it was the EIC that had rebelled against its feudal superior, whose vassal it technically remained.

between the 10th of May and 1st of October 1857, encourage, aid and abet, Muhammad Bakht Khan, Subadar of the Regiment of Artillery, and divers others, Native Commissioned Officers and Soldiers unknown, of the East India Company's Army, in the crimes of Mutiny and Rebellion against the State.

2nd — For having at Delhi, at various times between the 10th of May and 1st of October 1857, encouraged, aided and abetted Mirza Moghal, his own son, a subject of the British Government in India, and others unknown, inhabitants of Delhi, and of the North-West Provinces of India, also subjects of the said British Government, to rebel and wage war against the State.

3rd — For that he, being a subject of the British Government in India, and not regarding the duty of his allegiance, did, at Delhi, on the 11th of May 1857, or thereabouts, as a false traitor against the State, proclaim and declare himself the reigning King and Sovereign of India, and did then and there traitorously seize and take unlawful possession of the City of Delhi, and did moreover, at various times between the 10th of May and 1st of October 1857, as such false traitor aforesaid, treasonably conspire, consult, and agree with Mirza Moghal, his own son, and with Muhammad Bakht Khan, Subadar of the Regiment of Artillery, and divers other false traitors unknown, to raise levy and make insurrection, rebellion, and war, against the State, and further to fulfil and perfect his treasonable design of overthrowing and destroying the British Government in India, did assemble armed forces at Delhi, and send them forth to fight and wage war against the said British Government.

4th — For that he, at Delhi, on the 16th of May 1857, or thereabouts, did, within the precincts of the Palace at Delhi, feloniously cause, and become accessory to the murder of forty-nine persons, chiefly women and children of European and mixed European descent; and did moreover, between the 10th of May and 1st of October 1857, encourage and abet divers Soldiers and others in murdering European Officers, and other English subjects, including women and children, both by giving and promising such murderers service, advancement, and distinctions; and further, that he issued orders to different Native Rulers having local authority in India, to slay and murder Christians and English people, whenever and wherever found on their Territories; the whole or any part of such conduct being an heinous offence under Act XVI of 1857, of the Legislative Council in India.

When asked by the court whether he was 'guilty' or 'not guilty' of the charges preferred against him, Zafar stated: 'Not guilty'.

Harriott then opened the case for the prosecution with a detailed statement. Harriott informed the court that even if found guilty, Zafar's life would be spared because the government had extended this promise to him at the time of his surrender. Harriott also emphasized that the trial was 'of no ordinary interest' because thousands were awaiting the verdict. 'The magnitude of the crimes imputed to him [Zafar]', declared Harriott, 'or to his connection with events which will for ever remain recorded in the pages of history, must be of no ordinary interest'. It was therefore important, he argued, that every available evidence be collected and documented. Harriott argued that the trial was for history—the future will want to look at the heinous crimes Zafar perpetrated, and there must be a substantial amount of evidence to prove it. This vast body of evidence was presented under five heads: 'Miscellaneous Papers', 'Loan', 'Pay', 'Military' and 'Murder'.

The first witness was Ahsan Ullah Khan, Zafar's physician. He was called upon to identify the handwriting on the various orders submitted as evidence under 'Miscellaneous'. Ahsan Ullah Khan affirmed that they were in Zafar's own hand. The Royal Orders were then read out to the court in translation.

On Day Three we have the first major surprise. Zafar had appointed Ghulam Abbas as his lawyer on Day Two. When the third day's proceedings opened, the first witness was Ghulam Abbas—a strange situation where the defence lawyer is a witness for the prosecution!

This was a key witness. Ghulam Abbas describing 11 May in the palace told the court of the steps Zafar took on hearing of the arrival of the mutineers. He had ordered the gate to be closed, and sent the news to Captain Douglas immediately. He also prevented Douglas from speaking to the mutineers, arguing that they would kill him (Douglas) on sight. In fact, Abbas affirms that Zafar caught hold of Douglas' hand and said 'I won't let you go'. Zafar, claimed Abbas, immediately sought to ensure the European women's safety and sent them to Zeenat Mahal's chambers. When more mutineers entered the palace and asked for his protection since they had killed the Europeans at Meerut and were ready to fight for their faith, Zafar is said to have responded: 'I did not call for you, you have acted very wickedly.' But he eventually put his hands on the heads of the mutineers, an act that was, said Abbas 'equivalent to an acceptance of their allegiance and services'. Abbas also confirmed Zafar's handwriting on several documents. Coming to the key question of the murder of the Europeans in the palace (16 May) he informed the court that Ahsan Ullah had declared that the mutineers would not be restrained from the slaughter.

All the documents in Zafar's writing were treated as evidence of his collusion with the mutineers, that he corresponded with other native kings seeking support in the war against the English and so on.

Later (on day Six), Ahsan Ullah was asked a significant question: 'Did you know a man at Delhi of the name of Muhammad Hasan Askari, a priest by descent?' Ahsan Ullah admitted that Askari was a priest who often came to see Zafar. He then claimed that the contact with Persia—to unite in the battle against the firanghis—was initiated by Askari when he sent Sidi Kambar on a fictitious voyage to Mecca. He also claimed that Sidi Kambar carried some papers with Zafar's seal on them. Further, there were posters on Delhi walls calling all Muslims to 'unite under one banner' should there be need, said Ahsan Ullah during the course of his cross-examination.

Later, another witness, Jat Mall, on day Seven, would state that Askari, the priest, had seen in a dream

> a hurricane approaching from the West, which was followed by a great flood of water devastating the country; that it passed over, and that he noticed that the King suffered no inconvenience from it, but was borne up over the flood seated on his couch.

Jat Mall informed the court:

> The way in which Hasan Askari interpreted this dream was that the King of Persia with his army would annihilate the British power in the East, would restore the King to his ancient throne and reinstate him in his kingdom, and at the same time the infidels, meaning the British, would be all slaughtered.

(Askari, called as witness on day Ten denies all knowledge of either Sidi Kambar or the so-called prophecy involving the Persian king). This Persian connection will become an important part of Harriott's conspiracy theory involving Islam itself.

> *After a few days Jat Mall, who was a servant of the British Government, stationed on duty at the palace, enquired from me whether it was true that Sidi Kambar had proceeded on pilgrimage. He said he believed that the man had not gone on pilgrimage, but to Persia. I replied I know nothing about the matter; but having made enquiries privately, I ascertained from the eunuchs that the man had really gone to Persia... I enquired from Mirza Ali Bakht, who was a great friend of Mirza Najaf, whether the latter had carried any letter from the King of Delhi to the Sultan of Persia its contents to be to the effect that the King of Delhi had adopted the Shia creed, and the King of Persia should help him.*
>
> —Hakim Ahsan Ullah, at Zafar's trial

There were also, Jat Mall declared, frequent discussions regarding the disaffection of the troops and the cartridge question. There was a rumour that if the Meerut sepoys were court-martialled, they would come to Delhi and would be joined by the native troops there. Regarding any conspiracy, Jat Mall informed the court that the chappatis were variously interpreted by the people. One important interpretation was that they were 'circulated by the Government to signify that the population throughout the country would be compelled to use the same food as the Christians, and thus be deprived of their religion.' Jat Mall also claimed that Mirza Moghal, Zafar's son, 'was standing on the roof of his house overlooking the courtyard, and at the same time other sons and two grandsons of the king were standing on their houses, apparently for the purpose of witnessing the massacre.'

Jat Mall's, as can be gathered, was a crucial bit of evidence. It suggested the existence of disaffection, conspiracy, Persian connections, and a clear role for Zafar's sons (if not Zafar) in the massacre of the Europeans in the palace.

European witnesses began their depositions on day Eight. These were mainly eyewitness accounts of what happened in various quarters of the city after 11 May. Most witnesses described the acts of looting and murder committed by the natives. Officers such as Captain Forrest told the court that insolence had been rife among the native soldiers for some weeks prior to 11 May. Charles Theophilus Metcalfe described seeing notices on city walls exhorting all the 'faithful followers of the prophet Muhammad to join with him [the King of Persia who was fighting the English forces in *his* country] in extirpating the English infidels, and offering landed estates and other large rewards to all who would do so.' But Metcalfe was unable to state whether Zafar had any 'treasonable communication' with the native troops anywhere.

Some native witnesses like Makhan, a mace-bearer of Captain Douglas, and Kishan Singh, a 'chupprassy to the government', were called upon to describe the killing of the Europeans inside Zafar's palace rooms. A news-writer, Chuni Lal, deposing before the court admitted that at least one newspaper, the *Sadikul-Akhbar*, or the *Authentic News*, had published an article that 'evidenced decided enmity against the Government'. Chuni Lal testified that 'the King's personal armed attendants, and some of the mutinous soldiery were slaying the Europeans'—a crucial evidence against Zafar. In addition he affirms that the Europeans, prior to their massacre, were kept in dark, and pathetic rooms even though there was plenty of spare room with better facilities. No messenger interceded or tried to stop the killing, says Gulab, the next witness. Later, another native witness, Mukund Lal, Zafar's secretary, claims that he had heard talk of mutiny among the native soldiers in the palace.

Later, this charge of massacring the Europeans would be crucial for the prosecution. Ahsan Ullah Khan attested to the veracity of an entry in the court diary for 16 May:

The King delivered them up, saying 'The army may do as they please.'

This seems to suggest that Zafar knew what was to happen, and did nothing to prevent it.

Mrs Aldwell supplied crucial evidence. She described the treatment meted out by the natives—how they promised to protect the Europeans, reneged on their promises and finally even threatened to kill them. Mrs Aldwell was one of those imprisoned in the palace. She said in her deposition:

> The sepoys used to come with their muskets loaded and bayonets fixed, and ask us whether we would consent to become Mahomedans, and also slaves, if the King granted us our lives; but the King's special armed retainers from which the guard over us was always furnished, incited the sepoys to be content with nothing short of our lives, saying we should be cut up in small pieces, and given as food to the kites and crows.

Mrs Aldwell and her children escaped being slaughtered, she said in her testimony, by claiming to be Kashmiri Muslims. She did something else:

> Since the outbreak on Monday I had learnt and had taught my children the Mahomedan confession of faith, and we were all able to repeat it. It was from believing us Mussulmans that our lives were spared.

C.B. Saunders, Officiating Commissioner and Agent to the Lieutenant Governor, described the way in which the Company and the government had treated Zafar and his family.

> He was in receipt of a stipend of one lakh of rupees per mensem, of which 99,000 rupees were paid at Delhi, and

> 1,000 at Lucknow to the members of his family there. He also was in receipt of revenue to the amount of 1½ lakhs of rupees per annum from the crown lands, in the neighbourhood of Delhi. He also received a considerable sum from ground-rents of houses and tenements in the city of Delhi.

This testimonial suggests that Zafar had always been treated well by the government, something that would come up in Harriott's concluding remarks.

Also used as evidence were a large number of court orders, proclamations and news reports (the various 'papers' and appendices in the transcript of the trial). These included requests for help from native kings, Zafar's orders to Mirza Moghal and letters. Many of the letters from the native kings and merchants addressed Zafar as the new emperor (or rather the new power in India). Requests for help were therefore directed to him, as would be natural when a power has been identified and publicly acknowledged. News reports about Zafar accepting oaths of loyalty and fidelity were also used as evidence. A vast amount of instructions from Zafar's court to mutineers and native kings and feudatories was also produced.

Incidentally, many of the news items and proclamations asked for Hindus and Muslims to be united against the common enemy. One of Mirza Moghal's last orders, dated 13 September 1857 states:

> it is incumbent on all the inhabitants whether Hindu or Mahomedan, from a due regard to their faith, to assemble directly in the direction of the Cashmere Gate...

Once the witness testimonies have been recorded and the documentary evidence produced, Zafar's defence is read out in court.

> *From Bahadur Shah Zafar's defence at his Trial*
>
> *I had had no intelligence on the subject previously to the day of the outbreak ... though I again did all in my power to reason with the rebellious soldiery, they would not heed me, and carried out their purpose of slaying these poor people. I gave no orders for this slaughter ... They even declared they would depose me, and take Mirza Moghal king ... It is a matter for patient and just consideration then, what power in any way did I possess, or what reason had I to be satisfied with them? The officers of the army went even so far as to require that I should make over the queen Zinat Mahall to them that they might keep her a prisoner, saying she maintained friendly relations with the English ... I was helpless, and constrained by my fears, I did whatever they required, otherwise they would immediately have killed me. This is universally known. I found myself in such a predicament that I was weary of my life...*

And then Harriott began to sum up. Harriott's detailed exposition is a fascinating document in and of itself. The summing up (and the trial) constructed a narrative of Zafar's guilt, in which several themes coalesced. A quick summary would be as follows. It demonstrated that: several people in Delhi, including Zafar, had foreknowledge of the Mutiny; there appears to have been a Persian connection; the Europeans were massacred by the king's own personal bodyguard; there was always a possibility of rescuing the women and children; that Zafar knew Mirza Moghal or the native soldiers would kill them and yet did nothing; that he sought help on behalf of the mutineers from native kings; that the whole Mutiny was a Mohammedan conspiracy. Some of the problems with the trial's arguments, and its more significant emphases, are worth looking at.

Harriott did not lose any opportunity to mention that among the dead were women and children (described as 'young and delicate women' and 'tender children').

The trial was built on a wild speculation: that the eighty-two-year-old, weak and disinterested Zafar actively conspired with native rulers and Persia to overthrow the British.

> 'The King must have addressed the King of Oudh also, who was also a Shia, and that Mirza Haidar must have held out hopes of gain to the King of Delhi if he should unite himself with the King of Oudh.'
>
> —Hakim Ahsan Ullah, at Zafar's trial

> *'If we had no other evidence of a plot, no testimony indicative of a previous conspiracy, the very nature of the outbreak itself must have convinced us of the existence of one.'*
>
> —Harriott at Zafar's trial

Evidence was supplied in the form of letters and court orders purportedly written by Zafar himself, even though many of these (like the one to the Raja of Jaisalmer) did *not* carry his personal signature, and it was established that others in the palace (notably Mirza Moghal) had obtained access to his special seals. It was also common knowledge that Zafar himself was in fear of his life, and that he simply put his name and signature to documents because he was under pressure to do so. The prosecution ignored this factor.

Clinching evidence came in the form of Zafar's alleged letter to his son, Mirza Moghal. This long letter was declared (by Harriott) to be a 'written confession of the crime'. Harriott argued that Zafar in this letter 'actually makes merit of the slaughter of his Christian prisoners'. Zafar's letter does no such thing. What it actually says is:

> The troops first requested that the princes royal might be appointed to the different commands in the army, promising they would obey them. This was done. They next urged that it would afford them greater confidence, if dresses of honour should be bestowed on the princes to give a character of stability to their appointments as commandants, and if all the (European) prisoners should be killed at once. This was also complied with...

It does not, at *any* point, praise the mutineers for killing the Europeans. Nor does it suggest that Zafar asked them to commit murder. The rest of the letter is an attack on the behaviour of the mutineers—hardly evidence of Zafar's involvement in any kind of crime. It proves, in fact, that he was *not* in any control of the princes, the mutineers, or the events unfolding in the palace. The letter stated explicitly:

> The men of the army, whether cavalry or infantry, were prohibited going about armed through the city, and oppressing the inhabitants, yet one regiment of infantry has taken up its quarters at Delhi, another at the Lahore, and a third at the Ajmir Gate, within the walls of the city, and have thoroughly desolated several of the bazaars ... The officers of the army too make a practice of coming into court carelessly dressed, wearing caps instead of turbans and carrying their swords. Never during the British rule did any members of their profession behave in this way.

Zafar then actually threatens to abdicate:

> Wearied and helpless, we have now resolved on making a vow to pass the remainder of our days in services acceptable to God, and relinquishing the title of sovereign fraught with cares and troubles, and in our present griefs

and sorrows, assuming the garb of a religious mendicant, to proceed first and stay at the shrine of the saint Khwaja Sahib, and, after making necessary arrangements for the journey, to go eventually to Mecca.

None of these statements and orders, evidence that Zafar did not dictate or control the mutineers' actions, are taken into account in the court in what is a clear case of manipulated evidence.

In this same letter, also cited in the trial, Zafar had written: 'repeated injunctions have been issued prohibiting plunder and aggression in the city, but all to no purpose.' He also writes that the mutineers had been harassing the civilians, even though the worst raiders in history, Chengiz Khan and Nadir Shah had never troubled the civilian population. Everything seems to suggest that Zafar was not in control of the situation inside his own palace. On the contrary, the evidence points in the opposite direction—that even if the Mutiny was pre-planned Zafar had no idea of a plot.

Zafar provided one fascinating, and what ought to have been complete counter to this matter of documentary evidence. In his defence he pointed out that this so-called incriminating letter (even if they chose to trust its contents) was in *Urdu*. Zafar's court language had, by order, always been *Persian*—all official documents would therefore be in that language. What Zafar was saying that he could not have written the letter. The prosecution ignored this factor.

The trial reduced Zafar to a common criminal (he was referred to throughout the proceedings as 'the prisoner'). It argued that he had betrayed the protection offered by the British. That he had been ungrateful because he was the British government's pensioner. It ignored the fact that the Company was, technically, the Mughal emperor's vassal!

Finally, the prosecution argued that it was a Muslim plot to overthrow the British, perhaps with help from Persia. Harriott stated in his concluding remarks:

> If we now take a retrospective view of the various circumstances which we have been able to elicit during our extended enquiries, we shall perceive how exclusively *Mahommedan* are all the prominent points that attach to it. A *Mahommedan* priest, with pretended visions [Harriott is referring to Hasan Askari, a priest who seems to have had a great influence on Zafar], and assumed miraculous powers—a *Mahommedan* King, his dupe and accomplice—a *Mahommedan* clandestine embassy to the Mahommedan powers of Persia and Turkey resulting—*Mahommedan* prophecies as to the downfall of our power—*Mahommedan* rule as the successor of our own—the most cold-blooded murders by *Mahommedan* assassins—a religious war for *Mahommedan* ascendancy—a *Mahommedan* press unscrupulously abetting—and *Mahommedan* sepoys initiating the mutiny.

Harriott declared that the entire defence submitted by Zafar was unworthy of consideration.

> I do not mean to take the defence, paragraph by paragraph, and thus refute it.

But there was no other defence, and here was the prosecutor stating that there was no need to even look at what Zafar was saying. This silence around Zafar's defence meant the prosecution's evidence went unrefuted, and there were *no* counter-arguments!

After this farcical exercise, on 9 March 1858 the court finalized its verdict:

> The Court, on the evidence before them, are of opinion that the Prisoner Muhammad Bahadur Shah, Ex-King of Delhi, is Guilty of all and every part of the Charges preferred against him.

the raj rises again

The trial and the exile of Muhammad Bahadur Shah marked the end of one of the most illustrious dynasties in history. A dynasty whose kings built some of the most beautiful structures in the world, who patronized the greatest artistic talents of their age, whose contribution to unifying society and developing their chosen territories was unmatched.

> *A few days after the extinction of the East India Company had been publicly proclaimed there came to Allahabad "in a shabby palanquin, and surrounded by lancers with their weapons ready," the Great Moghul. He was a state prisoner on his journey to Calcutta, where he was to embark for Burmah.*
>
> —George W. Forrest,
> A History of the Indian Mutiny *(1893–1912)*

Perhaps the tragedy of the Mutiny, the helplessness of Zafar, the farce of the trial and the ignominious end of the great Mughals is nowhere better captured than in Zafar's own famous lines. Zafar wrote:

> *na kisi ki aankh ka nuur huun, na kisi ke dil ka qaraar huun.*
> *na kisi ke kaam aa sake, main vo ek musht-e-ghubaar huun.*
>
> *main nahin huun naghma-e-jaan fizaa; koi sun ke mujh ko karega kya?*
> *main bare biruug ki huun sada, kisi dil jale ki pukaar huun.*
>
> *mera rang rup bigar gayaa, mera yaar mujh se bichar gayaa,*
> *jo chaman khizaan se ujar gayaa, main usi ki fasl-e-bahaar huun.*
>
> *na to main kisi ka habiib huun, na to main kisi ka raqiib huun,*
> *jo bigar gayaa vo nasiib huun, jo ujar gayaa vo dayaar huun.*
>
> *pae faatihaa koi aae kyuun, koi chaar phuul chirhaae kyuun?*
> *zafar, ashk koi bahaae kyun, ke main bekasi ka mazaar huun.*

High Imperialism

One of the direct political results of the 1857 events was the end of Company rule. There were vigorous protests against the extinction of Company rule. John Stuart Mill defended Company rule by arguing in his essay on 'Representative Government' that free people (the British) could rule the 'semi-barbarous' (the Indians) only through an intermediate body of qualified administrators who had a 'special trust'.

After the 1857 events the Army's role as saviour and guardian was underlined as never before, though the Army had always had a crucial role to play in the Company's development of political sovereignty.[9] What the British government did was to change the composition of the Army. A commentator argued in *Fraser's Magazine* of August 1857:

> The Sepoy must ever be an invaluable auxiliary to the English soldier, but we must take care to keep him in his proper place as an auxiliary only.

In 1857 there were 34,000 European soldiers to 257,000 Indians. By 1863 there were 62,000 British soldiers to 125,000 Indians.

The police became the most important tool of control in India. An Auxiliary Force of India was raised. Every European male civilian was to be imparted part-time military training. No Indians were allowed to man field guns (this restriction lasted until the First World War). And yet Indians were given charge of

---

[9] For a study see Alavi (1995).

several companies in the Army, as a measure of British trust in them!

During recruitment and allocation care was taken to ensure that no particular caste or community dominated a regiment. The Peel Commission, appointed to look into India's military affairs, recommended that the native army should have various nationalities and castes mixed together. In addition to mixing companies the British drew the main population of the Army from communities it saw as 'martial': Rajputs, Deccan Muslims, Gurkhas, Rajputs and Sikhs. This was to prevent any particular Mutiny leader from garnering caste or community-based support.

On 1 November 1858 Queen Victoria proclaimed a new government for India, directly under the British monarch. The Proclamation was intended to placate the native fears of conversion and interference in matters of faith. The Proclamation emphasized this component mainly because it was so central to the Mutiny. It declared:

> None be in anywise favoured, none molested or disquieted, by reason of their religious faith or observances, but that all shall alike enjoy the equal and impartial protection of the law; and we do strictly charge and enjoin all those who may be in authority under us that they abstain from all interference with the religious belief or worship of any of our subjects on pain of our highest displeasure.

Though the East India Company existed till 1874, it did not have any powers. India, now the 'jewel in the British crown', was soon the only country in the world to be represented by a Secretary of State in England. London got its India Office under the new dispensation and Calcutta got Government House. The Governor General was now called 'Viceroy', and was answerable only to the monarch of Britain. The Executive Council and Legislative Council were meant to provide a monitoring and restraining mechanism.

Canning's regime introduced the durbars, where Indian princes, officials and landlords were bestowed titles, lands and money. It created the Star of India, a kind of Indian knighthood, to honour the most influential (and loyal) princes.

British presence in India moved into a new phase. Britain was now the unquestionable ruler of India. A reassertion of the superiority of the ruling race was integral to this phase, though the rulers were dependant on local elite (such as zamindars) for administration. The imperial idea eventually climaxed when Victoria was declared the 'Empress of India'.

A shift in attitude was perceivable: little attempts at reform, a reaffirmation of British supremacy and difference and absolute authority. James Fitzjames Stephen, one of the propagandists for this approach to government, argued that the careful application of force was crucial to the creation of civilized society. He argued that the trained civil services in India would be able to create such a society. A benevolent but firm government would quickly solve the problems created by the liberal rule of previous decades, he argued.

A grand Imperial Assemblage was held in 1877 to showcase the new imperialism. It is interesting to note how the Assemblage arranged itself: the British camps were pitched on the Ridge, the site from which twenty years ago they had fought for Delhi and the empire. One British commentator, J.T. Wheeler, described the arrangement feelingly:

> It was difficult to gaze upon the different camps without recalling some of the scenes in that famous siege.

Disraeli and company argued, instead, that the new title [Empress], would help Indian 'subjects' see a continuity between the splendour of Mughal glory and British power. This was the new conservatism of the Raj. The new conservatives—and Disraeli stands as the icon—emphasized continuity, tradition and permanence. India was a land of antiquity that had to be governed firmly because this was Britain's task and duty. This idea of imperial responsibility and the glamour of an empire slowly entered the imagination, and was soon linked with other ideas of patriotism and Englishness. That is, patriotism and pride in Englishness often meant a pride in the Empire.

The rising popularity of the Empire in the British imagination also meant that Britain began to distance herself from her 'subjects'. However, the zeal for reform was not entirely missing from this period of increasingly racialized colonialism. The reform of India was very much a part of the post-1857 British agenda. The Indian Councils Act of 1861 and the Local Self-government Act of 1882 were both measures that can be seen to have been 'reformist,' since they were attempts to include Indians in the government. The overarching ideology, despite all these, remained an authoritarian, if paternal, Raj.

There was an inherent paradox in Britain's dealings with India during this phase. India was projected as an integral part of the British empire, even as it argued for India's irresoluble difference from Britain. The ideology of empire negotiated the paradox by codifying the difference itself. The 'difference' between the subject Indians and the ruling British became more and more racialized.

What was the 'Mutiny'?

The exact nature of the Mutiny has been fiercely debated. Dozens of explanations have been offered, each based on select evidence, but none offering a total explanation.

Was it a purely military 'revolt', the result of the cartridge problem? Was it a 'popular uprising'? Or was it an anti-colonial movement, an incipient form of the nationalist revolt against foreign rule? What is certain is that it was not one thing alone, but rather a mix of circumstances, events and people, each contributing specific elements to 1857.

Technically the actions of the sepoys constituted 'Mutiny'—armed insubordination against direct orders from their superior officers. But that was merely a 'technical' issue. The events of 1857 stood for something larger, as observers across the world, from the early days to the end of the uprising, realized.

It was not that resistance to the Raj, or even armed resistance, was a new development. The Moplahs in Malabar (Kerala) had risen in 1849, 1851 and 1852 (and, even after the Mutiny in 1870). The Bhil tribes had fought the British in 1819, 1829 and 1844–46, as did the Santhals in 1855–56. The Wahabis, who were to prove influential throughout the later years of the nineteenth century, advised Indians that the British government's policies would destroy their (Indians') faith. What is fascinating about 1857 is the extent—most of northern India—and the structure of the revolt: military rebellion, furthered by and coalescing with popular and civilian movements.

There is evidence that the Mutiny might have been planned. Issuree Pandey, the jemadar who had refused to arrest Mangal Pandey and was hanged on 8 April 1857, admitted that a conspiracy existed, according to John Kaye's account. Sita Ram's account states:

> Agents of the Nawab of Oudh and also of the King of Delhi were sent all over India to discover the temper of the army. They worked upon the feelings of the sepoys, telling them how treacherously the foreigners behaved towards the king. They invented ten thousand lies and promises to persuade the soldiers to mutiny and turn against their masters, the English, with the object of restoring the Emperor of Delhi to the throne.

Sita Ram (whose account states that he was born in Tilowee village in Oudh) here suggests a wide-ranging conspiracy across the Oudh and the northern territories. Muslim reformers may have declared jihad in Muzaffarnagar. The actions of the England-educated Dr Wazir Khan, members of the Deobandi movement, and people like Haji Imdaullah, Muhammad Qasim and Rashid Ahmad suggest, according to at least one twentieth-century source, Ubaidullah Sindhi, the existence of an organization to rid India of the British (a claim disputed by Francis Robinson, 1993, on the ground that there is no evidence of the existence of such an organization).[10] Others such as Turrebaz Khan and Maulvi Ala-ud-din at Hyderabad (Deccan) denied any conspiracy.

The exact role of the chappatis—a phenomenon that points to a well-organized method of secret communication—has never been explained. The 'circulation' of itinerant maulvis and fakirs is also perhaps more than a coincidence. Accounts of the time indicate intrigues between native rulers and troops—and here, especially, Nana Sahib's role becomes crucial—which suggests careful planning and strategizing. In fact, V.D. Savarkar suggests that the fakirs were part of a secret organization that was plotting the rebellion, an organization in which Nana Sahib played a major role.

According to C.A. Bayly (1996) part of the reason for the unpreparedness of the British in 1857 was because they had stopped listening to the information being relayed through spies and native sources like the *harkaras* (literally meaning 'do all'). Bayly's influential—and amazingly documented—argument is that

---

[10]Imdaullah was in Thana Bhawan (Muzaffarnagar) when the jihad was declared. Muhammad Qasim were also in Thana Bhawan in August and September 1857, and Rahmatullah went up to Delhi on a mysterious mission. Imdaullah later migrated to Mecca, as did Rahmatullah. Qasim lived in hiding until the general amnesty of 1859. Rashid Ahmad was arrested in 1859, but released six years later because there was no evidence. Wazir Khan became governor of Agra briefly when British power collapsed.

after the 1840s the British relied on 'programmatic' information coming from statistical surveys, courts and reports on the vernacular press. This isolated the British from the native contexts. And when the disaffection and unhappiness of the sepoys came in through the spies, the British officers did not give the information much importance—an omission that cost them dear.[11]

The choice of the summer month, when the British troopers, officers and administration would be at their very worst in terms of energy in India's blistering heat seems significant. It was also certain that if a Mutiny erupted in summer, the top echelons of the administration would be far away—in Shimla, the summer retreat of the heat-beleaguered Briton—and would take time to respond, thus giving the rebels a head start. This was indeed exactly what happened: George Anson was away in Shimla.

James Wilson was appointed Special Commissioner to investigate the guilt or innocence of natives. His conclusion, detailed by John Kaye in *History of the Sepoy War in India* (1864), is that 31 May 1857 was fixed as the date for the uprising, thus suggesting premeditation and planning. Other documents from the period, memos filed by British officers and administrators (often drawing upon intelligence provided by native spies and sympathizers) suggest that sepoys had been meeting and discussing the possibility of uprising, especially after Meerut (in fact, Savarkar

---

[11]Bayly demonstrates how *throughout* the Mutiny the rebels and the British both fought to preserve their means of communication, since both sides quickly realized that the side controlling the transmission of information would win the war. The Punjab, and perhaps the empire itself, was saved, for instance, when the Bengal Army at Lahore was disarmed within twenty-four hours of the Meerut mutiny because of the quick relay of information. If the Punjab had been lost the British forces could not have gone to rescue Delhi within six weeks. The battle for the empire was therefore a battle for information, as Bayly's path-breaking book shows.

also believes that there was a series of secret meetings).[12] William Edwards in his *Personal Adventures during the Indian Rebellion* (1858) argues vehemently for a well-planned plot for the Mutiny. The aim, he claims, was to restore the Mughal empire.

Others have argued that the prophecy—that the British would have to leave India 100 years after Plassey—was influential in the Mutiny. Meadows Taylor in his history of India wrote:

> At last had arrived the Hindoo 'Sumbut 1914 (1857–58), the hundredth year after the battle of Plassey, when, on a certain conjunction of the planets, it had been declared by astrologers, that the raj, or reign, of the company, was to continue for a hundred years, but no more. It is impossible to overrate the effect of this strange prediction among a people who, ever credulous and superstitious in the last degree, look to astrological combinations for their guidance in every circumstance and action of life...

The element of conspiracy and planning may have involved both, the military (specifically the Bengal Army), and the civilian segment. The latter would be the Oudh angle, especially involving Nana Sahib, Ahmedullah Shah and perhaps others. Native officers of the Army worked with the sepoys and some even declared themselves rulers after the British abdicated.

Were the sepoys further provoked because of the excessive punishments meted out to their comrades elsewhere? One strand of thinking believes this was the case—that the court martials, public humiliations and gory executions further fanned the flames among the sepoys. Syed Ahmad Khan in a letter written a few

---

[12] Several of these documents have been compiled in the invaluable S.A.A Rizvi and M.L. Bhargava (ed) collection, *Freedom Struggle in Uttar Pradesh* (1957), six volumes.

years later to John Kaye argued that had the Meerut sepoys been given the option of resigning instead of being so severely punished for refusing to use the cartridges, they might have simply resigned.

The question of the local princes/rulers and their involvement in the rebellion is also a puzzling one. Did they actively support the British, as Gwalior's Scindia, Raja Sarup Singh of Jind and the Nizam of Hyderabad did? Were rulers Hurdeo Baksh in Oudh who refused to join the mutineers (in fact the Nawab of Farrukhabad had savagely criticized Buksh for being a 'Christian'—at that time both an insult and a crime), playing a wait-and-watch game, not wanting to antagonize the mutineers but also aware that if once the British returned to power any supporter of the sepoys would stand to lose all? Were they secretly siding with the rebels even as they promised support to the British? For instance, even as Scindia pledged his support to the British, he is purported to have congratulated the Nawab of Banda (as late as November 1857, by which time Delhi had been taken back by the British and it was obvious that the rebels were losing) for winning back his kingdom.[13]

If indeed it was a planned military revolt then wouldn't the sepoys have first put in place a chain of command with a central authority? Wouldn't there have been a single date for the army to rise in many places rather than the random eruptions through May and June? And, finally, why Meerut—a town which had the strongest *British* military presence? But then, if it was organized with a chain of command, would they not have lost the element of spontaneity and surprise—which gave them so much leverage against the British? With the explosive mix of populations,

---

[13] A more recent study, by Albert Pionke (2004), suggests that the British press presented the Mutiny as the result of a conspiracy of a handful of scheming Indians. It helped them to see the Mutiny as a limited revolt led by greedy Indians rather than as a large-scale insurrection by natives against foreign rule.

communities and faiths, would a central command have worked at all? (Bholanauth Chunder in his *Travels of a Hindoo*, 1869, declares: 'it was impossible that twenty uncongenial parties, divided by quarrels about caste, quarrels about religion, could long act together in undisturbed concert'). A chain of command would have been easier to attack—and the British would have tracked it down and destroyed it quickly. The mutineers' advantage was that the British never knew when or where the next troops would revolt—and this was their undoing.

The armies of the Bombay and Madras Presidencies stayed loyal during the Mutiny. It touched Assam, and only scattered incidents with little coordination were reported from southern India. It reached as far as Kolhapur, where the 27th Native Infantry and Nagpur where the sowars of the irregular cavalry mutinied. Disturbances were also recorded in Hyderabad and Karnataka, but were swiftly put down before they had any serious effect. Few princes joined the mutineers. The Raja of Assam was arrested and exiled—imagine this, if you can: the ruler of a province being exiled from his own province!—for allegedly inciting the 1st Assam Light Infantry to mutiny.

William Crooke collected and published several folk songs on 1857 in the 1911 issues of Indian Antiquary. *These were songs written in praise of Wajid Ali Shah, the Begum of Oudh, Rani Lakshmibai, Beni Madho and other rebel leaders and are an invaluable resource for understanding the popular base of 1857. One song ended with:*

Look! The Feringi merchants came
    And pillaged and plundered our land
    belong to the heavens, the heroes
    Who gave their lives for their land!

> *Ballads like* 'Ghadar di Var' *and* 'Jangnama Delhi' *were popular in the Punjab region. These ballads transformed 1857 into an epic battle, complete with gods, prophecies and magic. A ballad celebrating John Nicholson was also popular. The poem ended:*
>
> *Oh! Godlike chieftain Nicholson, our children lisp thy name*
> *Thou'lt not forget the Khalsa's prayers, their babies prate thy fame.*
>
> *Songs particular to uprisings in Ranchi were also collected.*

It is possible that if the revolt had touched the Bombay or Madras Presidencies, the rulers of Gwalior and Hyderabad may have thrown in their lot with the rebels. It would have also meant massacres and violence on a much greater scale. This last point was made forcefully by Karl Marx in his essay of 23 October 1857:

> If, however, the wavering princes of Central India should openly declare against the English, and the mutiny among the Bombay army assume a serious aspect, all military calculation is at an end for the present, and nothing will remain certain but an immense butchery from Cashmere to Cape Comorin.

Deposed rulers and landlords sided with the rebels. This included the Nawabs of Farrukhabad and Banda, Begum Hazrat Mahal of Oudh, Rani Lakshmibai, Nana Sahib and the rulers of Kolhapur and Sattara. Their argument was fairly simple. They were unlikely to get back their kingdoms and ruling status as long as the British governed India. Once their kingdoms had been annexed, through whatever means, it was wishful thinking to expect that the British would re-recognize native authority over the territory. They saw the rebellion as an opportunity to regain their kingdoms (after all they were *hereditary* rulers). The landlords and local chieftains—such as Kunwar Singh and the Raja of Mainpuri—sided with the rebels for the same reason: having lost enormous territory, they perceived in the rebellion a means of retrieving their villages and lands. Historians have argued that while 1857 may not have been a peasant rebellion against the British (in the sense of a class of peasants against the British), it was a 'set of patriotic revolts' that continued the older themes of land and kingship.'[14] Others believe that the sepoys mutinied, but had no clue as to what to do next. The civilians, who were troubled by the mutineers, did not support the rebels and only wanted peace to return (we have already noted the looting of cities and tradesmen by mutineers).

However, some of these landlords like the Bundelkhand thakurs, while rebelling against the British, often operated *independent* of the sepoys.[15] Others like Firoz Shah, Zafar's cousin, sided with the rebels too. Another relative of Zafar's, Waris Ali, was believed to have instigated rebellion among Muslims in Patna. He was hanged at Patna on 7 July. Golab Singh, the ruler of Jammu, may have corresponded with Nana Sahib before the Mutiny, and may even have contributed some money for persuading sepoys to join the Nana. Some like J.W. Sherer (1910), however, believes: 'of his [Nana Sahib's] individual influence there seems no trace throughout' [Sherer is referring to the betrayal of Wheeler]. Meadows Taylor (1904), on the other hand, is positive that 'the Nana Sahib ... had been busy with plots, for years.'

It is also likely that the sepoys were seeking another employer. Thus Indian officers were stepping into the shoes of the English officer. From this perspective there might have been several motivating factors. One was the general dissatisfaction in the

---

[14] Bayly (1998).

[15] An argument made by Tapti Roy (1993).

Army. It is significant that once the Mutiny had taken place leaders like Nana Sahib and Mirza Moghal (commanding the forces at Delhi) announced *revised* pay for the sepoys, prize money and other rewards. Bishwanath Sahi of Chhota Nagpur promised sepoys badshahi pay if they rebelled.

As noted in the opening chapter, the sepoys believed that there was little chance of progress within the Army. Their conditions had definitely worsened with each successive officer, their pay was poor and new regulations seemed to ignore their religious and cultural conditions and beliefs (their notions of purity and taboo or serving overseas, for instance). Further, when the Army began recruiting people from all castes and communities, it changed the demographic structure.[16]

> 'I consider that the native troops mutinied in the hope of worldly gain. The admixture of religion was only intended to disguise their real object.'
> —Hakim Ahsan Ullah, at Zafar's trial

F.W. Buckler proposed that the sepoys were seeking a shift of allegiance from the Company to the Mughal dynasty. Buckler argued that Zafar represented not only a political authority, but also a religious one. Hence the use of the term 'jihad' (signifying religious war) by the sepoys suggests that they were seeking a return of their religious and political head, one who had been wrongfully replaced by the Company.[17] Buckler was thus proposing an ingenious argument: that 1857 was a rebellion by the East India Company against its controlling authority, the British government.

---

[16] Philip Mason's argument about the influx of 'lower' castes into the Army (1974).

[17] F.W. Buckler, 'Political Theory of the Indian Mutiny', in Embree (1987).

The historian Eric Stokes argued that changing agrarian conditions and relations, initiated by the British, contributed massively to the spread of the Mutiny.[18]

The dominance of the Brahmins and upper castes was on the wane by the 1830s. Part of the motivation might have to do with this resentment (V.D. Savarkar highlights the fact that 'Shahid Mangal Pandey', was a Brahmin who, in Savarkar's words, 'took up the duties of a Kshatriya'). Karl Marx wrote:

> England has broken down the entire framework of Indian society, without any symptoms of reconstitution yet appearing. This loss of his old world, with no gain of a new one, imparts a particular kind of melancholy to the present misery of the Hindoo, and separates Hindostan, ruled by Britain, from all its ancient traditions, and from the whole of its past history.

This, mind you, is what Marx wrote in *1853*, in an essay titled 'The British Rule in India'. In a sense he had his finger on the pulse of the *social* causes behind the uprising.[19]

The British emphasis during the trial of Zafar was on a possible Persian connection too, as we have seen, and on the Mohammedan origins of the Mutiny. J. Gibbs, the Assistant Commissioner of Sindh, reported a conversation with a native, Seth Naomull, dated 7 June 1857, recorded in the Military Department, Printed Proceedings,[20] where Naomull was sure that 'the cause of the present crisis, is that Persian influence is at the bottom of it'. The influential *New York Times* agreed with this

---

[18] Stokes, 'Context of the 1857 Rebellion', in *Peasant and the Raj* (1978).

[19] Marx also believed that the British rule came to be established because, as he put it in a later essay from 1853, India was an 'unresisting and unchanging society.'

[20] Andhra Pradesh State Archives collection.

assessment and wrote of the 'Mahommedan Conspiracy for the Sovereignty of India' in its issue of 13 August 1857.

What seems certain is that rumours—of greased cartridges, conversions, British defeats and the rebels' victories—contributed substantially to the increasing participation in the Mutiny.

> 'Corps after corps caught the infection, excited and encouraged by the uncontradicted boast of the extermination of all Europeans.'
> —G.W. Williams, Special Commissioner, 15 November 1857

Some thinkers have proposed that the rumours were deliberately and selectively disseminated, and may have helped the spread of the mutinous spirit. Thus the Jodhpur legion sowars signed a petition, dated 29 May 1857, where they prayed that they might be allowed to 'evince and prove their zeal in the service of the state, by being led against any mutinous troops or other enemies that might be causing the British Government any trouble'. Two months later, perhaps on hearing of British reverses, they rebelled! Further, such rumours would have achieved something more: panic among the administration and the British. J.W. Sherer (1910) notes:

> If the transmission of these cakes was only intended to create a mysterious uneasiness, that object was gained.[21]

Rumours might well have been a native mode of communication, subverting the power of the colonial telegraph!

1857 has elements of a popular uprising, as Rudrangshu Mukherjee has demonstrated. It was neither a purely military

---

[21] Among those who see rumours as central to the events of 1857 are the postcolonial theorist, Homi K. Bhabha (1994), and the subaltern historian, Ranajit Guha (1986).

uprising nor a truly national rebellion (in the southern parts of the subcontinent incidents were isolated and sporadic and do not show any organized leadership or concerted effort). There seems to have been a certain pattern to the rebel movements in the north. For instance, the deliberate targeting of British structures and symbols of authority (government buildings, residences, cantonments) in every town across northern India suggests a plan of action rather than momentary madness (Mukherjee again). Some historians have proposed that the repeated use of the term 'Hindustan' in the proclamations of Nana Sahib and other rebel leaders suggests the creation of a national consciousness and patriotism. That is, the invocation of the term implies a definite attachment to a larger territory and identity and a blurring of regional and communal differences.[22] Proclamations such as the Azimgarh one (attributed to Zafar's grandson by Charles Ball in his *History of the Indian Mutiny*) called for unity among Hindus and Muslims, thereby building an effective if fragile platform during 1857.

Nandalal Chatterjee suggests that because of its popular element, 1857 was a national rebellion (cited in P.J.O. Taylor, 1996). R.C. Majumdar believes that it was neither a simple 'sepoy' mutiny nor a real 'national' struggle. One key argument that has been proposed by both Mazumdar and Surendra Nath Sen is that Nana Sahib, Rani Lakshmibai, Kunwar Singh, Begum Hazrat Mahal and others with *personal* grievances against the British were fighting for *their* territorial privileges rather than any national ideal.

However, it is almost definite that 1857 generated a fair amount of anti-colonial feeling. Netaji Subhas Chandra Bose, while admitting the failure of the rebellion, recognized its overall

---

[22]Historians who make this argument include Tapti Roy (1993), David Baker (1993) and Rajat Ray (1993).

significance. He described it this way: 'a grand example of national unity' where 'all sections of the people ... fought under the flag of Bahadur Shah, a Mohammedan.'

The events with their intense emotional output influenced *future* developments in the nationalist struggle. When the Hindus and Muslims came together to defend their faith in 1857, it may have been a moment when Indian nationalism itself originated. Nana Sahib, for instance, in his Proclamation announced that they were ordained by god to drive out the British kafirs. The language of the Proclamation suggests an attempt at unity of religious identities. Nana Sahib might have been proposing a return to the territorial structures of the old Mughal empire (which was termed 'Hindustan') here.[23] 1857, with its focus on Hindu–Muslim unity (thereby creating a larger community) and territorial attachments, might thus have given the nationalist movement a definite and sharp focus. And this may help us see the events of 1857 for what they are: **the first civilian-popular-military moments of Indian nationalism and the freedom struggle**.

*

What is clear is that the events of 1857 meant many things to many people, then and now, 150 years after the 'action'. It meant economic freedom from British systems for some, the restoration of the Mughals for others. It was an attempt to reclaim their hereditary kingdoms and jagirs for some, and the assertion of their faith in the face of real or imagined onslaught by the British for others. There was a sense of the local and the regional in many cases, as Rajas and Ranis proclaimed the return of their rule, while there was a sense of a larger, greater battle against the foreign

---

[23]For this proclamation see S.A.A. Rizvi and M.L. Bhargava (1957), vol. 4.

invader in others. Some were served by very local interests, others by issues that concerned 'Hindus' and 'Muslims' as communities in the subcontinent. It was facilitated by a remarkable sense of communal harmony, with both Hindus and Muslims recognizing the *Mughal* king as their leader (and the British as a common foe). In southern India the Muslims appear to have had played a larger part in mutinous actions and plots against the British, judging from records about the period in the Madras Records Office and histories of the freedom movement in Andhra Pradesh. Proclamations from both Hindu and Muslim local leaders and rebel chiefs pleaded for unity. This was, perhaps, the Mutiny's great achievement.

Thus, 1857: the most tumultuous year of the Raj, a spectacle of suffering, sacrifice and violence. 1857 in India cost lives, territories, honour and peace. It almost cost Britain the most profitable and prestigious corner of its Empire. 1857 taught the colonizers a great lesson: that empires may be earned by the gun, but they cannot always be *kept* by the gun. It taught the Indians a lesson too: that a muscled arm carrying the gun cannot defeat the Empire. It was a very valuable lesson. For the *winning* battle against the Empire would be fought at the point of a thin hand holding nothing more than a walking stick. If 1857 heralded the arrival of the nationalist idea in India, it also heralded the most unusual, the most spectacular, war in human history. If 1857 was the story of an experiment with violence, the winning battle climaxing in 1947 would be the story of an 'experiment with truth'.

Appendix 1
The Fiction of 1857

Expectedly, the events of 1857 India influenced the European literary imagination. The events were undoubtedly traumatic—such a massive challenge to the mighty British empire! Such massacres of innocent women and children! Such hatred!

As noted in the earlier chapters, numerous literary figures responded to the events unfolding in India. Martin Tupper, Christina Rossetti and Lord Tennyson wrote poetry about the Mutiny. The socialist leader, Ernest Jones produced a long, and rather rambling, poem unabashedly titled 'The Revolt of Hindostan'. Mary Leslie published *Sorrows, Aspirations and Legends from India*.

Dozens of plays were written around themes and characters of 1857 British India. Nana Sahib was the chief villain in *Keereda and Nena Sahib*, staged at the Victoria Theatre in November 1857. In 1863 the same stage saw *Nana Sahib, or A Story of Aymere*. Then there was *India in 1857* (1857), *The Fall of Delhi* (1857), *The Storming and Capture of Delhi* (1857) and Edmund Glover's *The Indian Revolt; or, The Relief of Lucknow* (1860). Charles Wood's *H, Being Monologues at Front of Burning Cities*, a play revolving around

Henry Havelock, was staged at the Old Vic in 1869. Patrick Brantlinger claims that Dion Boucicault's *Jessie Brown; or, The Relief of Lucknow*, first staged in New York on 22 February 1858 and later in Britain, was the most successful of the Mutiny plays. The British Library, London, lists a French play by Jean Richepin and dated 1884, on Nana Sahib. As late as 1998, theatre groups were staging the events of 1857. The English Drama Group at the University of Hildesheim performed *A Star Fell*, which explored the Nana Sahib legend. It included Wheeler, Margaret (Ulrica) Wheeler, her protector (Ali), Azimullah, the courtesan Oula and Begum Hossaini Khanum as characters. As we can see it focussed on Satichaura and Bibighar.

But it was the novel that really explored the Mutiny in detail. Even French authors were fascinated enough to write fiction based on 1857 India. For instance, Jules Verne revived Nana Sahib in his *The Steam House, or the End of Nana Sahib* (1881). This time, again, Nana Sahib is the key conspirator, returning from hiding to plot the overthrow of the Raj. Let us step into, for a brief while, the fictional worlds of 1857.[1]

*

The novel's theme was announced in its title itself: *practically every novel had 'a tale of the Indian Mutiny' as its subtitle.*

Many Mutiny novels were fictional recreations that adapted readily available descriptions from first-person accounts of the events. As S.D. Singh puts it, 'the ultimate and final picture of the Indian Mutiny from the books of history written by British authors is the same as that produced in English novels about them.'

One of the earliest of such fictional treatments of the Mutiny

---

[1] According to Patrick Brantlinger (1988), there were at least fifty Mutiny novels by 1900.

was by the novelist Charles Dickens. Dickens' 'The Perils of Certain English Prisoners', written in collaboration with Wilkie Collins, and published in his periodical *Household Words* (1857) is a tale that reads like a captivity narrative, and highlights the sufferings and heroism of the British. Though it is set ostensibly in Central America, its theme (and details) is very obviously drawn from the siege of Cawnpore and Lucknow. The focus on the supposed violation of women in Dickens sets the tone for the fiction of the Mutiny.

The contrast between the peaceful life in Indian towns and the violence of the Mutiny was dramatically highlighted in most fiction. The novelist often opened with descriptions of station life, the cantonments, the leisured lifestyle of the English men and women in India. It would be a quiet opening chapter where gossip, breakfasts and dinners, some dancing, youthful romance and official work would be detailed. There would then be passing references to disaffected natives and omens suggesting danger. And then the novel would move on to the events of the Mutiny itself. More often than not the novelist localized the Mutiny—situating it in a particular town, even though references would be made to other places and events.

Novelists added a dash of romance to the horrors of the Mutiny in their fiction (there are few Mutiny novels without a love interest). This served the purpose of adding an extra dimension to the characters, where even soldiers in danger of their lives retained their sense of chivalry and fair play. In order to achieve this the novelist placed the hero in sentimental situations, a romance, a family or even friendships. These explored questions of honour, commitment, duty versus sentiment, individual safety versus collective responsibility, and the question of choice.

Edward Money's *The Wife and the Ward* (1859) was perhaps one of the first full-length novels about the Mutiny. Set in Cawnpore, the novel mixes the personal and the political. It deals with the failing marriage of Edgington and Beatrice Plane, the relationship between Edgington and his ward, Marion, the Cawnpore siege and Satichaura. The novel is significant because it perhaps inaugurated the literary representation of Nana Sahib as demon/villain. In this novel, the young Marion is afraid of a fate 'worse than death'—that she might be forced to lose her honour to the Nana. This theme of the rape of European women by the mutineers, as critics have noted, is central to all commentaries on the Mutiny (Sharpe 1991; Paxton 1999), and may also have found its inaugural moment in Money's novel. In the tale, when the massacre at Satichaura begins, Nana Sahib notices Marion, who is a woman of rare beauty. Edgington honours his promise to Marion and shoots her dead to prevent her from falling into the hands of the mutineers (he is killed soon after). The suggestion that had Marion not been killed Nana Sahib would have captured her is clearly made in the novel.

While the novel adapts the stories of Amy Horne—Margaret Wheeler and the narratives of Cawnpore, it has little subtlety about it. It also inaugurates the theme of the Englishwoman's situation during the Mutiny—a subject that haunted the British imagination throughout the Mutiny and post-Mutiny period, as we shall see.[2] It is also significant that this, perhaps the first Mutiny novel, ends with a massacre (Cawnpore) rather than with British victory. Nana Sahib thus enters the European literary imagination as the ultimate villain of British India, and perhaps among the entire non-European parts of the world, with this novel.

In Forrest's *Eight Days* (1891) a particularly illustrative scene showcases the 'women's question' during 1857. A massively built butcher pursues the Hilton women up the stairs. The entire sequence of events is presented through the women's eyes, and

---

[2] S.D. Singh notes that this novel, inaugurating the theme of the possible rape of the Englishwoman in the Mutiny, was later reprinted in 1881 under the title *Woman's Fortitude: A Tale of the Cawnpore Tragedy*.

provides an excellent example of how the natives were demonized even in their physiognomies and facial expressions:

> The three women suddenly balance themselves in the act of putting their feet down on the first step, as they catch sight of that ferocious countenance and that huge naked frame coming round the curve in the middle of the staircase ... It is the terrible look on the man's face as he catches sight of them, which is like a stunning blow. And now the fellow shakes the knife at them, and salutes them with a ferocious grin...

The Awadh and Lucknow regions are often the setting for fictional towns in Mutiny novels. H.C. Irwin's novel *With Sword and Pen* (1904) explores the annexation of Awadh through the eyes of Malcolm Mainwaring. As expected, Wajid Ali Shah is the depraved despot in the novel, a situation that calls for annexation for the greater good of the people. There is also a fictionalized account of the siege of the Lucknow Residency, here cast as the siege of Nadirabad. Descriptions of retaken cities sometimes combine a triumphalist tone with some detail of the aftershocks of the battles.

When the last stronghold fell [Lucknow] and the English flag waved over the whole conquered city, a city of empty houses, deserted streets, silent bazaars, sacked and battered palaces, with shattered temples, wasted and trampled gardens, where pleasant orange-groves shed their blossoms over broken furniture, rich stiffs torn and soiled, and blood-stained corpses, and where marble fountains made a musical plashing in the ears of prowling thieves and beggars propped by blood-splashed statues.

—Maxwell Gray's In the Heart of the Storm

Delhi is the location of what may be the best-known Mutiny novel, Flora Annie Steel's *On the Face of the Waters* (1896). Steel's work combines a love story with the theme of the Mutiny. Jim Douglas who had worked with the Nawab of Oudh is now a spy. Set in Delhi for the most part, the novel is an adventure tale, where Douglas' daring exploits constitute the bulk of the action. It also uses a particular image common to many colonial writings: disguise. Douglas here masquerades as a native spy (inspired, no doubt, by real-life figures of the Mutiny like Thomas Kavanagh) and goes about the city at will. The suggestion here is that the colonial can pass easily through India, even a rebellious India. It seems to suggest complete colonial knowledge and power—to understand Indians and their behaviour, their mannerisms so well that the Briton could *pass off as a native*. The politics of mobility, as one may term it, exemplifies a colonial ideology: no lands are closed to the European.[3] Douglas rescues Mrs Erlton from the native soldiers and an unhappy marriage, and eventually marries her.

Steel's novel is more interesting than other, routine English novels about the Mutiny because she refuses to stereotype the native as lawless, villainous and evil. In fact, she paints the English men in India as being villainous, especially in matters of romance and marriage. Alice Gissing and Kate Erlton are both unhappy because the men they married are boorish and cruel. His compatriots do not accept Jim Douglas because he has had an

---

[3]The best example would be that of Richard Burton, who could travel among the Arabs, visit Mecca and other places passing off as a native because of his powers of disguise. The theme of disguise and European colonial mobility in Asian lands is explored in a fine study by Parama Roy (1998), and in Gautam Chakravarty (2004). Another Mutiny novel, *Jenetha's Venture* by A.F.P. Harcourt (1899) also has its hero, Roland Ashby, disguising himself as a native and gathering information inside Delhi.

adulterous affair with his officer's wife, and had later cohabited with a native woman. This is an interesting reversal of the routine image of the gentlemanly English man in most novels of the period. Steel shows how hypocritical the British are when it comes to morals—they easily classify the native men as lascivious and lustful when their own behaviour is hardly any better.

The novels are unabashedly propagandist in nature. While some like Irwin's *With Sword and Pen* might explore the political contexts of the Mutiny with a more even hand than the rest, the general tone of the fiction is unchanging. It is full of stereotypes and the plot predictable: a peaceful station life, a love affair, rebellion by sepoys, betrayal, battle, deeds of valour, and finally escape and victory.

The natives are invariably villainous and treacherous. Several novelists evidently believed that the Mutiny was a planned one. Conspiring natives and plans are the subject of many novels of the time. James Grant's *First Love and Last Love* (1868) centres the conspiracy in Bahadur Shah Zafar's palace. Here Nana Sahib's confidante Azimullah and Mangal Pandey's brother, Ferukh Pandey conspire to overthrow the British. There is the usual theme of the threat to the English woman (Polly, in this case, desired by both princes, Mirza Moghal and Abu Bakr). Hodson's shooting of the Mughal princes, it is suggested, was an act of revenge for the public humiliation and murder of Polly near one of the Gates in Delhi. Another novel, Robert Sterndale's *The Afghan Knife* (1879), suggests a conspiracy between the Wahabis (here represented by Haji Sahib) and Zafar's palace. Nana Sahib and Ahmedullah Shah are seen meeting and planning the Mutiny inside the Lal Qila in Hume Nisbet's *The Queen's Desire* (1893).

In some, like Philip Meadows Taylor's *Seeta* (1872), it is the Brahmin, Azrael Pande (no doubt an echo of Mangal Pande) who is the villain. This Brahmin has forgotten his basic profession and character—rituals and piety—and taken to mutiny, robbery and murder.

> '*I have heard but one cry—a cry that comes from the very souls of the people—deliverance from the English!*'
>
> —*Azrael Pande* in
> Philip Meadows Taylor's *Seeta*

The natives in these novels also seem to need large numbers to show any kind of courage, whereas the Englishman is willing to face the enemy alone. Thus in Alice Jackson's *A Brave Girl* we have the girl narrator say: 'no attack was made that night. Perhaps the natives didn't think themselves strong enough.' In *Rung Ho!* (1914) by Talbot Mundy [pseudonym of Sylvia Anne Matheson] Ralph Cunningham is able to put down the uprising in his state single-handedly. Ralph and his ever-present Mohammed Gunga are clearly modelled after John Nicholson and his faithful Pathan.

The natives are rarely identified by name or physiognomies— and represented as hordes or nameless assistants (manning guns or serving the men) to the British. When they do possess an identity it is usually as versions of Nana Sahib—untrustworthy, lascivious and despotic. Or they are snarling, vicious-looking men, as seen in dozens of visual representations from the period. Here is a particularly typical representation (from R.E. Forrest's *Eight Days*):

> And now the rushing stream has reached the Bank-house ... Mr Hilton ... [is] simply borne away as if he were a bit of wood in front of a mass of rushing water. The marauders have poured into the long hall in the middle of which is the square underground cellar of vault ... The leader of the dacoits and two or three men he has selected rapidly descend into the vault ... And so a groan, and then a howl, goes up from the crowd ... and so the roughs grapple with the robbers—they have no boots on their feet with which to kick them—and there is fierce wrestling and furious struggling all round the

ring, and the huge hall resounds with yells and cries... It is as if a wounded deer had fallen down to the bottom of a pit, and a pack of wolves had rushed down upon it there...

The British are courageous and generous in times of siege, and chivalrous to the very end. Maxwell Gray's Mutiny novel *In The Heart of the Storm* (1891) is subtitled 'a tale of modern chivalry'. The women, delicate and innocent, find resources of courage and stamina—true British grit—in times of crises. Rather than the routine image of the hysterical and vulnerable woman of standard Victorian novels, we find many of them playing the role of the brave woman who stands by the men in England's hour of need. Occasionally, however, they pose problems for the men with their vacillations and tendency to fall into dangerous situations. In Lucy Taylor's *Sahib and Sepoy, or Saving an Empire* (1897), native women are located on a rooftop (In Lucknow) hurling 'boiling water, sticks, and stones down on the troops'. One woman 'in her uncontrollable frenzy flung the child from her arms down upon the serried ranks of bayonets below!' A British soldier, Dick, catches the falling child, and carefully places it inside a window. Turning, he is shot and dies immediately. The image of the native woman flinging down her child to certain death and the British soldier's rescue reinforces the difference between the two races: the native abdicates all responsibility for her child, the Englishman saves the women and children at all costs.

> '*A hero's death too, for he died saving that tiny brown rebel.*'
> —Oswald on Dick's death in
> Lucy Taylor's Sahib and Sepoy

The novels are essential heroic narratives, as a result. The men are of course icons of masculine courage—it must be remembered that masculinity is a persistent theme in almost all adventure fiction of this period—and resourcefulness. They bear pain and suffering stoically and never lose faith in their ability to survive and win. They also actively seek action, and want to go out and battle the rebels and win. Harry in Henry Seton Merriman's *Flotsam* (1896), is situated on Delhi Ridge in September 1857, one of the English soldiers waging the crucial battle to win back Delhi. There was, Merriman informs us, fighting, but it was 'not of the description to satisfy Harry.' He is irritated at his commander, General Barnard, and he 'grumbled sorely at the lack of enterprise displayed by his chief.' Here is a typical British soldier—longing to go out and wage battles to win back the empire. The first chapter of Lucy Taylor's *Sahib and Sepoy or Saving an Empire* is a novel about the most well-known British hero of the Mutiny—Henry Havelock. Given the trend of Mutiny fiction it does not surprise us to see the first chapter of a novel on Havelock titled 'The Making of a Hero'. The conclusion, which is a description of Havelock's death, is full of lavish praise. Havelock is described as 'the now famous warrior who had done so much to save our Indian empire.'

An interesting genre within the Mutiny novel focusses on British children in India. Hume Nisbet's *The Queen's Desire* uses a boy-hero, Sammy Tompkins, who even masquerades as a native spy, gathers information about sepoy movements and informs General Hewitt (the man in charge at Meerut, as we know). In F.P. Gibbon's *The Disputed VC* (1909) we again have the boy's adventure novel—a genre popularized by G.A. Henty, R.L. Stevenson, R.M. Ballantyne and several others in the nineteenth century—set in a colonial context.[4] Ted Russell is the boy at the centre of the story that is divided between Delhi and Lucknow,

---

[4]The adventure fiction genre for boys had a sub-category: empire adventure, which, set in Asia and Africa, often used themes of imperial responsibility, racial purity, and militarism, thereby inculcating such values in the British schoolboy. For a study see Bristow (1991).

with an early section on 'Aurungpore'. These tales are perhaps significant for a not-so-subtle theme: even a British *boy* can, because of his resourcefulness and courage, inherent to his race, survive events such as the Mutiny, and maybe even alter the course of events. In Augusta Marryat's *Lost in the Jungle* (1877) young Harry Brisbane survives a turbulent time in the jungle somewhere outside Delhi when all about him native sepoys kill Europeans. Harry also has his British sense of justice, fair play and values in place at his young age. The Brisbane family have been looked after by natives and Mr Wilson, a missionary. When they are about to leave the village where they have been staying Harry's father mourns the fact that he has no money to pay his debts to the natives, and that this is very bad for a British gentleman. He has only a gold watch (a 'gold repeater') which he has promised Harry. Harry, because it is now his watch, gives it to Wilson (to eventually benefit the natives) to prove that he is also a gentleman at his age.

> *'I am a gentleman also, and we must pay our debts.'*
>
> — young Harry Brisbane in
> Augusta Marryat's Lost in the Jungle

As a counterpart to such a stereotype of racial masculinity, we have Alice Jackson's *A Brave Girl* (1899) where we have young Joan keeping her nerve and shooting a rebel sepoy even as her younger sister has fainting spells from sheer terror!

There is little attempt in these novels to explore the multiple dimensions of British rule in India. When Henry Kingsley summarizes the Mutiny in his *Stretton* (1869) he reduces it to the battle of the evil Indians with the good British. He concludes his novel with the following statement:

Like all ill-considered and causeless revolutions, it failed.

It was evil against good, and good won.

The social and political effects of British policies are rarely discussed. When they do foreground the impact of British rule in India, it is mostly represented as harsh but beneficial. Such novels emphasize the theme of a benevolent empire. As late as 1947 C. Lestock Reid's *Masque of Mutiny* revisits the Mutiny and argues that the natives are incapable of governing themselves. Further, there is no attempt to examine the nature of British retribution. In rare cases there are scattered descriptions of post-1857 ruined state of towns in India. Villainy is, apparently, the prerogative of the natives alone! There is, as Patrick Brantlinger suggests, a 'widening chasm' in such fiction: the natives as absolute villains and the British as absolutely innocent.

Mutiny novels are also sagas of British nationalism. What is interesting is the way in which the defence of the empire becomes a defence of British national and cultural identity itself. The emphasis on British valour and stoicism in the face of the rebel attacks makes this clear: when you defend the fort or Residency, you are in fact defending Britain itself.

*

Central to this theme of the defence of the empire was the role of the English woman in the period of the Mutiny. The British woman becomes the symbol of the nation's purity and innocence. She stands at the boundary between a protected, safe empire/nation and a ruined, conquered one. The conquered English woman represented a conquered Britain.

After the Cawnpore massacres the key question (often unspoken, but visible beneath the debates in the novels and other writings) was: what if the women are raped? This fear haunts almost every Mutiny text—both fiction and non-fiction, incidentally—from the period. This fear is linked to and is the logical consequence of a theme in Western writing about Indians and the Asians: the native male has always been stereotyped as hypersexual and lascivious, with a secret lust for the white woman (a theme that figures, in a more complicated fashion, in E.M. Forster's *A Passage to India*, 1924). If the hypersexual native male was indeed attracted to white women then, given the context of the loss of British power, wasn't it possible that the Englishwomen would be at the mercy of the natives?

> '[The British] are near enough, and strong enough, to strike and to bring you and your brother to your knees if you harm a British woman.'
>
> —Rosemary McClean to Jaimihr in Talbot Mundy's Rung Ho!

The men in these novels are portrayed as concerned about two things: their empire and their women. In many cases these two merge—the successful defence of their women, where they are protected from the villainous natives, becomes a symbol for the defence of empire itself. The threat of rape and dishonour figures prominently in many contemporary novels on the Mutiny. Flora, in J.E. Muddock's *The Great White Hand* (1895), is taken away as a prisoner to Nana Sahib's palace and later to Delhi. She however manages to escape. In H.M. Greenhow's *The Bow of Fate* (1893), Lilian, who has been abducted by Secunder Khan, consumes poison and dies to prevent her rape by the native. Miss Marshall is abducted by the rebels but is saved by her countrymen before she is dishonoured in C.R. Fenn's *For the Old Flag* (1899). When Mrs Hilton pleads with her husband to abandon the Bank in R.E. Forrest's *Eight Days*, he refuses. Hilton says: 'I shall be able to manage much better by myself, when you are away.' The suggestion is that the woman's safety must be ensured so that the man is free to do his duty for Britain and empire. Britain's prestige, identity, honour are all invested in the women, apparently, and hence this anxiety and fear about the dishonouring of the women.[5] Further, the actions of the Memsahibs themselves become symbols of British courage. In J.F. Fanthome's *Mariam* (1896) Mangal Khan abducts the Lavater family, and wants to marry Mariam, who manages to evade the issue of marriage until they are rescued. When they leave Mangal Khan's house, she actually gives him testimonials for having taken care of them (not unlike Amy Horne's deal with her Muslim abductor–protector in her autobiographical account). James Grant's three-volume *First Love and Last Love* is an unusual novel in the sense it is one of the few that does not refrain from stating the rape and dishonour of English women. In a particularly graphic passage Grant writes:

> [English women were] always stripped of their clothing, treated with every indignity, and then slowly tortured to death, or hacked at once to pieces ... Delicate women were stripped to the skin, turned thus into the streets, beaten with bamboos, pelted with filth, and abandoned to the vile lusts of blood-stained miscreants, until death or madness terminated their unutterable woe...

---

[5] At least part of this anxiety stemmed from the fear of racial mixing. Englishmen in India often had Indian 'bibis'. Racial mixing and such liaisons were not always happily accepted. In fact, in Taylor's *Seeta*, the key relationship is that between Cyril Brandon and Seeta. The question of racial purity, interracial sexual relations and the role of Eurasian offspring were connected to the theme of empire in many writings of the period. The role of British women in imperialism has been exhaustively studied by critics like Pat Barr (1976), Macmillan (1988), Sharpe (1993), Jayawardane (1995) and Indrani Sen (2002), among others.

Later he describes one such incident of the public humiliation of English women, and the rape of Polly Weston. Madelena Weston in the novel escapes capture and dishonour by natives by disguising herself as a native woman. Keeping the general theme of British (masculine) chivalry and courage in the foreground, Grant focusses on the efforts of the heroes, Rowley Thompson and Jack Harrower, to protect the elder Weston sisters, Madelena and Kate.

In some cases the novels also portray a bond between natives and the English, born from sympathy, loyalty, or in some cases a shared gender. The native woman often helps the English woman to escape and survive, as in the case of Fazilla in Sterndale's *The Afghan Knife* where the former stays as Grace's companion. In E.M. Field's *Bryda* (1888), Lottie stays with the women in the palace of the Raja of Bundi. Phillip Randall lives in the house of Gossanjee Bhose, and is cared for by the family in Maxwell Gray's *In the Heart of the Storm*. In Muddock's *The Great White Hand* it is the ayah, Zeemith, who brings news of Flora's kidnapping. Eventually Zeemith enables Flora to scape from Moghal Singh's palace. Native women in Delhi give Kate Erlton refuge in Steel's *On the Face of the Waters*. In *Eight Days* a Brahmin guard helps the English survivors of Khizrabad to escape from the Nawab's clutches. In F.S. Brereton's *A Hero of Lucknow* (1905) Ikand, the faithful servant of the Watsons, stabs a guard and helps Mrs Heaton and her daughters to escape.

The women in Mutiny writings—both fiction and non-fiction—move mostly between two roles: victim and heroine. Built, perhaps, on the story of Miss Wheeler defending herself against the sepoys, the woman is harassed, in fear of her life and has lost her loved ones. And yet she is no whiny, neurotic woman always seeking help from the male. She is resourceful, courageous, responsible and is willing to contribute her share to the cause of the empire. Thus Mrs Hilton, threatened (along with her daughters) by a large butcher climbing the stairs manages to grab a spear. This is how the description goes:

> At the dart of the bright point towards him makes the man quickly descend a couple of steps: then Mrs Hilton goes down two steps after him, the spear held down at the charge; and the man continues to retreat, and she continues to press upon him; and that she does so affords the highest proof of her courage ... he glares up at her and shakes the knife at her ... shouts out 'I will bring some others with me, and we will then cut your throat...'

One frail Englishwoman successfully defends her daughter and herself, even as the native (who is described, as noted earlier, as massively built) requires more people to overcome her. This is a prototype of the narratives of the Mutiny, where the woman's courage is constantly underlined. This suggests, for the British public back home, that their women are holding their own in the empire.

There are no European accounts of the British treatment of Indian women, though many women were killed (often with their infant children) during the reprisals.[6]

*

It is obvious from the corpus of writings that the fiction of 1857 contributed to the image of the infamous Kipling image of the 'white man's burden'. Here the burden was not only the protection

---

[6] On the theme of British savagery against Indian women a few passing references are all we have. Among these are W.H. Russell's *My Indian Mutiny Diary* (1860), T.R. Holmes' *History of the Indian Mutiny* (1898). See Surendra Nath Sen (1957).

and improvement of the natives, but also the bolstering of the Raj's legitimacy. The Mutiny had questioned the legitimacy of the Raj, it had challenged its image of invulnerability. The novels, by portraying British courage leading to British victory, reinforce the self-confidence and legitimacy of the Raj, even though some reveal reservations about the exact nature of British policy in India.

Non-fictional accounts dealing with particular Indian rebels like Nana Sahib also exist. G.O. Trevelyan's *Cawnpore* (1865) was of course the best-known non-fictional account of the period. Trevelyan used a vast amount of documentary evidence—eventually collated in G.W. Forrest's *Selections from Letters, Despatches and State Papers*, 1893–1912—to recreate the events at Cawnpore in June 1857. The chapter titles speak for themselves: 'The Station', 'The Outbreak', 'The Siege', 'The Treachery', 'The Massacre'. The epigraph to the book is a part of the inscription on the memorial wall over the Bibighar well: 'Sacred to the Perpetual Memory of a Great Company of Christian People Chiefly Women and Children, 16th Day of July 1857'. A later account is Perceval Landon's *Under the Sun: Impressions of Indian Cities, with a Chapter dealing with the Later Life of Nana Sahib* (1906).

In 1897 a reviewer noted in the respected *Blackwood's Edinburgh Magazine* that the Indian Mutiny seems to have inspired a great deal of fiction. This is, in retrospect, a truism. For the Mutiny has indeed continued to haunt imaginations and languages in Europe. The London *Times* covering the English cricket team's tour of India in 1989 made it a point to refer to Kanpur as the setting of the mutiny's 'more gory events' (The *Times*, 24 October 1989). When the Indian cricket team threatened to boycott the third test match in 2001 as a protest against referee Mike Denness's decisions, the *Express* (London) titled the news report 'Indian mutiny threatens tour' (24 November 2001). And when Britain quit the European

Exchange Rate mechanism the *Independent* (London) compared the decision and the Tory party's fortunes to the execution of mutineers—strapped to the cannon's mouth and fired—and the damage wrecked by mutineers (16 September 2002).

The Mutiny was over in 1859.

And it lives on.

Appendix 2
British India, A Chronology

Year	England/The World	India
1599	EIC founded	
1603	James I becomes King	
1605		Jahangir becomes emperor
1612		Factory at Surat
1625	Charles I becomes King	
1627		Shah Jehan becomes emperor
1641		Fort St. George, Madras
1649	Charles I executed	
1658		Aurangzeb becomes emperor
1660	Charles II becomes King	
1665		Bombay as dowry to Charles II
1668	French EIC	
1685	James II becomes King	
1689	William of Orange becomes King	
1690	Calcutta founded	

british india, a chronology

Year	England/The World	India
1702	Queen Anne ascends throne	
1707	Bahadur Shah I becomes emperor	
1712	Farruksiyar becomes emperor	
1714	George I becomes Emperor	John Surman's mission to Mughal court
1720		Muhammad Shah becomes emperor
1726		Presidencies get Mayor's court
1727	George II becomes King	Maratha chieftains acquire power
1739		Marathas conquer Malwa, Persians conquer, ransack Delhi
1742		French Dupleix becomes Pondicherry Governor
1744	Austrian war	
1746		French capture Madras
1748		Ahmad Shah becomes emperor
1749		Madras restored to English
1750		Deccan and Carnatic wars of succession
1751		Arcot siege
1754		Dupleix recalled, Alamgir II becomes emperor
1756		Siraj-ud-Dowla takes Calcutta, Black Hole
1757		Plassey
1759		Shah Alam becomes emperor
1760	George III becomes King	
1765		Clive becomes Governor of Bengal
1767		War with Hyder Ali

Year	England/The World	India
1772		Hastings as Governor
1773		Regulating Act
1774		Rohilla War
1775		First Maratha war
1776	American Declaration of Independence	
1779		Second Mysore war
1784		Pitt's India Act
1789	French Revolution begins	
1790		Third Mysore war
1793		Permanent Settlement of Bengal
1795		Deccan Nizam defeated by Marathas; Hastings acquitted
1799		Fourth Mysore war; Tipu dies
1800		Fort William College founded
1803		Second Maratha war
1805		Shah Alam dies, Wellesley recalled
1806		Vellore Mutiny, Akbar II becomes emperor
1809		Haileybury College opened
1814		War with Nepal
1817		Pindari campaign
1819		Central India controlled
1820	George IV becomes king	Coal mined at Raniganj
1824		Burma war
1829		Sati banned in Bengal, Thugi campaign
1830		Sati banned in Bombay and Madras

british india, a chronology

Year	England/The World	India
1833		EIC Charter renewed
1835		Macaulay's Minute on Education
1837	Victoria becomes Queen	Bahadur Shah II becomes king of Delhi
1839		Ranjit Singh dies, Afghan invasion
1840		Dost Mohammed deposed
1841		First tea planted in Darjeeling
1842		Kabul retreat
1843		Sind conquered
1845		First Sikh war
1848		Second Sikh war
1849		Punjab annexed
1852		Second Burmese war
1853		Nagpur annexed, Bombay–Thana railway line opened
1854		Serampore jute mill, Bombay cotton mill opened
1856		Oudh annexed
1857		'Mutiny'
1858		Crown of England assumes charge of India
1860		Indian Councils Act, Macaulay's penal code becomes law
1861	American Civil War	
1863		Simla becomes summer seat of Government
1864		Bhutan war
1867		British Reform Bill
1869	Suez Canal opened	Gandhi born

Year	England/The World	India
1877		Victoria declared 'Empress' of India
1878		Second Afghan war
1883		Ilbert Bill
1885		Third Burmese war, Indian National Congress founded
1886		Upper Burma annexed. Communal riots in Delhi
1891		Age of Consent Act, Tilak begins agitation
1892		Indian Councils Act
1897		Bombay Plague
1900		North-West Frontier Province
1901	Edward VII becomes King	Delhi Durbar
1904		Co-operative Societies Act
1905		Bengal Partition
1906		Muslim League formed
1909		Morley–Minto reforms
1910		George V becomes king
1911		King Emperor's visit, Delhi Durbar; Delhi becomes capital; Bengal Partition revoked
1914	First World War begins	
1915		Gandhi returns to India
1916		Besant's Home Rule League
1918	First World War ends	Montagu–Chelmsford Report, Rowlatt Report
1919		Jallianwallah Bagh massacre, Third Afghan war

british india, a chronology

Year	England/The World	India
1920		Hunter Commission Report on Jallianwallah Bagh
1921		Prince of Wales' visit, with riots in Bombay
1922		Gandhi imprisoned for civil disobedience
1928		Simon Commission
1930		Salt Satyagraha, Round Table Conference
1931		Gandhi–Irwin Pact
1932		Civil Disobedience begins again
1935		Government of India Act
1936		Nehru becomes President of Congress
1937		Congress wins majority of provincial elections
1939	Second World War begins	Congress ministries resign, Jinnah calls for Thanksgiving Day
1942	Singapore falls	Subhas Bose arrives in Japan, Cripps Mission, 'Quit India'
1943		Bengal famine
1945	Second World War ends	Labour government in Britain
1947		Independence, Pakistan inaugurated
1948		Gandhi assassinated

Bibliography

PRIMARY SOURCES

Non-Fiction, First Person Accounts and Histories

Anonymous [Sambhu Chandra Mukherjee]. *The Mutinies and the People, Or Statements of Native Fidelity Exhibited during the Outbreak of 1857–58, by a Hindu*. Calcutta: Sanskrit Pustak Bhandar, 1969 (1859).

Anonymous. [Mrs G. Harris?] *A Lady's Account of the Siege of Lucknow, written for the Perusal of Friends at Home*. Delhi: Rupa, 2002 (1858).

Anonymous. *England's Great Mission in India*. Lucknow: London Printing, 1879.

Ball, Charles. *The History of the Indian Mutiny*. London: London Printing and Publishing Co., 1858–59. 2 vols.

Barter, Richard. *The Siege of Delhi: Mutiny Memories of an Old Officer*. London: The Folio Society, 1984.

Bartrum, Katharine Mary. *A Widow's Reminiscences of the Siege of Lucknow*. London: J. Nisbet, 1858.

Blomfield, David. *Lahore to Lucknow: The Indian Mutiny Journal of Arthur Moffat Lang*. London: Leo Cooper, 1992.

Bonham, John. *Oude in 1857: Some Memories of the Indian Mutiny*. London: Williams and Norgate, 1928.

bibliography 259

Bose, Subas Chandra. 'Free India and Its Problems'. *The Essential Writings of Netaji Subash Chandra Bose.* Ed. Sisir Kumar Bose and Sugata Bose. Delhi: Oxford University Press, 1998.

Campbell, Colin. *Narrative of the Indian Revolt.* London: George Vickers, 1858.

Case, Adelaide. *Day by Day at Lucknow: A Journal of the Siege of Lucknow.* London: Richard Bentley, 1858.

Chalmers, John. Letters *Written from India during the Mutiny and the Waziri Campaigns.* Edinburgh: T. and A. Constable, 1904.

Chick, N.A. *Annals of the Indian Rebellion of 1857–58, containing Narratives of the Outbreaks and Eventful Occurrences and Stories of Personal Adventures.* Calcutta: Sanders, Cones and Co., 1859.

Chunder, Bholanauth. *The Travels of a Hindoo to Various Parts of Bengal and Upper Bengal.* London: N. Trübner, 1869. 2 vols.

Collier, Richard. *The Sound of Fury: An Account of the Indian Mutiny.* London: Collins, 1963.

Mrs Coopland [R.M. Coopland] *A Lady's Escape from Gwalior, and Life in the Fort of Agra during the Mutinies of 1857.* London: Smith, Elder, and Co., 1859.

Dalhousie, Lord. *Private Letters of the Marquess of Dalhousie.* Ed. J.G.A. Baird. London: William Blackwood, 1910.

Diver, Maud. *The Englishwoman in India.* Edinburgh and London: William Blackwood, 1909.

———. *The Unsung: A Record of British Services in India.* Edinburgh and London: William Blackwood, 1945.

Dobrolyubov, Nikolai. *The Indian National Uprising of 1857: A Contemporary Russian Account.* Tr. Harish C. Gupta. Calcutta: Nalanda, 1988 (1858).

Doyley, Charles. *The European in India, from a Collection of Drawings by Charles Doyley*, engraved by J.H. Clark and C. Dubourg. New Delhi: Asian Education Services, 1995 (1813).

Dunlop, Robert Henry Wallace. *Service and Adventure with the Khekee Ressalah or Meerut Volunteer Force during the Mutinies of 1857-58.* London: R. Bentley, 1858.

Dutt, Romesh C. *England and India: A Record of Progress during A Hundred Years 1785–1885*. New Delhi: Mudgal, 1985 (1897).

Edwards, William. *Personal Adventures during the India Rebellion in Rohilcund, Futtegarh, and Oude*. London: Smith, Elder and Co., 1858.

Forrest, George W. *A History of the Indian Mutiny*. Edinburgh: William Blackwood and Sons, 1912. 3 vols.

———. *Selections from Letters, Despatches and Other State Papers Preserved in the Military Department of the Government of India 1857–58*. (1893–1912) Chennai: Asian Educational Services, 2006. 4 vols (1893–1912).

Gandhi, M.K. 'The Proclamation of 1858'. *Collected Works*, http://www.gandhiserve.org/cwmg. Vol. 3: 134–36.

———. 'Talk with Seva Dal Workers'. *Collected Works* http://www.gandhiserve.org/cwmg. Vol. 53: 197–99.

Germon, Maria Vincent. *Journal of the Siege of Lucknow*. Ed. Michael Edwardes. London: Constable, 1958.

Ghalib, Mirza Asadullah Khan. *Dastunubuy: A Diary of the Indian Revolt of 1857*. Tr. Khwaja Ahmad Faruqi. Delhi: NP, 1992.

Godse, Vishnu Bhatt. *Majha Pravas*. Pune: Venus, 2000.

Gough, Hugh. *Old Memories*. Edinburgh and London: Blackwood and Sons, 1897.

Griffiths, Charles John. *The Siege of Delhi, with an Account of the Mutiny at Ferozepur in 1857*, ed. Henry John Yonge. London: John Murray, 1910.

Guernsey, A.H. 'The English in India'. *Harper's New Monthly Magazine*, 25.149 (1862): 685–91.

Hearn, G.R. *The Seven Cities of Delhi*. London: W. Thacker, 1906.

Hewitt, James. Ed. *Eye-witnesses to the Indian Mutiny*. Reading: Osprey, 1972.

Holmes, T.R. *History of the Indian Mutiny*. London: Macmillan, 1898.

Hutchins, Francis. *The Illusion of Permanence: British Imperialism in India*, Princeton, NJ: Princeton University Press, 1967.

Mitra, J.M. Ed. *Press-List of 'Mutiny Papers' 1857*. Calcutta: Superintendent Government Printing, 1921.

Inglis, Lady [Julia]. *The Siege of Lucknow: A Diary*. London: James R. Osgood, McIlvaine & Co., 1893.

Ireland, William W. *A History of the Siege of Delhi by an Officer who served there*. Edinburgh: Adam and Charles Black, 1861.

Kavanagh, T.H. *How I Won the Victoria Cross*. Ward and Lock, 1860.

Kaye, John. *History of the Sepoy War in India, 1857-1858*. London: W.H. Allen, 1875 (1864). 3 vols.

Keith, A. Berriedale. Ed. *Speeches and Documents on Indian Policy, 1750–1921*. London: Oxford University Press, 1922.

Khan, Syed Ahmad. *An Essay on the Causes of the Indian Revolt*. Benares: Medical Hall Press, 1873.

Lawrence, John. *Lawrence of Lucknow: A Biography*. London: Hodder and Stoughton, 1990.

Leckey, Edward. *Fictions Connected with the Indian Outbreak Exposed*. Bombay: Chesson and Woodhall, 1859.

Macaulay, Lord. *Life and Letters*. Ed. G.O. Trevelyan. Oxford: Oxford University Press, 1978 (1876). 2 vols.

Mackintosh, William. *Travels in Europe, Asia and Africa*. London: J. Murray, 1782. 2 vols.

Maharashtra Archives. *Bulletin of the Department of Archives, No. 9 and 10: The Legend of Nana Saheb*. Ed. V.G. Khobrekar. NP: Maharashtra Archives, nd.

Marx, Karl and Frederick Engels. *On Colonialism*. Moscow: Progress Publishers, 1959.

———. *The First War of Indian Independence 1857-1859*. Moscow: Progress, 1975.

Metcalfe, Charles Theophilus. Tr. *Two Native Narratives of the Mutiny in Delhi*. London: Archibald Constable, 1898.

Military Department. *Printed Proceedings. 1857*. Andhra Pradesh State Archives.

Thomson, Mowbray. *The Story of Cawnpore*. London: Np, 1859.

Muir, William. *Records of the Intelligence Department of the Government of the North-West Provinces during the Mutiny of 1857*. Ed. William Coldstream. Edinburgh: T.T. Clark, 1902 (originally published as William Muir, *Agra Correspondence during the Mutiny*, Edinburgh: T.T. Clark, 1898).

Muter, Mrs [Dunbar Douglas]. *My Recollections of the Sepoy Revolt (1857-58)*. London: John Long, 1911.

Norton, John Bruce. *The Rebellion in India: How to Prevent Another*. London: Richardson, 1857.

Parkes, Fanny. *Wanderings of a Pilgrim in Search of the Picturesque*. London: P. Richardson, 1850. 2 vols.

Proceedings on the Trial of Muhammad Bahadur Shah, Titular King of Delhi, before a Military Commission, upon a Charge of Rebellion, Treason and Murder. Calcutta: John Gray, Office, 1858.

Raikes, Charles. *Notes on the Revolt of the North-Western Provinces of India*. London: Np, 1858.

Rees, L.E. Ruutz. *A Personal Narrative if the Siege of Lucknow*. London: Longman, Brown, Green, Longmans and Roberts, 1858.

Roberts, Fred. *Letters Written during the Indian Mutiny*. New Delhi: Lal, 1979.

———. *Forty-One Years in India: From Subaltern to Commander-in-Chief*. London: Bentley, 1897. 2 vols.

Russell, W.H. *My Indian Mutiny Diary*. London: Cassel, 1860.

Scott, John. *A Vindication of the Hindoos*. London: R. and J. Rodwell, 1808.

Shepherd, J.W. *A Personal Narrative of the Outbreak and Massacre at Cawnpore during the Sepoy Revolt of 1857*. London: 1886. (also extracted in Forrest, *SLDSP* 2)

Sherer, J.W. *Daily Life during the Indian Mutiny: Personal Experiences of 1857*. London: Sonnenschein, 1898.

———. *Havelock's March on Cawnpore*. London: Nelson, 1910.

Sherring, M.A. *The Indian Church during the Great Rebellion*. London: James Nisbet, 1859.

Sita Ram. *From Sepoy to Subedar, Being the Life and Adventures of Subedar Sita Ram, a Native Officer of the Bengal Army, written and related by Himself.* Ed. James Lunt. London: Papermac, 1988 (1873).

Steel, Flora Annie and G[race] Gardiner. *The Complete Indian Housekeeper and Cook.* London: William Heinemann, 1909 (1888).

Taylor, Meadows. *A Student's Manual of the History of India.* New Delhi: Asian Educational Services, 1986 (1904).

Thompson, Edward. *The Other Side of the Medal.* New Delhi: Sterling, 1989 (1925).

Thomson, Captain Mowbray. *The Story of Cawnpore.* London: R. Bentley, 1859.

Trevelyan, G.O. *Cawnpore.* Chennai: Asian Educational Services, 2006 (1865).

———. *The Competition Wallah.* Delhi: HarperCollins, 1992 (1866).

Twain, Mark. *Following the Equator: A Journey Around the World.* Hartford, Conn.: American Publishing Company, 1897.

Twining, Thomas. *A Letter, to the Chairman of the East India Company, on the Danger of Interfering in the Religious Opinions of the Natives of India.* London: J. Ridgway, 1807.

Tytler, Harriet. *The Memoirs of Harriet Tytler.* Ed. Anthony Sattin. Oxford University Press, 1986.

Waring, Scott. *A Letter to the Conductors of the Christian Observer.* London: James Ridgway, 1809.

Wheeler, J.T. *The History of the Imperial Assemblage at Delhi.* Delhi: R.N. Ahuja, 1982 (1877).

Wilberforce, Reginald G. *An Unrecorded Chapter of the Indian Mutiny.* London: John Murray, 1894.

Young, Keith. *Delhi—1857: The Siege, Assault and Capture as Given in the Diary and Correspondence of the Late Colonel Keith Young.* Ed. Henry W. Norman and Mrs Keith Young. Delhi: Gian, 1988.

Select Fiction and Literary Works

Brereton, F.S. *A Hero of Lucknow: A Tale of the Indian Mutiny*. Blackie and Son, 1905.

Field, E.M. *Bryda: A Story of the Indian Mutiny*. London: Wells, Gardner Dayton and Co., 1888.

Fenn, George M. *Begumbagh: A Tale of the Indian Mutiny, and other stories*. London and Edinburgh: W. and R. Chambers, 1879.

Forrest, R.E. *Eight Days: A Tale of the Indian Mutiny*. London, Edinburgh and New York: Thomas Nelson, 1891.

Grant, James. *First Love and Last Love: A Tale of the Indian Mutiny*. London: Guilford, 1868. 3 vols.

Greenhow, H.M. *The Bow of Fate*. London: Allen and Co., 1893.

Gray, Maxwell. *In the Heart of the Storm: A Tale of Modern Chivalry*. New York: F.M. Lupton, 1891.

Harcourt, A.F.P. *Jenetha's Venture: A Tale of the Siege of Delhi*. London: Cassell, 1899.

Irwin, H.C. *With Sword and Pen: A Story of India in the Fifties*. London: T Fisher Unwin, 1904.

Jackson, Alice F. *A Brave Girl: A True Story of the Indian Mutiny*. London: Society for Promoting Christian Knowledge, 1899.

Marryat, Augusta. *Lost in the Jungle: A Story of the Indian Mutiny*. London: Griffith Farran, Okeden and Welsh, 1877.

Merriman, Henry Seton. *Flotsam*. London: Longmans, Green and Co., 1896.

Muddock, J.E. *The Great White Hand, or the Tiger of Cawnpore: A Tale of the Indian Mutiny*. London: Hutchinson, 1895.

Mundy, Talbot [Sylvie Anne Matheson]. *Rung Ho!*. Indianapolis: Bobbs-Merrill, 1914.

Nisbet, Hume. *The Queen's Desire: A Romance of the Indian Mutiny*. London: F.W. White, 1893.

Penn, Clive Robert. *For the Old Flag: A Tale of the Mutiny*. London: Sampson, Low, Marston, 1899.

Reid, C. Lestock. *Masque of Mutiny*. London: C. and J. Temple, 1947.

Steel, Flora Annie. *On the Face of the Waters*. New Delhi: Arnold-Heinemann, 1985.

Sterndale, R.A. *The Afghan Knife*. London: Sampson Low, 1879. 3 vols.

Kingsley, Henry. *Stretton*. London: Tinsley, 1869. 3 vols.

Taylor, L. [Lucy]. *Sahib and Sepoy, or Saving an Empire: A Tale of the Indian Mutiny*. London: J.F. Shaw, 1897.

Taylor, Meadows. *Seeta*. New Delhi: Asian Educational Services, 1989 (1881).

Tracy, Louis. *The Red Year: A Story of the Indian Mutiny*. London: FW White, 1907.

Thomas, D.H. [RET Forrest]. *The Touchstone of Peril: A Tale of the Indian Mutiny*. London: T. Fisher Unwin, 1886. 2 vols.

Williamson, John. *Fallen Heroes of the Indian War: A Poem. In Memory of Havelock and other Britons Gloriously Fallen in Defence of England's Supremacy in Asia during the Sepoy's Rebellion of 1857-8*. London: Lindsey, 1858.

Wood, J. Claverdon [Thomas Carter]. *When Nicholson Kept the Border*. London: Boy's Own Paper, 1922.

SECONDARY SOURCES

Allen, Charles. Ed. *Plain Tales from the Raj: Images of British India in the Twentieth Century*. London: Futura, 1978.

———. *Soldier Sahibs: The Men Who Made the North-West Frontier*. London: Abacus, 2000.

Baker, David. *Colonialism in an Indian Hinterland: The Central Provinces, 1820-1920*. Delhi: Oxford University Press, 1993.

Ballhatchet, Kenneth. *Race, Sex and Class Under the Raj: Imperial Attitudes and Policies and their Critics, 1793-1905*. London: Weidenfeld and Nicolson, 1980.

Barr, Pat. *The Memsahibs: The Women of Victorian India*. Delhi: Allied, 1978 (1976).

Bayly, C.A. Ed. *The Raj: India and the British 1600-1947*. London: National Portrait Gallery, 1990.

———.*Empire and Information: Intelligence Gathering and Social Communication in India 1780-1870*. Cambridge: Cambridge University Press, 1996.

———.*Origins of Nationality in South Asia: Patriotism and Ethical Government in the Making of Modern India.* New Delhi: Oxford University Press, 2001 (1998).

Bhabha, Homi K. 'By Bread Alone: Signs of Violence in the Mid-nineteenth Century'. In *The Location of Culture*. London and New York: Routledge, 1994. 198–211.

Bhadra, Gautam. 'Four Rebels of 1857'. *Subaltern Studies, IV* Delhi: Oxford University Press, 1985. 229–75.

Blunt, Alison. 'Embodying War: British Women and Domestic Defilement in the Indian 'Mutiny', 1857-8', *Journal of Historical Geography* 26.3 (2000): pp. 412–14.

———.'Spatial Stories under Siege: British Women Writing from Lucknow in 1857', *Space, Place and Culture* 7.3 (2000): pp. 229–46.

Bolt, Christine. *Victorian Attitudes to Race*. London: Routledge and Kegan Paul, 1971.

Bora, Mahendra. *1857 in Assam*. Gauhati: Lawyer's Book Stall, 1957.

Brantlinger, Patrick. *Rule of Darkness: British Literature and Imperialism, 1830–1914*. Ithaca: Cornell University Press, 1988.

Bristow, Joseph. *Empire Boys: Adventures in a Man's World*. London: HarperCollins, 1991.

Bryne, James. 'British Opinion and the Indian Revolt'. In P.C. Joshi (ed) *Rebellion 1857: A Symposium*. Calcutta and New Delhi: K.P. Bagchi, 1986 (1957). pp. 291–312.

Chakravarty, Gautam. *Indian Mutiny and the British Imagination*. Cambridge: Cambridge University Press, 2004.

Chaudhuri, S.B. *Theories of the Indian Mutiny 1857-1859*. Calcutta: World Press, 1965.

———.*Civil Rebellion in the Indian Mutinies (1857-1859)*. Calcutta: World Press, 1957.

———. 'The Union of the Civil and Military Rebellions'. In Ainslie T. Embree (ed) *India in 1857*. Delhi: Chanakya, 1987. pp. 127–33.

Dalrymple, William. *The Last Mughal: The Fall of a Dynasty, Delhi, 1857*. New Delhi: Penguin-Viking, 2006.

David, Saul. *The Indian Mutiny*. Delhi: Penguin, 2003.

Das, Gurcharan. *Larins Sahib*. London: Oxford University Press, 1970.

Devi, Mahasweta. *The Queen of Jhansi*. Tr. Sagaree and Mandira Sengupta. Calcutta: Seagull, 2000.

Devi, Ritambhari. 'Outbreak of the "Mutiny" in Muzaffarpur'. *Proceedings of the Indian Historical Congress* 33 (1972): pp. 475–77.

Dirks, Nicholas B. 'The Ethnographic State'. In Saurabh Dube (ed) *Postcolonial Passages: Contemporary History-writing on India*. New Delhi: Oxford University Press, 2004. 70–88.

Dutta, Kalikinkar. 'Some Unpublished Papers Relating to the Mutiny of 1857-59', *Indian Historical Quarterly* 12 (1936).

Edwardes, Michael. *Battles of the Indian Mutiny*. London: T. Batsford, 1963.

———. *Red Year: The Indian Rebellion of 1857*. London: Hamish Hamilton, 1973.

Embree, Ainslie T. Ed. *India in 1857: The Revolt Against Foreign Rule*. Delhi: Chanakya, 1987.

Ghose, Indira. Ed. *Memsahibs Abroad: Writings by Women Travellers in Nineteenth Century India*. Delhi: Oxford University Press, 1998.

Goswami, Manu. 'Englishness' on the Imperial Circuit: Mutiny Tours in Colonial South Asia', *Journal of Historical Sociology* 9.1 (1996): pp. 54–84.

Gregg, Hilda. 'The Indian Mutiny in Fiction', *Blackwood's Edinburgh Magazine* 161 (1897): pp. 218–31.

Guha, Ranajit. *Elementary Aspects of Peasant Insurgency in Colonial India*. Delhi: Oxford University Press, 1986 (1983).

Gupta, J.K. 'The Uprising of 1857 in Sirsa District'. *Proceedings of the Punjab History Conference*, 20th Session (1986): p. 226.

Habib, Irfan. 'The Coming of 1857', *Social Scientist* 26. 296–99 (1998): pp. 6–15.

Harris, John. *The Indian Mutiny*. Hertfordshire: Wordsworth, 2001.

Hibbert, Christopher. *The Great Mutiny India 1857*. London: Allen Lane-Penguin, 1978.

Jain, Vipin. *The Indian Mutiny of 1857: An Annotated Bibliography*. Delhi: Vintage, 1998.

Jayawardene, Kumari. *The White Woman's Other Burden: Western Woman and South Asia during British Colonial Rule*. New York: Routledge, 1995.

Jha, P.C. 'The Battle of Chatra'. *Proceedings of the Indian Historical Congress* 42 (1983): 602–09.

Judd, Denis. *The Lion and the Tiger: The Rise and Fall of the British Raj, 1600-1947*. Oxford: Oxford University Press, 2004.

Kumar, P. 'Hare Krishna Singh—The Prime-Mover of 1857 in Bihar'. *Proceedings of the Indian Historical Congress* 42 (1983): 610–17.

Lahiri, Nayanjot. 'Commemorating and Remembering 1857: The Revolt in Delhi and its Aftermath', *World Archaeology* 35.1 (2003): 35–60.

Lawrence, John. *Lawrence of Lucknow: A Biography*. London: Hodder and Stoughton, 1990.

Luther, Narendra. *Hyderabad: Memoirs of a City*. Hyderabad: Orient Longman, 1995.

Macmillan, Margaret. *Women of the Raj*. London: Thames and Hudson, 1988.

Mason, Philip. 'Fear and its Causes'. In *A Matter of Honour: An Account of the Indian Army, its Officers and Men*. London: Cape, 1974.

Mazumdar, RC. *The Sepoy Mutiny and the Revolt of 1857*. Calcutta: Firma K.L. Mukhopadhyay, 1957.

Morris, Jan. *Stones of Empire: The Buildings of British India*. Harmondsworth: Penguin, 1994.

Mukherjee, Rudrangshu. *Awadh in Revolt: A Study of Popular Resistance*. Delhi: Oxford University Press, 1984.

———.'The Sepoy Mutinies Revisited'. In Mushirul Hasan and Narayani Gupta (ed) *India's Colonial Encounter: Essays in Memory of Eric Stokes*. New Delhi: Manohar, 2004 (1993). pp. 193–204.

———.*Mangal Pandey: Brave Martyr or Accidental Hero?* New Delhi: Penguin, 2005.

Nagai, Kaori. 'The Writing on the Wall: The Commemoration of the Indian Mutiny in the Delhi Durbar and Rudyard Kipling's "The Little House at Arrah" ', *Interventions* 7.1 (2005): pp. 84–96.

Narayan, Badri. 'Popular Culture and 1857: Memory Against Forgetting', *Social Scientist* 26.296–99 (1998): pp. 86–94.

Norman, Dorothy. Selected and Edited. *Nehru: the First Sixty Years*. New York: John Day, 1965.

Palmer, J.A.B. *The Mutiny Outbreak at Meerut in 1857*. Cambridge: Cambridge University Press, 1966.

Paxton, Nancy L. 'Mobilizing Chivalry: Rape in British Novels About the Indian Uprising of 1857', *Victorian Studies* 36.1 (1992): pp. 5–30.

———.*Writing Under The Raj: Gender, Race, and Rape in the British Colonial Imagination, 1830-1947*. New Brunswick, NJ: Rutgers University Press, 1999.

Pionke, Albert. *Plots of Opportunity: Representing Conspiracy in Victorian England*. Columbus: Ohio State University Press, 2004.

Randall, Don. 'Autumn 1857: The Making of the Indian "Mutiny" ', *Victorian Literature and Culture* 31 (2003): pp. 3–17.

Ray, Rajat K. 'Race, Religion and Realm: The Political Theory of the "Reigning India Crusade", 1857'. In Mushirul Hasan and Narayani Gupta (eds), *India's Colonial Encounter: Essays in Memory of Eric Stokes*. Delhi: Manohar, 2004 (1993). pp. 205–54.

Rizvi, S.A.A. and M.L. Bhargava. Ed. *Freedom Struggle in Uttar Pradesh: Source Material*. Lucknow: Publications Bureau, Information Department, 1957–1961. 6 vols.

Robins, Nick. *The Corporation that Changed the World: How the East India Company Shaped the Modern Multinational*. Hyderabad: Orient Longman, 2006.

Robinson, Francis. 'The Muslims of Upper India and the Shock of the Mutiny Rustkhez-i-beja'. In Mushirul Hasan and Narayani Gupta (eds), *India's Colonial Encounter: Essays in Memory of Eric Stokes*. Delhi: Manohar, 2004 (1993). pp. 255–71.

Robinson, Jane. *Angels of Albion: Women of the Indian Mutiny*. London: Viking, 1996.

Roy, Parama. *Indian Traffic: Identities in Question in Colonial and Postcolonial India*. Berkeley and London: University of California Press, 1998.

Roy, Tapti. 'Visions of the Rebels: A Study of 1857 in Bundelkhand', *Modern Asian Studies* 27.1 (1993): pp. 217–26.

———. *The Politics of a Popular Uprising: Bundelkhand in 1857*. Delhi: Oxford University Press, 1994.

Savarkar, V.D. *The Indian War of Independence, 1857*. New Delhi: R. Granthagar, 1970 (1909).

Scholberg, Henry. *The Indian Literature of the Great Rebellion*. New Delhi: Promilla, 1993.

Sen, Indrani. *Woman and Empire: Representations in the Writings of British India (1858–1900)*. Hyderabad: Orient Longman, 2002.

Sen, Surendra Nath. *Eighteen Fifty Seven*. New Delhi: Publications Division, 1957.

Sharpe, Jenny. 'The Unspeakable Limits of Rape: Colonial Violence and Counter-Insurgency', *Genders* 10 (1991): pp. 25–46.

———. *Allegories of Empire: The Figure of the Woman in the Colonial Text*. Minneapolis and London: University of Minnesota Press, 1993.

Singh, Ajit. 'Jind State and the Sepoy Mutiny of 1857'. *Proceedings of the Punjab History Conference*, 20th Session (1986): pp. 227–31.

Singh, K.S. 'Tribals in 1857', *Social Scientist* 26. 296–99 (1998): pp. 76–85.

Singh, Rai Jasbir. 'An Analysis of Punjabi Ballad regarding the Uprising of 1857'. In *Proceedings of the Punjab History Conference*, 20th Session (1986): 232–36.

Singh, Shailendra Dhari. *Novels on the Indian Mutiny*. London: Arnold Heinemann, 1980.

Singh, Zabar. 'Mutiny of the Jodhpur Legion (1857)'. *Proceedings of the Indian Historical Congress* 32.2 (1970): pp. 73–78.

Spear, Percival. *The Nabobs: A Study of the Social Life of the English in Eighteenth Century India.* London: Curzon, 1980 (1963).

Stepan, Nancy L. *The Idea of Race in Science: Great Britain, 1800-1960.* Hamden, Conn.: Archon Books, 1982.

Stokes, Eric. 'The Context of the 1857 Rebellion'. In *The Peasant and the Raj: Studies in Agrarian Society and Peasant Rebellion in Colonial India.* Cambridge University Press, 1978.

———. *The Peasant Armed: The Indian Revolt of 1857.* Oxford: Clarendon Press, 1986.

Taylor, P.J.O. Ed. *A Companion to the 'Indian Mutiny' of 1857.* Delhi: Oxford University Press, 1996.

———. *What Really Happened during the Mutiny: A Day-by-Day Account of the Major Events of 1857-1859 in India.* Delhi: Oxford University Press, 1997.

Toler, Pamela D. Untitled essay on Rani Lakshmi Bai. *Military History* 23.6 (2006): pp. 17–18.

Trollope, Joanna. *Brittania's Daughters: Women of the British Empire.* London: Hutchinson, 1983.

Venkatarangaiya, M. Ed. *The Freedom Struggle in Andhra Pradesh (Andhra).* Vol. 1 (1800-1905 A.D.). NP: Andhra Pradesh State Committee appointed for the Compilation of a History of the Freedom Struggle in Andhra Pradesh, 1965.

Wilkinson, Theon. *Two Monsoons: The Life and Death of Europeans in India.* London: Duckworth, 1987.

Index

Abbas, Ghulam, 204
Abu Bakr, Mirza, 97, 99, 141, 156, 240
Act of 1813, 42
Act of Union between England and Scotland, 4
Act XVI of 1857, 203
Afghan War (1878–80), 24
Agra, 103, 104; mutiny, 71, 90, 168; rebels defeated, 144, 157–58; back in British control, 166
Ahmad, Rashid, 221
Ahmedullah Shah, Maulvi of Faizabad, 59, 80, 166, 167, 223, 240
Ahsanullah Khan, Hakim, 86, 87–88, 153, 204–07, 211, 228
Akbar, 2, 54, 79
Ala-ud-din, Maulvi, 94, 221
Aldwell, Mrs, 86, 208
Aligarh: sepoy discontent, 89
Allahabad, 118–20, 125, 164, 178; mutiny, 71, 108, 117, 130
Allen, A.S., 64
Allen, Charles, 36
American reactions and responses to the mutiny, 191, 195–97

American War of Independence, 15
Anglo-Mysore Wars, *see* Mysore wars
Anson, George (1797–1857), 55–56, 70, 75, 91, 92, 222
Arcot: battles, 5–6; Subsidiary Alliance system, 11
armies in three Presidencies, 20, 43
Arnold, Thomas, 145
Arrah, siege, 133–34
Asiatic Society of Bengal, 13, 44
Askari, Muhammad Hasan, 205, 214
Assam, Raja of, 225
Auckland, Lord, 21
Auxiliary Force of India, 216
Azeezun, 114
Azimgarh, 231
Azurda, Mufti Sadruddin, 42n[1]

Babur, 79, 153
Badli-ki-Serai, 71, 96
Baji Rao Peshwa II, 111
Bala Rao, 101–2, 125
Ball, Charles, 121, 188, 191, 231
Banda: battle, 194; Nawab of, 224, 226
Bareilly, 167; sepoy discontent, 89

index 273

Barnard, Henry (1799–1857), 91, 92, 96, 144, 243
Barrackpore, 31, 43, 45, 49, 102; mutiny/discontent, 62, 64–66, 70, 195; sepoys revolted (1824), 53
Barter, Richard, 147, 150, 157
Bartrum, Dr William, 135
Bartrum, Katharine, 135, 160
Bashiratganj, 138
Batson, Dr, 85
Bayly, C.A., 221–22
Belgaum, 94
Belsare, Pandurang Mahipat, 175
Benares: mutiny, 71, 107, 116–17, 124–25, 178
Bengal, 106, 194; Company's procurement of Indian goods, 5; indigo plantations, 23; trade, 63
Bengal Army, 40, 43, 45, 46, 49, 70, 91, 223
Bengal Renaissance, 9
Beni Madho, 134, 225
Bennett, William, 123
Bentham, Jeremy, 15
Bentinck, William, 14, 15, 17, 18–19
Berhampore: discontent, 62, 64, 65–66, 70
Best, Thomas, 2
Bhadra, Gautam, 200
Bhawani Prasad, 174
Bheem Rao, 95
Bhil tribes, uprisings, 220
Bhola Singh, 101
Bibighar, massacre, 71, 102, 112, 122, 125–31, 235
Birch, J.H., 65
Birjis Qadr, son of Wajid Ali Shah, 71, 113, 167, 176

Bithur, 101, 112, 126, 138; *see also* Nana Sahib
Black Hole, 5
Blackwood's Edinburgh Magazine, 180, 181, 184, 250
Blunt, Alison, 160n^3
Bose Netaji Subhas Chandra, 199, 231
Brendish, William, 84
Briggs, Major S.C., 94
British: commercial venture in India, 23-24; life in India, 25–38; policy of non-intervention, 10, 22, 42; reactions and responses to the mutiny, 179–200
Brydon, William, 137
Buckler, F.W., 201n^8, 228
Bundelkhand, 227
Burke, Edmund, 10, 79
Burmese War (1885), 24
Buxar, 1, 134; war (1764), 5

Calcutta, 30, 45, 52, 63, 64, 91, 161, 164, 195
Calcutta Book Society, 19
Calcutta Madrassa, 13
Campbell, Colin (1792–1863), 124, 134, 136–37, 144, 161–65, 166, 167
Campbell, George, 107, 149–50
canals, role in rousing natives, 60
Canning, Lady, 31, 129n^{10}
Canning, Lord (1812–62), 21, 47, 49, 50, 61, 69, 71, 90, 106–07, 129, 131, 181–83, 218
Carey, William, 14, 17, 42
Carmichael-Smyth, George Munro, 72–75, 78
Carnatic, Nawab, 5
cartridges issue, 46, 54–55, 61, 62,

63–64, 66, 69, 70, 72–74, 79, 198, 199, 219, 224
Case, Adelaide, 136, 159
caste system, 29, 42, 43–44, 48, 61, 102, 196
Cawnpore (Kanpur), 56, 92, 101, 102, 107, 124–26, 138, 143, 144, 175; mutiny, 71, 90, 111, 114, 116–17, 130, 132, 164, 168; back in British control, 166, 187; siege, 236, 237
Chalmers, John, 86
chappati movement, 56–58, 59, 141, 221
Charles II, 3
Charter Act (1793), 9; (1833), 22
Chatterjee, Nandalal, 231
Chaudhuri, S.B., 199
Chengiz Khan, 213
Chester, Colonel, 76
Chhota Nagpur, 101, 228; mutiny, 142
Chingleput, 94
Chinhat, 59, 136
Christianity, 17, 21, 65, 189–90, 195
Christians, 96, 105, 123, 133, 168; native, 77
Chunder, Bholanauth, 152, 225
Chuni Lal, 207
Clapham Sect, 44
Clive, Robert, 5–6, 7, 39
Collins, Wilkie, 236
colonialism, 60, 219
Colvin, John (1807–57), 104–06
conservatism/conservatives, 11, 218
conservative attitude (towards India), 10
conversions, 42, 45–46, 65–66, 188, 195

Coopland, R.M., 42, 89, 103, 180, 181
Corbett, Brigadier Stuart, 109
Cornwallis, Lord (1785–93), 8, 12, 191
corruption, 17
Craigie, Captain H.C., 72
Crooke, William, 51, 134, 225
Cuddapah, 94
Culpee (Kalpi), 166, 172–74
cultural misunderstanding, 35, 47

Dalhousie, Lord (1812–60), 14, 16–17, 46–51, 53, 118, 168, 191
daroga system, *see* police system
Davidson, Colonel, 93
Dawes, Lt Col, 201
Debi Singh, 103
Delhi, 56, 106, 108, 115, 178; mutiny, 71, 79, 81–85, 90, 91, 96–100, 111, 140–42; rebels defeated, 144–59; back in British control, 166, 181, 224; post-battle looting, 193
Delhi Field Force, 144
Deobandi movement, 221
despotism, 10–12, 15, 47, 193–94
Dickens, Charles, 112, 183, 236
Dinapore, 133, 138
Dirks, Nicholas, 196
discontent, 49–50, 56, 61, 62*ff*, 195
Disraeli, Benjamin (1804–81), 23, 181, 187–88, 191, 218
Diver, Maud, *The Englishwomen in India*, 31, 156
Dobrolyubov, Nikolai, 193–94
Doctrine of Lapse, 16, 47
Dost Mohammed, 19
Douglas, Captain, 82, 86, 204, 207

Doyley, Charles, *The European in India*, 27
Dum Dum, 63, 102
Dundasena, 95
Dunlop, Robert, 180
Dupleix, François, 5
Dutt, Romesh, 197

East India Company (EIC), 1–11, 13, 20, 22, 25, 39, 41, 45–48, 64–66, 82, 179, 187, 202, 217, 228; administrative structure, 7–9, 11; Court of Directors, 4; monopoly ended, 13; power transferred to Crown of England, 166, 176, 189
economic freedom from British system, 232
education, 16–19, 22
Edwardes, Michael, 120
Edwards, William, 223
Elizabeth, Queen, 2, 6
Ellenborough, Lord, 21, 182
Elphinstone, Mountstuart, 12, 18
Enfield Rifle, 54
Engels, Frederick, 192
The Englishman, 180, 190
Entract, John, 72
Erskine, W.C., 169
European, Europeans: privilege over Indians, 18; reactions and responses to the mutiny, 169, 179–80, 191, 197
evangelicalism, 37
Ewart, John Alexander, 56, 129
Eyre, Vincent (1811–81), 133–34

Faizabad, 133
farming system, 7
Farrukhabad, 100, 101; Nawab of, 224, 226

Fatehgarh, 101; mutiny/sepoy discontent, 71, 89
Ferozepur, 109
fidelity statements (by natives), 195, 204–10; *see also The Mutinies and the People*
Finnis, Colonel John, 75
Firoz Shah, 80, 177, 227
Fitchett, John, 121
Foote, Samuel, *The Nabobs*, 26
Forrest, George W., 139, 207, 215, 237, 250
Forrest, R.E., 241, 246
Forster, E.M., 31
Forsyth, Nathaniel, 15
Fort St. George (Madras), 3, 140
Fort William College, Calcutta, 9, 14
Francis, Philip, 12
Fraser, Simon, 81, 86
French Revolution, 75

Gandhi, M.K., 38, 182, 198–99
gender barrier, 36
General Service Enlistment Act (1856), 45
Germon, Maria, 159–60
Ghalib, Mirza, 79, 97, 99, 152, 154, 155, 195
Gibbon, F.P., *The Disputed VC*, 243
Gibbs, J., 229
gift system, 7
Glover, Edmund, 234
Godse, Vishnubhatt, 171n[5]
Golab Singh, ruler of Jammu, 207, 227
Gomm, William, 54
Gordon, Sergeant Major, 83
Goswami, Manu, 187n[1]

Gough, Hugh (1833–1909), 76, 83
Grant, Charles, 15, 44
Grant, Hope, 78–79, 132, 151, 167
Grant, James, 240, 247–48
Gray, Maxwell, 242
Greathed, Edward, 144, 157–58
Griffiths, Charles, 146
Gubbins, Martin (1812–63), 58n^4, 113, 117, 118, 131, 132–33
Gujarat, 175; disturbances, 92–93
Gujjars, 142, 155
Gulab Shah, 87
Gurkhas, 37, 217
Gwalior, 102–3, 226; siege, 42; mutiny, 71, 90

Halhead, N.B., 8
Hardinge, Lord, 21, 124
Harriott, F.J., 189, 201, 203, 205, 210–11, 213–14
Harris, Lord, 140
Hassan Khan, Mainoddin, 56, 83, 88, 96–97, 141
Hastings, Warren, 7–8, 10, 18
Havelock, Henry (1795–1857), 71, 107, 124, 126, 130, 138–39, 143, 144, 158–61, 165, 235, 243
Hawkins, William, 2
Hazewell, Charles Creighton, 196
Hazrat Mahal, Begum of Oudh (d. 1879), 52, 80, 100, 113, 134, 167, 176–77, 226, 231
Hearsey, John, 65, 67
Hearsey, John Bennet, 45, 49, 64–65, 67–69
Hewitt, Major General W.H., 75, 76, 78, 84, 91, 243
Hewson, Sergeant General, 67
hierarchy among British India, 35–36

Hindu College, Calcutta, 17
Hindu Dharma Sabha, 58
Hindus, 44, 45, 51, 101, 106, 195, 196, 209, 231–33; responses to mutiny, 187
Hingun, 101
Hodson, William (1821–58), 56, 81, 100, 144, 145, 147, 156–57, 163, 187, 240
Holwell, J.Z., 5
Horne, Amelia (Amy), 121, 123, 237, 247
Hossaini Khanum, 126, 130, 235
Hurdeo Baksh, ruler of Oudh, 224
Hutchins, Francis, 21
Hyderabad, 11, 58; discontent, 93–94, 221, 225–26; Nizam of, 5, 94, 195, 224; Subsidiary Alliance system, 11

Ilahi Baksh, Mirza, 156
Imdaullah, Haji, 221
Imperial Assemblage, 218
imperialism, 19–20, 37, 127, 216, 247n^5
Indian Army, 6–8, 41, 217; role as saviour and guardian, 216
Indian Civil Service, 22–23
Indian Councils Act (1861), 219
Indian National Congress, 38
Indian responses to Mutiny, 152, 154, 154–55, 169
Indore, 168
industrialization, 24
Inglis, John, 137–38
Inglis, Julia, 159–60
Innes, Peter, 109
Irwin, H.C., 238, 240
Ismail Khan, Mohammed, 123

Jackson, Alice, 241
Jackson, Coverley, 118, 131
Jahangir (Mughal Emperor), 2
Jama Masjid, 149–50, 153, 193
James I, 2
Jat Mall, 88, 205–06
Jawan Bakht (1841–84), son of Bahadur Shah Zafar, 80, 81
Jhansi, 103; British annexation, 47, 50; mutiny, 71, 168–74, 178
Jiwan Lal, Munshi, 88, 98
Jodhpur, 230
John, Charles, 50
Jones, Ernest, 190, 234
Jones, William (1746–94), 44, 149, 153
Jubbulpore, 89
Jung Bahadur, 102, 113, 134, 176
Jwala Prasad, 115

Kambar, Sidi, 205–06
Kavanagh, Thomas, 161–62, 239
Kaye, John, 48, 58, 118, 127, 129, 190, 220, 222, 224
Khan Bahadur Khan, 167
Khan, Azimullah, 112–14, 177, 235, 240
Khan, Muhammad Bakht, 99, 100, 142, 146–47, 202
Khan, Syed Ahmad, 197–98, 223
Khan, Turrebaz, 94, 221
Khan, Wazir, 221
Khizr Sultan, 156
Kingsley, Henry, 186–87, 244
Kolhapur, 226
Kunwar Singh (d. 1858), Raja of Jagdishpur, 133–34, 166, 172–73, 227

A Lady's Diary of the Siege of Lucknow, 132, 159

Lahore Chronicle, 180, 183
Lahore, mutiny, 110
Lakshmibai, Rani of Jhansi (1828–58), 112, 113, 165, 166, 168–74, 187, 200, 225, 226, 231
lawlessness, 97, 148
Lawrence, Henry, 20–21, 49, 70, 90–91, 113–14, 117–18, 131–33, 135–37, 165
Lawrence, John, 20–21, 106, 107–08, 110, 113, 156
Lawrence, Richard, 149
Lawrence, Stringer, 6
Leslie, Mary, 234
Liaqat Ali, 123, 177
liberalism, 16
Lloyd, George, 133
Local Self-government Act (1882), 219
London Missionary Society (LMS), 15
Longfield, Brigadier, 149
Low, John, $47n^2$
Lucknow, 108, 113, 131, 132, 178, 187; first relief, 136, 144; second relief, 136, 144; mutiny/sepoys discontent, 70, 71, 90, 135–39; siege, 71, 158–65, 166, 194, 236, 238; post-battle looting, 193

Macaulay, T. B., 16, 18–19, 43
Mackenzie, Lieutenant, 77
Mackintosh, William, 29
Madras, 140; discontent, 94
Maganlal, 93
Majumdar, R.C., 231
Malcolm, John, 12
Malgonkar, Manohar, 72
Malleson, G.B., 173
Man Singh, Raja of Narwar, 160, 175

Marathas, 11
Marshman, Joshua, 17
Martin, Montgomery, 181
Marx, Karl, 20, 89, 154, 191–93, 226, 229
Masulipatnam, 95
Mathura, 103
Maude, F.C., 139
Maulvi of Faizabad, see Ahmedullah Shah
maulvis and fakirs (itinerant), 58–59, 92, 101, 191, 221
Mayhew, W.A.J., 45
Mazumdar, R.C., 231
Meerut, discontent/mutiny, 58, 62, 71, 72–79, 81, 84, 85, 110, 111, 115, 131, 168, 204, 222, 224
memorials (to dead Europeans), 25, 128, 186
memsahibs (Englishwomen), 36, 41, 129, 179; during mutiny, 237–38, 242, 247n[5], 248–49; dishonoured, 129–30; everyday life, 29–31, 34
Merriman, Henry Seton, 243
Metcalfe, Charles Theophilus (1828–83), 12, 18, 49, 82, 83, 141, 155, 207
Mhow: mutiny, 168
Middleton, Sir Henry, 2
Middleton, Thomas, 14
Military and Civilian Management Committee, 97
Mill, James, 15–16
Mill, John Stuart, 16, 216
Mir Jafar, 6
missionaries in India, 14–17, 39, 44
Moghal, Mirza (1828–57), 87, 96, 98–99, 141, 148, 156, 202, 206, 209–11, 228, 240

Mohan Lal, Munshi, 98
Money, Edward, 236
Montgomery, Robert, 108, 110
Moore, Kate, 77
Moplah uprisings, Malabar, 21–22, 220
Morar, 172
Mughal power, decline, 9
Muir, William, 130
Mukherjee, Rudransghu, 37–38, 165, 230–31
Mukund Lal, 207
Muller, Max, 196
Munro, Thomas, 10, 12
Muslims, 45, 51, 93, 101, 106, 154, 195, 209, 231–33; responses to mutiny, 187
Muter, Captain, 149
Mutinies and the People, by Sambhu Chandra Mukherjee, 140n[11], 194
Muzaffarnagar, 221
Mysore (and Seringapatnam), 95
Mysore wars (1767–69, 1780–84, 1790–92, 1799), 5, 9

Nabobs, 7, 26, 37
Nadir Shah, 155, 213
Nadirabad, 238
Nagpur: British annexation, 47, 50, 175
Naikdas, 93
Nana Sahib (Dhondu Pant), Raja of Bithur, 48, 71, 95, 101–02, 107, 111–14, 116–19, 122, 124–27, 130, 142, 164, 166, 170, 175, 186, 200, 221, 223, 226, 227–28, 231, 232, 234, 235, 237, 240, 241, 246, 250
Nanuckchand, 114

index 279

Naomull, Seth, 229
Napier, Charles (1782–1853), 19, 20n[1], 45, 49, 81
Napoleon, 9–10
Napoleonic wars, 13, 24
Nimuch: sepoy discontent, 89, 144
Nehru, Jawaharlal, 199
Neill, James (1810–57), 107, 116–17, 124–27, 129, 130, 138–39, 178, 187
Nicholson, John (1821–57), 20, 108–10, 124, 143, 144–51, 154, 180, 186, 187, 226, 241
Nisbet, Hume, *The Queen's Desire*, 240, 243
North-West Provinces, 40, 59, 60, 101, 104, 109, 202
Norton, John Bruce, 190

opium trade, 13–14
Orientalism, Orientalists, 13–14, 19, 36, 44
Oudh (Awadh), 11, 70, 133, 138, 139, 161, 164, 165, 166–67, 220–21, 223; annexation, 50–51, 131, 197; Subsidiary Alliance system, 11
Outram, James (1803–63), 138–39, 144, 158, 159, 160, 163

Palmer, J., 101
Palmer, J.A.B., 79
Paltu, Shaikh, 67–68
Pandey, Issuree, 67, 69, 220
Pandey, Mangal, 62, 66–68, 70, 186, 198, 229, 240; trial of, 68–69, 220
Pandey, Sita Ram, 110, 220
Panduranga, Ramchandra, *see* Tope, Tatya

Parkes, Fanny, 31, 36
paternalism, 12
Paxton, Nancy, 237
Peel Commission, 217
Peer Shah, 94
Peile, Mrs, 85
Permanent Settlement, 8, 12
Peshawar, 108, 109
Pilkington, J.W., 84–85
Pindaris, 11
Pitt, William, 10
Plassey, battle (1757), 5, 6, 39, 48, 223
Police Act (1861), 20n[1]
police system, 8–9
political context of the mutiny, 240
postal system, 57, 60
press censorship, 18
princes/rulers: indirect rule of Company, 12, 39; role in mutiny, 101, 191, 194–95, 224–32
Punjab Moveable Column, 144
Punjab, 81, 108–10, 156; British annexation, 50, 53
Purvis, A., 96

Qasim, Muhammad, 221n[10]

racial aspect of the mutiny, 107
racism/racial prejudices, 36, 37, 244
Rahmatullah, 221n[10]
Rajamundry, 95
Rajputs, 37, 217
Ranchi: uprisings, 226
Rango Bapuji, 93
Ranjit Singh, Maharaja of Punjab, 20
Reddi, Subba, 95
Reform Act (1832 and 1833), 15
Regulating Act of 1773, 7; 1784, 7

Reid, Major, 148–49
religious beliefs of natives, 106–07
religious tolerance, 21
Renaud, Sydenham, 124
Roberts, Fred, 85, 112, 145, 150, 191
Robinson, Francis, 155, 221
Roe, Thomas, 2, 25
Rohillas, 94, 95
Rohtak: sepoy discontent, 89
Rose, Hugh (1801–85), 170–72, 174
Ross, 165, 166
Rosser, Charles, 78
Rossetti, Christina, 168–69, 234
Roy, M.N., 197, 199
Roy, Raja Rammohan (1772–1833), 9, 44
Ruiya, 167
rule of law, 8, 11, 12
Russell, William, 35, 160
Ryotwari Settlement, 12

Sahi, Bishwanath, 142, 228
Salar Jung, Nawab of Hyderabad, 91, 93, 195
sanads (patents) system, 21, 195
Sanskrit College, Benares, 13
Sanskrit College, Calcutta, 17
Santhal rebellion, 22, 49, 220
Sarup Singh, Raja of Jind, 194, 224
sati, 36, 44
Satichaura, massacre, 56, 71, 102, 112, 119, 121, 123, 125, 129, 131, 154, 235, 237
Sattara, 226; British annexation, 47, 50
Saunders, C.B., 123, 208
Saunders, Mrs, 155
Savarkar, V.D., 69, 198, 221, 222, 229

Scindia, 172, 224; Raja of, 103
Sen, Surendra Nath, 193, 231
Serampore missionaries, 42
Shahjahanpur: sepoy discontent, 89
Sharp, Jenny, 237
Shepherd, J.W., 117, 121
Sherer, J.W., 187–88, 200, 227, 230
Shorapur, 95
Sikhs, 37, 45, 217
Sind, occupied by Britain, 19
Sindhi, Ubaidullah, 221
Singh, Hare Krishna, 134
Singh, K.S., 199
Singh, Kishan, 207
Singh, S.D., 235, $237n^2$
Singh, Teeka, 125
Siraj-ud-Daula, Nawab of Bengal, 5–6
Sirsa, 101
Sitapur, 135
Sivaji, 3
Skene, Alexander, 168–69, 170
slavery, 17; anti-slave trade movement, 18
Sleeman, Colonel W.H., 17, $47n^2$
Smith, Baird, 151
social interaction, 36–37
social order of British India, 29
social transformation, 14
Spear, Percival, 37; *The Nabobs*, 32
Steel, Flora Annie, 239–40
Steel, Flora Annie (and G. Gardiner), *The Complete Housekeeper and Cook*, 30–31
Stephen, James Fitzjames, 218
Stephen, Thomas, 2
Stokes, Eric, 229
Subsidiary Alliance system, 11
Surat, 3
Sutherland, Mrs 102

Tayler, William, 92
Taylor, Lucy; *Sahib and Sepoy*, 242–43
Taylor, P.J.O., 89n[4], 114, 231
Taylor, Philip Meadows, 17, 223, 227, 240–41
Tennyson, Alfred Lord, 112, 184–86, 234
Thompson, Elizabeth (Lady Butler), 137
Thomson, Mowbray, 117, 120
Thornhill, Mark, 103–4
Thuburn, F.A.V., 178
thugi (thuggee), 17–18
Timur, 79, 153
Tipu Sultan, 9, 41
Todd, Charles, 84–85
Tope, Tatya (Ramchandra Pandurang), 116, 125, 144, 164, 165, 166, 170–72, 175
Trevelyan, G.O., 32, 107; *Cawnpore*, 129, 143, 186, 250
tribal uprisings, 24, 220
Tukoji Rao Holkar II, Maharaja, 93
Tupper, Martin, 183, 234
Twain, Mark, 195
Tytler, Captain Robert, 82, 155
Tytler, Harriet, 82, 85, 92, 155

utilitarianism, 15, 19

Vellore, 41; mutiny (1806), 53
Verne, Jules, 235
Verney, G.L., 72
Vibart, Edward, 85, 155
Victoria, Queen, 19, 107, 129, 155, 182, 188, 218; Proclamation (1858), 22, 113, 176–77, 217
Vizianagaram, sepoy discontent, 62, 69–70

wage discrimination between native and European sepoys, 46
Wahabis, 92, 220, 240
Wajid Ali Shah (1822–87), Nawab of Oudh, 51–52, 113, 133, 225, 238
Walpole, Brigadier, 167
Wellesley, Lord (1798–1805), 9–10, 11, 14
Wentworth, Patricia, 72
Western system of medicine, 44
Wheeler, Hugh (1789–1857), 71, 90, 111, 114, 115, 116–19, 227, 235
Wheeler, J.T., 218
Wheeler, Margaret, 121–22, 235, 237
Wheler, Colonel S.G., 43, 64, 67
Whish, G.P., 74
Whitlock, General, 194
widow remarriage, 45
Wilayati, Allah Dad, 87
    Hurdeo Buksh, 224
Wilberforce, Reginald, 109
Williams, G.W., 101, 114, 119–21, 126, 230
Willoughby, George, 83
Wilson, Archibald, 195
Wilson, Brigadier Archdale, 72, 78, 91, 99, 144, 145, 147, 149–52
Wilson, Horace H., 17
Wilson, James, 222
Wilson, T.F., *The Defence of Lucknow*, 133
Windham, Charles, 144, 164, 166
women's education, 44
Wood, Charles, 43, 234
World War I, 23

Yernagudem, 95

282 index

Zafar, Bahadur Shah (Muhammad Bahadur Shah II, 1775–1862), 41, 47, 54, 71, 79–80, 82, 86, 88, 95–100, 140–41, 144, 146, 153, 156, 179, 186, 227, 228, 231, 232, 240; trial, 87, 96, 165, 189, 200–19, 228

Zanool-ab-deen, 94
Zeenat Mahal, Begum (1821–82), 80, 81, 86, 156, 204, 210